RELIABILITY AND RISK

HIGH RELIABILITY AND CRISIS MANAGEMENT

Series Editors: Karlene H. Roberts and Ian I. Mitroff

RELIABILITY AND RISK

The Challenge of Managing Interconnected

Infrastructures

Emery Roe and Paul R. Schulman

Stanford Business Books
An Imprint of Stanford University Press
Stanford, California

Stanford University Press
Stanford, California

Special discounts for bulk quantities of Stanford Business Books are available to
corporations, professional associations, and other organizations. For details and
discount information, contact the special sales department of Stanford University
Press. Tel: (650) 736-1782, Fax: (650) 736-1784

Printed on acid-free, archival-quality paper

Printed and bound in Great Britain by
Marston Book Services Ltd, Oxfordshire

Library of Congress Cataloging-in-Publication Data

Names: Roe, Emery, author. | Schulman, Paul R., author.
Title: Reliability and risk : the challenge of managing interconnected
    infrastructures / Emery Roe and Paul R. Schulman.
Other titles: High reliability and crisis management.
Description: Stanford, California : Stanford Business Books, an imprint
    of Stanford University Press, 2016. | Series: High reliability and crisis
    management | Includes bibliographical references and index.
Identifiers: LCCN 2015048591 (print) | LCCN 2015050243 (ebook) |
    ISBN 9780804793933 (cloth : alk. paper) | ISBN 9780804798624
    (electronic)
Subjects: LCSH: Infrastructure (Economics)—Management. | Risk management. |
    Reliability (Engineering) | Infrastructure (Economics)—California,
    Northern—Management—Case studies. | Risk management—California,
    Northern—Case studies. | Reliability (Engineering)—California, Northern—
    Case studies.
Classification: LCC HC79.C3 R643 2016 (print) | LCC HC79.C3 (ebook) |
    DDC 363.6068/1—dc23
LC record available at http://lccn.loc.gov/2015048591

Typeset by Newgen in 10.5/15 Adobe Garamond

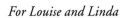

For Louise and Linda

CONTENTS

ILLUSTRATIONS

FIGURES

MAP

TABLES

PREFACE

Not long ago a California statewide emergency manager, with wide public- and private-sector experience in infrastructure operations, made a remarkable statement to us: "These infrastructures are more interconnected than we can imagine." We have discovered the profundity and at the same time the practicality of his insight in writing this book.

Our argument here is that modern infrastructures, which are among our greatest sociotechnological achievements, providing vital services that underpin much of our conception of social modernity, are precarious in newer and more troubling ways than experienced in the past or explained by current theories, analytic frameworks, and advanced computer modeling.

We as a society have evolved a complexity in these systems—in particular their complex interconnections—that makes them difficult to understand. Even operators, risk analysts, regulators, and policy makers, both inside and outside infrastructure organizations, can themselves scarcely anticipate all system-to-system vulnerabilities and the likelihood of reciprocal failure. When such failure happens, we often discover causes only after the fact, and even then much debate attends what caused what.

This is the challenge addressed in this book: We, as citizens and consumers, have become extraordinarily dependent on large sociotechnical systems whose complexity experts, politicians and policy makers, and the public do not adequately comprehend. Yet system performance and failure affect life and death more than ever before in modern society. In tackling this challenge, our book addresses the question, How can policy makers, specialists, and the informed public better understand the nature of both reliability and risk in interconnected systems whose interactions may be very difficult to foresee?

At the same time this book seeks to advance our understanding of organizational reliability in the management of complex sociotechnical systems. For quite some time an important part of the research into this subject has been polarized around two competing perspectives. One, reflected in what has been termed "normal accident" research, argues that, given the technical characteristics of large, complex, and tightly interconnected physical systems, their failure is inevitable, with potentially catastrophic social effects. Their technical properties make organizational design and managerial strategy ineffective in preventing these failures. These complex technical systems are accidents waiting to happen, and they will happen given enough time for the systems to fully express themselves.

The competing perspective has been reflected in high reliability organization (HRO) research. This research, based on case studies in selected organizations—originally a nuclear aircraft carrier, a nuclear power plant, and an air traffic control center—argues that special organizational features and demanding managerial practices could forestall Murphy's Law and prevent catastrophic events from happening.

This debate between these two views has been going on for over two decades and seems to have a life of its own. A number of attempts have been made to reconcile the arguments or provide alternatives to them (e.g., Rijpma 1997 or, more recently, Leveson et al. 2009; Shrivastava, Sonpar, and Pazzaglia 2009a; and Amalberti 2013). This book offers our own, third perspective. It is founded on the argument that the two main approaches have rested on an insufficient understanding of *both* reliability *and* risk. Both prior perspectives were focused on only two divergent conditions, or states, for technical systems: normal operations or major system failure and its disastrous effects. Reliability meant maintaining the first state while preventing the second. Many formal risk assessment methodologies assume primarily these two states.

But we demonstrate that interconnected infrastructures can assume system states in between and beyond normal operations and failure. We identify and provide examples of the states of normal operations, disruption, restoration, failure, recovery, and the establishment of a new normal. "Reliability" has different meanings not just for normal and failed operations but also for system disruption and its restoration, recovery, and the establishment of a new normal. This is so because each system state presents its own distinctive forms of risk. In our third perspective, ensuring reliability and managing risks are themselves interconnected because they vary across different system states. To insist that reliability and risk are in tension because the acceptance of risk too often degrades and rarely enhances reliability no longer captures the full picture. As we show, interconnected systems are too complex with respect to reliability and risk to understand them through that polarity.

Our descriptions and analysis, based on our years of firsthand observations, interviews, documents, and case studies across multiple infrastructures (see the appendix), establish the impact of interconnectivity and how the character of interconnectivity itself *changes* across different states. We highlight the role of infrastructure operators in managing this interconnectivity and promoting different forms of reliability across multiple system conditions. We also explain how current definitions of "the infrastructure crisis" go wrong and how policies and regulatory approaches following from this misperception intensify infrastructure vulnerability and undermine different forms of reliability. We conclude with an assessment of the future of infrastructure reliability, given increasing interconnectivity and the managerial, policy, and regulatory challenges that high reliability poses. Accordingly, our analysis starts as largely descriptive and explanatory with respect to present conditions and shifts later to the wider implications and suggestions for the future.

ACKNOWLEDGMENTS

Over the course of four years, we talked to many key informants in infrastructures for the California Bay-Delta and discussed our findings with fellow project members of the Resilient and Sustainable Infrastructures (RESIN) team at the University of California, Berkeley. We are very grateful to them, and at the same time, none of them is responsible for any errors of interpretation or analysis that may remain in this book. Any lapses in fact or interpretation are our responsibility alone and not those we thank here. This material is based on work supported by the National Science Foundation under Grant No. 0836047. Any opinions, findings, and conclusions or recommendations expressed in this material are ours and do not necessarily reflect the views of the National Science Foundation.

It has been our privilege to work closely with Bob Bea (RESIN leader), Sonny Fong (California Department of Water Resources), Don Boland (California Utility Emergency Association), and Scott Humphrey (Coast Guard) on different aspects of the enterprise. We thank our RESIN team members Bas Jonkman and Rune Storesund for their discussions and points. We appreciate the comments of Dr. Ingrid Brouwer Utne on a draft of the book's case study on the interconnected water pumping in the California State Water

Project. Special thanks go to Benjamin Baker, who proofread an earlier version and did the data runs and initial analysis from which the Chapter 8 case study was developed (along with the earlier assistance of Doanh Do and Robin Torres). Anna Tumanova helped us greatly in a literature search and review, Jude Berman was an insightful developmental editor, and the two reviewers of our manuscript deserve special thanks. We benefited from comments arising out of our participation at an April 2012 workshop sponsored in large part by Boise State University's Energy Policy Institute, where we first presented some of the material discussed in this book. The early assistance of Karlene Roberts and Kathleen Tierney is gratefully acknowledged as well. At Stanford University Press we are grateful to Margo Beth Fleming and James Holt for their assistance throughout, and we thank Mary Ann Short for her excellent copyediting and Jay Marchand for creating the index. We likewise thank individually the following persons grouped by affiliation where possible:

RESIN: Kristi Black, Cheryl Bly-Chester, Henri de Corn, Howard Foster, Hamed Hamedifar, Kofi Inkabi, Jessica Ludy, Mary Matella, and John Radke

California Emergency Management Agency (now California Office of Emergency Services) State Operations Center: Jim Brown, Mitch Miller, and Steve Sellars

California Independent System Operator (CAISO): Steve Berberich, Joan Berglund, Jim Detmers, Bill Ellard, Bob Emmert, Greg Fishman, Jim McIntosh, Greg Tillitson, Tim Van Blaricom, and Greg van Pelt

Coast Guard: Rich Brewer, Gabriel Flesher, Joe Ford, Scott Humphrey, Sean Kelley, Leanne Lusk, Darin Mathis, Don Montoro, Michael Roja, Jeff Rubini, Greg Rule, Douglas Samp, Robert Steward, Stacey Ward, and Abdulrahman Zedan. We also thank Jerry Bynum, Paul Martin, Jerry Pitken, and Kara Satra.

Contra Costa Water District: Jimmie Abbott, Doug Beckstrand, Dave Huey, Shelley Mays, Mary Miller, Leah Orloff, and Pete Schoemann

California Utilities Emergency Association: Selby Mohr and John Spitler

California Department of Water Resources (DWR): Luis Carrillo, Andy Chu, Kevin Elcock, Sheila Green, Jerry Johns, Robert Lanini, John Leahigh, Chris Mattos, Dave Mraz, John Rizzardo, Maury Roos, David Samson, Glenn Solberg, Carl Torgersen, and Tio Zasso

East Bay Municipal Utility District: Andy Enos and Steven Frew

PG&E: Ben Almario, Kathy Bradshaw, John Fagnani, Lessly Field, John Gillio, Bruce Henry, Lauri Jones, Michael Lang, and Keith Slibsanger

Port of Stockton: Gary Gentry, Steve Larson, George Lerner, Mike Tyler, and Jeffrey Wingfield

Sherman Island Reclamation District: members of the reclamation district board, Bryan Brock, and Henry Matsunaga

Union Pacific Railroad: Ray Perry and Robert Schafer

URS Corporation: Mike Forrest, Ram Kulkarni, and Said Salah-Mars

U.S. Bureau of Reclamation and Army Corps of Engineers: Monte Bowman, Paige Caldwell, Wayne Johnson, David LeBlanc, Mike McKay, and Tuy Washburn

Verizon Wireless: Robert Spinelli

Beyond those mentioned here, others were of great assistance to us at CAISO, within the Coast Guard, among the ranks in the Contra Costa Water District, at DWR, and at Union Pacific Railroad. We also thank Ron Baldwin, Cliff Bowen, Bill Darsie, Agnieszka Fortmann-Roe, Miriam Heller, Paul King, Todd LaPorte, Eric Luiijf, Cindy Matthews, Geoff McDonnell, Chris Neudeck, John Searle, Jon Espen Skogdalen, Bob Whitley, and Rae Zimmerman—vital supporters along the way.

MAJOR ACRONYMS

CAISO: California Independent System Operator (California's primary transmission manager of the statewide high-voltage electricity grid)

Cal Fire: California Department of Forestry and Fire Protection

Caltrans: California Department of Transportation

Cf: Consequences of failure

CIS: Critical infrastructure system

CPS2:   Control Performance Standard 2, used by CAISO as a grid management performance standard

DWR: California Department of Water Resources

EBMUD: East Bay Municipal Utility District, a major water utility in the San Francisco Bay region and surroundings

ICIS: Interconnected critical infrastructure system

Pf: Probability of failure

PG&E: Pacific Gas and Electric, a major California energy utility

SWP: State Water Project of the DWR

VTS: Vessel Traffic Service of the U.S. Coast Guard

USBR: U.S. Bureau of Reclamation

RELIABILITY AND RISK

CHAPTER I

THE INFRASTRUCTURE
SOCIETY

Knowing how something works is not the same as knowing how it
can fail.
—Giandomenico Majone, "Technology Assessment
  in a Dialectic Key"

History teaches us that a crisis often causes problems to correlate in
a manner undreamed of in more tranquil times.
—Warren Buffett, "What Worries Warren Buffett"

IF ALEXIS DE TOCQUEVILLE HAD DROWNED
on a late-November night in 1831, we would have no *Democracy in America*, let alone the other works of that first great interpreter of the
American setting. He, along with some two hundred others, was a passenger
on a steamboat, the *Fourth of July*, when it hit a rock or sandbank in the Ohio
River near Wheeling, West Virginia. "The cry 'we sink!' immediately rang
out," Tocqueville wrote. "The ship, crew, and passengers together began their
journey toward eternity. I have never heard a nastier noise than the noise the
water made as it rushed inside the boat" (quoted in Jardin 1988, 165). Nearly
drowned, he was rescued along with others a couple of hours later.

Memories of the incident preyed on Tocqueville, and in early 1832, while
still traveling, he pressed Joel Roberts Poinsett, U.S. politician and statesman,
as to why steamboats weren't better made. Poinsett told Tocqueville,

There is a general feeling among us [Americans] that prevents our aiming at the durable in anything: there reigns in America a popular and universal faith in the progress of the human mind. They are always expecting that improvements will be discovered in everything, and in fact they are often right. For instance, a few years ago I asked the builders of steamboats for the North River why they made their vessels so fragile. They answered that, as it was, the boats would perhaps last too long because the art of steam navigation was making daily progress. As a matter of fact, the vessels, which steamed at 8 or 9 miles an hour, could no longer a short time afterwards sustain competition with others whose construction allowed them to make 12 to 15. (Quoted in Kammen 1997)

Sound familiar? If we were to bring this part of the story up to the present, it would show not only how risk taking—more neutrally, technological innovation—has always been a key part of developing America's critical infrastructures (and not just shipping) but also how infrastructure reliability in terms of safety and dependability has increased since Tocqueville. This would be a story about how *taking risks actually improves reliability*.

But that story is true only as far as it goes, and we need to take it a good deal further if we are to understand reliability and risks in today's infrastructure. Even by the time Tocqueville got there, Wheeling, West Virginia, was a transportation hub of the Americas. In 1818, the National Road, the first major highway in the United States, connecting the Potomac and Ohio Rivers, had reached Wheeling, thereby enabling goods and services to move from the Ohio Valley eastward as well as westward into the frontier (the Ohio River flows into the Mississippi River). Today it is estimated that more than 230 million tons of cargo are shipped on the Ohio River each year, mostly coal and much of it by barge (including fifteen-barge tows of a thousand feet or longer).

Originally a shallow river, the Ohio has been deepened through a large infrastructure of dams, reservoirs, and locks that connect the more than 975 miles of that river (and its adjacent cities, major ports, and terminals) to the deepwater ports of New Orleans, Louisiana, and Mobile, Alabama, and beyond. Five million people depend on the river for their drinking water, and some twenty-five million people or more, nearly 10 percent of the U.S. population, are said to reside in the Ohio River Basin.[1] By the time Tocqueville's steamboat sank, the Ohio had already been interconnected with the country's nascent infrastructure sectors and was well on its way to being interconnected to ever more important infrastructures. Reliability and risk have also been transformed by this interconnectivity, not just by technological innovation alone. It is that story—the wider story with its implications of our having become an infrastructure society—that we tell in this book.

OUR STORY

This is a book about the capabilities of humans to manage complex and increasingly connected infrastructure systems that supply clean water; provide communications, transportation, electricity, flood protection, and financial services; and ensure major emergency response. It is about our capacity to operate these systems at levels of dependability and safety that match the intensive, continued, and predictable operation we now expect of them within modern society. We argue that interconnected infrastructures are reaching limits in the degree to which these systems can be managed reliably.

We know that in the modern world of infrastructures, reliability cannot be a property of single infrastructures and their managing organizations but rather must be the property of relationships among very different infrastructures producing very different services. If we think of reliability as the safe and continuous provision of a critical service, then it must be interinfrastructural today. Any critical service, such as water and energy, cannot be provided reliably without those water and energy supplies relying on other infrastructures such as telecommunications or transportation. Reliability depends on networks of networks and on a complex physical and organizational interconnectivity that even many experts do not fully appreciate. These networks, moreover, are at risk.

That much we know, but it is far from certain that we know how to manage interinfrastructural reliability across multiple systems and organizations. Because of the increasing complexity of interconnections, the world seems riskier and prone more to catastrophic and near-catastrophic events. The global financial crisis in 2008 and its aftermath may well be a harbinger of things to come (Roe 2013). The Indonesian and Fukushima tsunami disasters are other examples of interconnected failures with catastrophic consequences.

Worldwide pandemics and the more pointed effects of global climate change may be the next megachallenges for humanity in the coming decades.

INFRASTRUCTURES AND SOCIAL MODERNITY

In important ways our infrastructures *define* modern society (Ascher 2007; Huler 2010). Advances in communication and transportation, by way of example, have led to profound changes in social organization ranging from shifting residential patterns to the evolution of family structures. Long-linked infrastructures of water supply and storage and large-scale pumping and irrigation capacity have fueled high population concentrations in deserts and across floodplains and in other geographical areas that prevented such dense settlements in the past.

Our capacities for transportation, communication, health care, financial transactions, and reliable water and energy so shape contemporary life and are so intimately interwoven with its pace, possibilities, and widely shared expectations and aspirations that their failures assume crisis proportions. The major electricity blackouts in the northeastern United States in August 2003 not only led to deaths. They also disrupted air traffic (shutting down regional airports because of inability to screen passengers and process electronic tickets) and automobile traffic because of signal light failures, and they stopped Amtrak rail transportation throughout the regional corridor. The blackouts interrupted cellular and telephone communications and cable television, and they affected water supplies through reducing pumping pressure and increasing contamination as a result of purification and sewage treatment plant failures. The blackouts likewise affected hospital and emergency medical services, as well as the food service sector and a wide variety of other services. It has been estimated that these blackouts cost between $6 billion and $7 billion in lost production, wages, spoilage, and the like (ELCON 2004).

When infrastructure failures occur in conjunction with an earthquake, major storm, or tsunami, they become an integral part of the catastrophe— adding to the death toll and hobbling recovery. Our infrastructures simultaneously create the capacities of modern society and introduce the possibility for catastrophic risks to its continuance (Beck 1992; Giddens 2002; Graham

2009). Both reliability and risk have become integral features of modern infrastructures, the former even contributing to the latter.

PROPERTIES OF INFRASTRUCTURES

Physically, infrastructures consist of structural elements and material designs that enable them to function as major social and capital assets. Such large systems include the nation's many dams, reservoirs, generators and transmission lines, levees, and roads and bridges. But our critical infrastructures also consist of organizations and their management and thus are more than technical systems. For this reason, we refer to them as large sociotechnical systems rather than as technical or physical systems only.

Organizationally, these critical systems incorporate a framework for management and control. This framework consists of the roles, rules, procedures, and protocols prescribing their operation and the skills their personnel (managers and operators) need to operate them. These systems also include the design assumptions and analytic models covering their operation and the data networks to monitor and assess their real-time condition.

Moreover, these infrastructures are not just organizations in addition to their technologies: critical infrastructures function as institutions in society. Institutionally, infrastructure systems include the laws, regulatory agencies, and public subsidies that constrain and support their operation through time. Together these technical *and* organizational *and* institutional dimensions make up an infrastructure as a whole system that, unlike other systems, is meant to operate and be maintained continuously, safely, and for the foreseeable—and unforeseeable—future.

As we demonstrate, the organizational and institutional factors are just as palpably critical as the technical factors. Wherever you see railcars and tracks, electrical generators and transmission lines, or dams, reservoirs, and pipeline systems you find they have control rooms for real-time management of the physical assets.[2] These control elements are often distributed over significant distances, and many are in separate organizations, separately operated and managed. Without managed control elements, the technical elements would have little chance to function reliably.

The networked property of infrastructures makes coordination of activities required for their operation and maintenance a significant and constant managerial challenge. No management challenge in infrastructures is solved solely by investing in new technology, including more sophisticated computerized and automated control systems or physical assets such as new transmission lines or large generators. To the contrary, designs and technologies have needlessly increased that management challenge, a point this book underscores with numerous examples. As we show, the geographical and organizational dispersion of critical infrastructures also leads to more complexity and a wider set of potential system conditions or states than is typical with simpler technical systems under unitary command and control.

While infrastructures are quite specialized in structure and service, they are highly generalized in terms of the foundations they provide for a huge variety of follow-on capabilities. Thus electrical grids allow for communication, transportation, health care, and many other services. In these enhancements that they extend to other capacities, infrastructures become the means to multiple ends. As one analyst (Frischmann 2005) puts it, our infrastructures generate enormous positive externalities that create an unbounded set of potential benefits. They act as economic growth multipliers by providing capacities that generate and facilitate economic transactions and improvements that lead to growing new industries. More than ever before, major industries and economic sectors rest on high-speed, worldwide communication and transportation capabilities. Fast-acting global supply chains remain core to today's international economy (Sheffi 2005).

Infrastructures have additional attributes that distinguish them from other technologies and human interventions. They are designed for large-scale public uses, not individual or solely private uses. Even though infrastructures such as airlines, telecommunication networks, and power grids may be privately or investor owned, their operation provides a distinctively public service (Frischmann 2005).

Large sociotechnical systems also have distinctive histories with respect to their system components. Infrastructures evolve as different parts wear out and are replaced; improvements are made selectively over extended periods. Consequently, many infrastructures are hybrids of technical, organizational, and institutional elements. An electrical grid, for instance, must rely on many generators of different ages, start-up (ramp) rates, and generation capacities and highly differentiated transmission lines with varying electrical load limits and differing vulnerabilities to weather conditions such as wind and temperature. So too, in their own fashion, do railroads and water supplies.

As a result of these variegated factors, it becomes unlikely that a single formal analytic model or approach could adequately portray for management purposes the full behavioral diversity of these infrastructures. Efforts to automate key operations often fail to adjust for this variety and complexity. They then create surprises for their modelers and designers (that they had not predicted or prepared for). On this analysis, the experience, background, and memory of system operators move center stage in the reliable performance of these large sociotechnical systems.

Finally, infrastructures feature complex interconnections and relationships, both internally and with one another. This complexity enlarges dramatically with the expansion of the number of technical, organizational, and institutional components of infrastructures. The interactive possibilities for a set of elements increase mathematically as a multiple of those elements. This in turn can and often does create new system conditions, or states. New types or arrangements of energy users, for example, have changed the expected profile for electricity demand at different times during the day.

Our research underscores that the character of interconnections among elements within single or among multiple infrastructures differs quite considerably under conditions of failure compared with normal operation, so there may be at least two additional configurations (manifest and latent) for each added element. For example, two separate transportation infrastructures, highways and rail transit, operate independently during normal operations, but if one fails during rush hour it can overload the other. A flood takes out a roadway and in turn affects the ability of repair vehicles to reach downed electrical power lines. Managing this complex interconnectivity challenges human ability to anticipate manifold permutation possibilities under differing conditions of operation.

INFRASTRUCTURES AND RELIABILITY

A major pillar of modernity is that the social pace, pattern, and scale of contemporary life have evolved largely to match if not drive current infrastructure capacities (McLuhan 1966). This means that modern social life is closely attuned to, not merely dependent on, the functioning of its infrastructures. We rely so heavily on our infrastructures that it would be hard to imagine what life would be like without them. Always-on infrastructure reliability is not just taken for granted; it is a prerequisite of up-to-the-minute social life.

Lapses in infrastructure reliability are simultaneously disorienting on multiple levels and especially so when the lapses ramify to other infrastructures and throughout other diverse critical-service systems. We don't just lose water and electricity when nothing comes out of the tap and the fridge shuts off; routine social practices are disrupted, and widely accepted standards and expectations for social life and everyday experience are threatened.

When infrastructures fail, their failures assume distinct normative dimensions. Our reliance on infrastructures has in fact transformed a variety of services into presumed rights to delivery. When California underwent a series of blackouts in 2001 on the heels of its wholesale electricity market restructuring, it quickly became evident in public reactions that always-on electricity had been elevated to the status of a public entitlement, a core part of the definition of contemporary California. Indeed, public unrest over the electricity crisis played a significant role in the recall of California's governor in 2003.

As others have also asserted, an infrastructure crisis is under way and not just in the United States. The crisis we describe differs in major respects, however. To many, the reliability and risk of infrastructures are properties that lie primarily within the design of physical systems. In this view, the structural brittleness or robustness of the constituent elements of these systems define their overall reliability, determined as they are by structural features such as materials strength or the redundancy of key elements. In contrast, we do not identify the infrastructure crisis narrowly in terms of degrading or out-of-date assets; the crisis we focus on in this book lies in the real-time management of the hardware and software assets we have.

Our research has revealed that reliability is as much a function of managerial skill as of technology and physical structure (Roe and Schulman 2008). One engineer estimated that up to 85 percent of all infrastructure failures result from human and organizational factors rather than technical failures (Bea 2006). We highlight these organizational and management factors and their importance in infrastructural and interinfrastructural reliability.

The following chapters make clear that safeguarding the reliability of many modern social activities and technical capacities lies in recognizing and managing our interconnected critical infrastructures as valued social institutions.

SOLVING THE INFRASTRUCTURE CRISIS

Commonly proposed solutions to the infrastructure crisis, such as finding new financing mechanisms to generate the trillions needed for new assets, are inherently ill advised, we argue, when the real organizational and institutional dimensions of the reliability challenge have not been recognized. Likewise, technical innovations that undermine rather than enhance the flexibility of real-time control operators to respond to inevitable technical shortfalls and rude surprises are fatal at their core. The infrastructure crisis this book highlights is the one caused by design undermining better managerial practice and by innovation that assumes management will always adapt, whatever the situation. We show why a design solution to these problems must take seriously the management of unavoidably incomplete designs or design errors and their inadvertent consequences.

Yet as important as they are, the reliability and risks of our interconnected infrastructures are not well understood and not accurately reflected in risk assessment and risk management methodologies currently applied to infrastructures. This argument stands in marked contrast to much current thinking about the threats to critical infrastructures—namely, that their risks are self-evident, ranging from all too obvious aging structures to vulnerabilities visible to the determined terrorist. Given this diagnosis, risk analysis and modeling are now widely argued for, applied, and said to be getting better and better (Ostrom and Wilhelmsen 2012). Our argument, on the other hand, is that these methods are seriously flawed when compared with the unique real-time risk assessment and management skills of control operators in the critical infrastructures themselves. Moreover, many policy makers, regulators, and system designers display a studied indifference to this fact, if not silent dismissal of it. Policy makers and system designers also do not appreciate the challenges to operator skills imposed by faulty technical designs, misdirected policy, and regulatory error (all of which are described in this book). At the same time, our infrastructures have become interconnected in ways far more complex than even their operators and support staff fully understand.

Since a good many of the presumed infrastructure problems and methods of risk analysis have been misidentified, it is unsurprising that technical, policy, and management prescriptions applied are not just wrong but at times dangerously counterproductive. Whereas a crisis of critical infrastructures has been described in terms of underinvestment and overutilization of the nation's physical structures, we insist that better understanding the management crisis opens up an entirely new terrain for more cost-effective remedies.

In framing our argument, we must take reliability beyond a single infrastructure, such as electricity transmission, which was the focus of our earlier research (Roe and Schulman 2008). Here instead, we frame and analyze risks of interconnected operations and failure among electricity, telecommunications, ports, water supply, levees, marine navigation, roads, and railroads infrastructures in the San Francisco Bay–Sacramento River–San Joaquin River Delta, our case study area. This research has been part of the larger 2009–2013 Resilient and Sustainable Infrastructure Networks (RESIN) initiative, funded by the National Science Foundation and housed in the Center for Catastrophic Risk Management at the University of California, Berkeley (for other results from the RESIN project, see Hamedifar 2012). Since our findings offer a new way of understanding the complex interrelationships among these systems, we develop and considerably extend our earlier framework on high reliability management (Roe and Schulman 2008). In so doing, we build on the research and literature of other scholars and practitioners on networked reliability among infrastructures (e.g., de Bruijne 2006; van Eeten et al. 2011).

THE HIGH RELIABILITY RESEARCH CONTEXT

Any *tour d'horizon* of the reliability literature must necessarily be incomplete, but for our purposes the beginning lay in the research into high reliability organizations (HROs). The hazardous organizations studied were mandated to maintain reliable (safe and continuous) operations even during peak periods and simultaneously guard against accidents or other events that must not happen with such systems (LaPorte and Consolini 1991; Roberts 1993). The early research was largely taxonomic in seeking to identify key HRO features or factors (e.g., Rochlin 1993; Schulman 1993), and much HRO research has been contrasted with the normal accidents theory of Charles Perrow (Perrow [1984] 1999; Rijpma 1997).

Subsequent studies built on this base or extended it in diverse ways, including contributions to management practice (e.g., Weick and Sutcliffe 2001), the field of safety science (e.g., Hopkins 2014; Amalberti 2013), resilience theory and practice (e.g., Hollnagel, Woods, and Leveson 2006; Boin and van Eeten 2013), networked reliability (e.g., de Bruijne 2006), and the statistical analyses of high reliability as a continuous quantifiable variable in the operations of health care, nuclear power, and other industries (Vogus and Sutcliffe 2007; Schöbel 2009; May 2013; O'Neil and Kriz 2013).

As for this book's contribution, it is the latest chapter in an evolving story for us. It began with over seven years of research at the California Independent System Operator (CAISO), the organization charged with responsibility for managing the California high-voltage transmission grid. We studied its struggle to maintain reliable electrical service operations for California in the midst of its 2001 electricity crisis and in the years afterward. This book takes its point of departure from that study and adds four more years of a much expanded analysis of varying forms of reliability challenges among interconnected infrastructures.

OUR POINT OF DEPARTURE

The question of the reliability of infrastructures across their interconnections takes us to the edge of our understanding of high reliability itself. This book examines in detail what happens when large-scale infrastructures turn out to be far more complexly interconnected than their designers, managers, and even operators have conceived on the basis of formal design and the experience of normal operations.

To summarize, we are at high reliability's edge in these systems for several reasons. First, a single infrastructure's reliability and its risks are no longer a self-contained property (this has important implications, as we see later, for infrastructure resilience and robustness). Second, the interconnected system failures we are concerned about are likely to be those that lie outside prior analysis and experience within any individual system. Last, reliability cannot simply be about normal operation and avoiding the risks of failure. It must also include the probabilities of successful restoration and recovery. "Reliability" under these conditions has a different meaning than that attached to it in earlier HRO literature. Our intent here is to examine and illustrate alternative meanings for reliability, given the variety of system states and conditions that interconnected infrastructures assume.

These new reliability challenges give rise to an authentic infrastructure crisis, which, while unreported or underacknowledged, should be the paramount one of concern to society. This crisis revolves around threats to the managerial dimension of reliability—the skills and strategies that have up to this point contained risks, limited the spread of interconnected failures, and provided new options and resources for interinfrastructural reliability. No arguments about the state of infrastructures can ignore the daunting nature of their ever more complex interconnectivity. Better appreciation of this challenge, and how it has hitherto been misunderstood, is the first step to understanding risk and reliability in our modern infrastructure society. Consequently, we begin with an analysis of modern interinfrastructure connectivity.

CHAPTER 2

THE INTERINFRASTRUCTURE CHALLENGE

THE VENUE: THE CENTER FOR CATASTROPHIC Risk Management at the University of California, Berkeley. The occasion: a presentation by officials from a state Department of Education on the location of public school facilities near major overhead power lines, underground natural gas pipes, large dams, and other infrastructure elements like rail tracks. The problem: the potential risks posed to schools by these structures. Our question: How can school districts and other organizations, including regulators, better understand infrastructure risk and risk management beyond the simple physical proximity of individual infrastructure elements?

To highlight their concerns about risks, the Department of Education officials showed photos of schools located near potentially dangerous assets and facilities. Each photo (see Figures 2.1–2.5) has been given a title to illustrate what we took to be the primary concerns. For ease of exposition and from this point on, each figure refers not to a specific case but to an illustrative problem of interconnectivity.

When the education officials described concerns represented by such photos, they saw—as many readers can now see—immediate connections of cause

FIGURE 2.1   Major water reservoir and dam northeast of urban area with public schools in the floodplain. *Source:* Google.

FIGURE 2.2   Transmission pylon and overhead power lines located next to school with major road on the right. *Source:* Google.

FIGURE 2.3   School play fields and buildings bifurcated by rail tracks. *Source:* Google.

FIGURE 2.4   School adjacent to underground gas pipelines. *Source:* Google.

and effect, where the dam breaches, the transmission pylon collapses, a derailment occurs, or the gas pipeline or the underground gas reservoir explodes, each with cascading knock-on effects for close-by people and property, not least of which being the public schools.

But we propose that there are at least six distinctive analytic frames of reference for understanding infrastructure interconnectivity, only a few of which

FIGURE 2.5   School adjacent to underground natural gas reservoir, which is in turn adjacent to rail line, levee, and waterway on the left. *Source:* Google; image by Bluesky.

directly hinge on spatial proximity. The differences largely revolve around distinguishing infrastructure systems from their elements and distinguishing different types of interconnectivity, including latent interconnections that become evident only under certain conditions. These different frameworks for interconnected critical infrastructure systems (ICISs) are summarized in Table 2.1 and discussed in more detail in the following sections.

SIX INTERCONNECTED CRITICAL
INFRASTRUCTURE SYSTEMS

ICIS1

Let's call the school disaster scenario of cascading cause and effect across the infrastructures ICIS1. Often termed a common mode failure, the actual sequence in any such disaster scenario varies, but all share the same feature of elements fully stressed to the point of failure, creating an unmanaged system that poses an unacceptable threat to people and property. For education officials, "no child should die in school" defines an event they are mandated

TABLE 2.1 Alternative analytic frames on interconnected infrastructures

Frame	Scope	Management strategy	Risks	Reliability challenge
ICIS1	Individual infra-structure elements	Unmanaged failure	Cascading failure to other elements	Robust design for each element
ICIS2	Comparative practices for same elements in other places	Better practice; risk management	Cascading failure to other elements	Early warning; careful monitoring and maintenance
ICIS3	Each element in an infrastructure system	Contingency plan-ning; restoration resilience	Loss of system as-sets and service	High reliability in operations and maintenance
ICIS4	Elements shared by two or more systems	Interinfrastruc-ture information sharing	Disruption or loss of service in two or more systems	Well-coordinated maintenance
ICIS5	Control variables connected to two or more systems	Coordinated in-terinfrastructure operations	Compounding control error; loss of recovery ca-pacity	Continuous in-formation com-munication and planning
ICIS6	Latent intercon-nections among two or more infra-structure systems	Emergency re-sponse planning and management	Cascading failure across infrastruc-tures	Anticipatory mod-eling of connec-tivity shifts from normal to failure

and committed to prevent. Their challenge is made all the more formidable because the disaster scenarios are so varied.[1]

Seeing the photos from this ICIS1 perspective may be required by regu-lation, mission statement, and politics. Officials often have no choice but to depict threats in this manner. Yet those interested in ICISs and the reliability and risk challenges posed by them must quickly move beyond ICIS1 disas-ter scenarios. To see this, think of risk as the product of the probability and consequences of a failure and reliability as the safe and continuous provision of critical services through the prevention of failure. There are, just as impor-tantly, other system-level ways of looking at the visuals in Figures 2.1–2.5 when it comes to such reliability and risk. The other perspectives include not only different takes on the ICIS at issue but also different scenarios of how the op-erations of infrastructures are connected to each other for reliability and risk management purposes. Here we present the five other such perspectives also discussed in the chapters ahead.

ICIS2

Return to Figure 2.1, our illustrative photo of the dam whose floodplain incorporates the adjacent urban area in which public school buildings are located. When it comes to infrastructure reliability and risk, one important question has to be, Since this can't be the first time or the only place a large dam or major water reservoir is close to essential public facilities, like schools and large population centers, what better practices have evolved over time for managing the risks involved at other similar sites and cases?

To be specific, what are the managers of the large water system within which a dam is located doing to mitigate the reservoir's probability of failure (Pf) and consequences of failure (Cf)? What are district school officials and others doing to protect the school in such an eventuality? How do these respective reliability and risk management practices compare to those that have emerged across many other cases of such spatial adjacency?

There are around 14,500 school districts in the United States alone, and doubtless some face the same or a comparable problem, so what has this subsample of school districts done, and done better, that schools in such a photo could adopt and modify? We call this subsample of reference systems and their risk management practices ICIS2. (Think here of the so-called basket of institutions that an organization compares its salary levels and benefits against for assessing its own remuneration.)

The question of what ICIS2 schools have done is very significant because, given reliability and risk management practices across cases like the one of interest, the analyst and manager will have a much better idea of what are considered *acceptable risks* in these cases against which to compare the case in the photo. These practices may include quite specific types of designs, inspections, and emergency procedures that both establish and reflect what are or are not acceptable risks for communities next to large water facilities. Why is such a baseline of acceptable risks and practices in like situations so crucial? Quite simply, because Figure 2.1 may show a *managed* ICIS2, meaning risks have been determined to be institutionally or socially acceptable and their management includes specific anticipatory and preventive practices rather than solely a disaster scenario in the making involving *unmanaged* connections and *unacceptable* risks (as in ICIS1).

If analysts or managers of reliability and risk were to cast the net for better ICIS2 management practices further afield, they may end up with conclusions opposite to the ICIS1 disaster scenario first posed in Figure 2.1. In parts of Asia, frequently traveled paths and roads are located alongside major irrigation waterways and reservoirs in ways that ensure that many more eyes and ears are available to detect indications of something going wrong with the irrigation infrastructure early on. Someone having *that* perspective might well conclude from Figure 2.1, "My gosh, look at all the people available around the clock, every day, to monitor this reservoir!" Such a recasting means treating an urban population as their own reliability managers and a resource to reduce Pf and Cf rather than only the source of an inevitably large Cf.

ICIS3

Return to Figure 2.5, the photo of the underground natural gas reservoir and adjacent structures. For our purposes, the figure illustrates, from left to right, a waterway protected by a levee next to which runs a rail line that abuts an underground reservoir next to which, on the lower right, lies the public school facility. Again, various legal and regulatory requirements can demand that officials imagine some disaster scenario in which the waterway floods, the levee breaches, the railbed is washed out, the mechanical equipment operating the underground reservoir malfunctions, a leak or explosion follows, and the school is destroyed. Yet in concatenating a scenario this way, we are in fact focusing solely on the spatial intersection or adjacency of *elements* of different infrastructure systems (e.g., *that* stretch of levee next to *that* track of rail). This raises immediately another question for the analyst and manager of reliability and risk: How is each infrastructure element managed within its respective infrastructure system?

Just because an element is spatially adjacent to elements of other infrastructures does not entail that the cluster of elements must be managed as its own system or as a choke point of interconnected cause and effect. The reason is that one or more of the infrastructure systems whose elements are displayed in any such photo could have been designed to lose a single element (or more) without adversely affecting the system-wide operation and critical service provision. (For example, the electricity transmission grid has been designed to a standard of $N - 2$ contingencies—that is, a failure in one of its transmission lines would not necessarily interrupt overall power flows, since alternative routing exists.) Our research on multiple interconnected infrastructures underscores that it is the infrastructure system that is being managed, often by control operators and support staff in their respective control rooms, not necessarily this or that individual element we may be looking at in a photo. Let's call the way a larger system is managed, and the implications of that management for any of its own elements and in turn the elements of other collocated infrastructures, ICIS3.

That many critical infrastructures are managed as systems rather than element by element is worth underscoring when it comes to the much-discussed role of human, or operator, error in infrastructure failures. It may well be that human, organizational, or informational mistakes lead to the loss of an infrastructure element (e.g., a given levee stretch was poorly constructed or maintained), but as subsequent chapters demonstrate again and again, it is also human, organizational, and informational factors that maintain reliability of the larger infrastructure as a system despite loss of elements or temporary disruption of service.

What does this mean for a system such as in Figure 2.5? Officials would be asking: What larger flood protection management system is this stretch of levee part of? What larger rail system is this section of track part of? What larger natural gas system is this underground reservoir part of? What larger education district or region is this school part of? It may be that only the natural gas reservoir and possibly the waterway have control centers undertaking operational risk assessments in real time. Clearly, the utility gas infrastructure has a very different control room than, say, a school district, whose infrastructure doesn't have any such control center.

A California Delta Example

Let's consider an extended California Delta case of how easy it is to confuse ICIS1 and ICIS3 for the purposes of assessing and managing reliability and risk. The Delta has been termed California's infrastructure crossroads, and Sherman Island, a major western Delta island of roughly forty square kilometers and with twenty-nine kilometers of levees, has been called the Delta's cork in the bottle because of the many structures that pass under, on, and over it. These

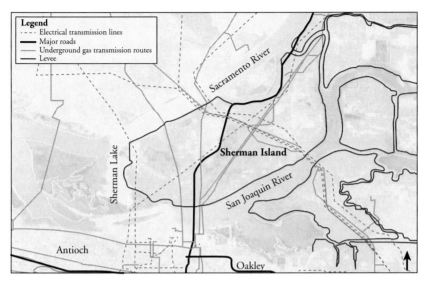

MAP 2.1   Sherman Island, in the western part of the California Delta.

include natural gas pipelines, regional and inter-regional electricity transmission lines, two deepwater shipping channels that run alongside the north and south sides of the island, and State Highway 160 (a short-cut to California's state capitol and regional hub). Since no overhead photo can show all this, Map 2.1 presents a schematic of these infrastructures.

In an ICIS1 analysis, it is a fairly simple matter to imagine scenarios of escalating failure. An earthquake ruptures the underground gas lines below Sherman Island and causes levee breaches above. Or a major storm and rising water levels overtop the levees directly, causing them to breach, leading then to the closure of the adjacent deepwater shipping channels. Levee failure causes island flooding, which disrupts road transportation, including maintenance trucks for the overhead power lines and transport for crews to repair and strengthen the levee. A tanker accident on one deepwater shipping channel passing Sherman Island might also lead to levee and related infrastructure failures. And so on, all seeming to instantiate Sherman Island as its own very major multi-infrastructure choke point.

"Who manages this choke point?" becomes the immediate question, and its answer, "Well, actually, no one," becomes very chilling—that is, until we ask the more relevant ICIS3 question "Does the failure of the spatial cluster of infrastructure elements on Sherman Island trigger the functional failure of the infrastructure systems that intersect there?"

Only after our research was well under way did we understand that an ICIS3 scenario was at work when it came to Sherman Island. Save for two very important exceptions discussed in the next paragraph, that critical infrastructure elements passed under, across, and over the island did not make each element equally strategic to its respective infrastructure system. Road traffic would be detoured if that section of highway 160 were lost, shipping traffic would be rerouted to ports other than Sacramento or Stockton were those sections of the deepwater shipping channel closed, electricity would be redirected to other transmission lines to ensure grid service reliability, and so on. The economic consequences of doing any of this might very well be substantial, but the infrastructure systems as systems have been designed or could be managed to accommodate such one-off contingencies.

In contrast, the two infrastructure *systems* that would be highly threatened by a levee breach on Sherman Island are the California State Water Project (SWP) and the federal Central Valley Project. A breach would directly endanger the continued operation of these large-scale freshwater systems, disrupting the flow of freshwater to urban, agricultural, and environmental users in and south of the Delta. A levee breach on the island could trigger a massive intrusion of saltwater from the west (San Francisco Bay) into the freshwater Delta as the island's below-sea-level area flooded. If such a "big gulp" occurred, saltwater and freshwater would mix in the Delta, necessitating the indefinite closure of the major state and federal pumps and suspending operations for the transfer of contracted freshwater, other things being equal.

In this system-level scenario, Sherman Island is indeed a choke point—not in the sense of the island as the site of failure of collocated infrastructure elements that intersect there but rather as a major choke point within the large-scale state and federal water supply systems. In fact, California's Department of Water Resources (DWR), which operates the SWP, has taken over management of Sherman Island and made major levee improvements there over the years for these very system-level reasons (and in the process protecting the other infrastructure elements intersecting there).

Even so, the scenario of Sherman Island as a system-level choke point for the state's water system is subject to a host of contingencies that render the choke point status less or more consequential. Were one of the island's levees to breach, intrusion of saltwater into the Delta would depend on whether it occurred at low or high tide, what time of year it occurred (wet season or dry season with higher or lower flood levels), amount and timing of reservoir releases from major dams upstream (to push the saltwater back toward San Francisco Bay), and time to repair the levee breach in question, among other factors. "It's . . . not [just] about weak levees, but it depends on whether the tides are high or low, where the winds are coming out of, what's happening with respect to waves—what is the weakest link depends on all of that," summed up a state emergency manager we questioned.[2]

ICIS4

If we were to stop with the preceding three ICIS perspectives, we would have covered a good deal of how infrastructures are interconnected. But our research findings show that system interconnections arise in other ways. Now that we are at the system rather than element level of analysis, three other ICIS perspectives move to the foreground, each with its own set of implications for analysts and managers of infrastructure reliability and risk.

Look closely at Map 2.1 and you see that the island's southeast levee also serves there as the bank of the San Joaquin River deepwater shipping channel. That single stretch keeps the water in the channel and out of the island. The same physical structure, in short, is shared by two different infrastructure systems. Let's call this an example of ICIS4. In this case, infrastructure elements are not spatially adjacent as in ICIS1, but two infrastructure systems are interconnected by virtue of having the very same element. A section of highway 160 roadbed is itself a stretch of levee on Sherman Island, while other stretches of the levee structure provide ecosystem services, such as fish habitat. Infrastructure elements having multiple purposes are in fact common for this area: the large reservoirs leading into the Delta are for flood control as well as electricity generation and water supply (for other examples of double-functioning elements in architecture and engineering, see Venturi 2002).

The systems also do not have to be interconnected through the same physical structure. Elements of one infrastructure may end up in the system definition of another. A levee stretch may have a higher probability of a breach caused by seepage because a gas or water pipe runs through that levee section. In an engineering sense, a gas pipeline segment becomes as much part of the levee system definition when calculating seepage failure as it is part of the gas line system definition (or vice versa; at that intersection the levee system becomes part of the gas line system definition). So too for the case in which wetlands that moderate the effect of wind and waves on the abutting levees are part of the levee system definition, just as those levees that protect these freshwater wetlands from saltwater intrusion are part of the Delta ecosystem definition (Ludy, Matella, and Roe 2010).

This need not be a static or fixed interconnectivity: in a storm emergency a single stretch of road on Sherman Island may become an essential part of access for repairing PG&E's transmission lines as well as access for the DWR's flood-fighting crews to repair or reinforce weakened or failing levees. In this case, a single stretch of roadway becomes part of the emergency response of two infrastructures. Similarly, a roadway between wildlands on one side and electricity distribution lines on the other side of the road becomes a firebreak in the emergency response system for approaching wildfires. Much of this has to do with interconnectivity shifting between positive and negative roles depending on the scenario. The bridge that passes over an aqueduct's spillway enables access for its repair and maintenance, but when the bridge collapses into that spillway, the systems in disrupted or failed operations—road and aqueduct—now look quite different. Indeed, a chief characteristic of emergencies is to change the system definitions of infrastructures from normal operations. We take up this point again when we discuss latent and manifest interconnections.

ICISs

In a very practical sense, infrastructures as systems depend on the operation of other infrastructures as systems, and that interconnectivity needs to be captured as well. When it comes to such system-to-system linkages it is tempting to cast these links as the output of one infrastructure being the input of another—for example, water pumps run on electricity, and electricity runs on natural gas. It is more complicated than that, however, when it comes to system-to-system reliability and risk.

In important cases—and we spend considerable time in this book on such situations—different infrastructures may have interconnected control variables or even share some. For our purposes, control variables are the actionable features of an infrastructure (e.g., voltage and frequency for an electrical grid, water release rates for a dam or reservoir) used to alter the overall condition or state of the infrastructure. For instance, controlling Delta water flows matters in varying degrees to the Port of Stockton's reliable operations, the U.S. Army Corps of Engineers (responsible for federal levee standards and the selected dredging of deepwater shipping channels), the state and federal water projects (and adjacent water districts) that rely on that water, and the Coast Guard Vessel Traffic Service (VTS), which is responsible for real-time management of navigation in San Francisco Bay up to and through major parts of the California Delta. These water flows and their major characteristics (amount, rate of flow, and periodicity) are control variables, either because those infrastructures directly control them (e.g., the SWP through its pumps or the port through having its waterway dredged) to maintain the reliability of their systems or because the infrastructures have to manage reliably in response to them.

An important issue arises when infrastructures are managing or responding to the same control variables, now connecting the infrastructures' reliability management in ways not fully known or recognized by their respective control rooms responsible for real-time operations. Efforts of one infrastructure to manage its control variables in circumstances in which it does not know or cannot know that the other infrastructure is also trying to manage the same variable may cause additional risks for one or both infrastructures. Such interconnectivity has profound implications for each infrastructure's robustness and resilience.

When infrastructures with shared control variables operate in periods that stress or otherwise disrupt their processes, we say the infrastructures are interconnected at the system-to-system level. We call this form of interconnectivity ICIS5. This system-to-system focus highlights how different an ICIS5 conception is from the ICIS1 scenario of a fully stressed, unmanaged set of elements with interconnections at the point of failure. In that perspective, failure is precisely when infrastructure elements, like a breached levee and the school building behind it, are not managed. It may, however, be that such individual elements are not fully reliable for the very reason that their wider infrastructures *are* reliable; that is, resources for control and management have been allocated to alternative elements for overall system reliability or resilience and not to clusters of infrastructure elements spatially collocated, whose failure each of the systems can work around by redundant devices or managerial strategy.

The potential for committing a huge analytic mistake in reliability and risk management when ignoring system-to-system ICIS5 interconnectivity should be evident. Focusing on making this or that stretch of levee more robust (e.g., by bringing it up to Army Corps of Engineers standards) or making it more resilient (e.g., reducing recovery time after a breach occurs), need in no way be the same thing as making the levee *system* robust or resilient as an entire infrastructure. The latter depends on the way the system and its control variables are managed, and a great deal of this book describes the way infrastructures are actually managed for reliability and risk by their respective control rooms.

ICIS6

Control operators of infrastructure systems have to not only manage their interconnections with other systems but reliably manage those interconnections in both latent and manifest states. One main finding of our research is that the connections differ in normal operation from what they are in failure. Manifest interconnections are those that attend infrastructures in normal operations. Latent interconnections are those that emerge and become visible only when one or more of the infrastructures are disrupted or fail. The focus on managing latent and manifest interconnectivity increases the complexity of ICIS reliability management but makes the understanding and management of risks more realistic.

Take a hypothetical example, which we extend later, of oceangoing vessels coming into the San Francisco Bay on their way to the Port of Stockton with shipments to be off-loaded there onto railcars for onward and outward transportation. The Coast Guard's normal operating strategy is based on a pooled or mediated interconnection among all major ships in the bay, with the VTS as the communication hub for them. The vessels receive guidance in relation to one another through VTS as the focal infrastructure. If, however, all VTS communication systems fail, the Coast Guard has to rely on vessel-to-vessel (pilot-to-pilot) communication and coordination to ensure reliable navigation in and through the bay. Under these conditions ships are no longer in a pooled interconnection but in direct interactive or reciprocal interdependency.[3]

Once a vessel reaches Stockton, the port's preferred strategy is assisting the vessel to dock, with prior arrangements having been routinely made by vessels and railroads themselves for on-site union labor to off-load and with railcars waiting and ready to move on. We were told, however, that in a disruption or emergency the port defaults to a more hands-on role, one of mediating between ship, union labor, and rail transportation to coordinate schedules in nonroutine ways. The port takes on an active coordination function it does not normally assume as long as the disruption lasts. Once the cargo is loaded onto rail, the preferred strategy, at least for the rail system we studied, is to route shipments in routine linear sequence to their destinations. If something goes wrong (again, for the system we studied), the default is for shipments to be rerouted through a variety of alternative routes and sequences.

In these cases—Coast Guard, port, and rail—what had been latent configurations of interconnectivity become activated, under stress conditions, as manifest configurations of interconnectivity. We call this ICIS6. We cannot emphasize sufficiently the importance of the ICIS6 perspective, if only because it singles out and highlights the management of latent and not just manifest interconnections. From this perspective, an accident (such as a ship colliding into a bridge) that is averted through management is as much an event as an accident or collision itself. An actively prevented event, through managing shifting interconnectivity configurations, is as real an event as one that could not be prevented. While such a perspective complicates the ICIS picture, these key shifts from latent to manifest make both vulnerabilities and resilience in infrastructures most visible at the ICIS level, as we see later. It is a perspective crucial for the management of reliability and risk across infrastructures.

SUMMARY IMPLICATIONS FOR THE REST OF THE BOOK

The following chapters set the context and framework for drawing out the different ICIS perspectives and their consequences for reliability and risk management at the level of the system of systems and network of networks. The argument and framework are built step by step and block by block (conceptual and empirical). To that end, subsequent chapters detail more fully what is meant by high reliability management and other forms of reliability management under shifting infrastructure conditions or states, the unique organizational niche of control rooms and their operators as reliability managers and risk assessors, the importance of uncertainty and other unpredictabilities in management, the role and types of latent and manifest interconnections among infrastructures, and the implications of our analytic framework for regulation, planning and evaluation, leadership, and finally, for understanding alternative standards of infrastructure reliability.

In the process, we demonstrate that conventional risk analysis is frequently limiting if not misleading when it comes to understanding reliability and risk at the ICIS level. Event- and fault-tree analyses for assessing risk typically have only two states, normal and failed operations. Yet there are equally important additional states—temporary disruption of service that is neither normal nor failed operation, restoration to normal operation after disruption before it worsens to failure, recovery if failure actually happens, and establishment of a new normal afterward—each of which poses its own reliability challenges, gives rise to differing forms of system resilience, and provides a test of how reliable operator risk management strategies may be.

When moving from the element level to the system level, current analytic models of infrastructures connected to each other to form a system of systems often seem an incomprehensible cat's-cradle in which everything is connected to everything else. Yet when we zoom in on any specific set of these interconnections, we are just as apt to find that the links are not comprehensive enough—that is, they do not reflect latent and manifest interconnections but only individual elements that are, at best, correlated with one another.

Much of the more sophisticated network analysis of interinfrastructural interconnectivity suffers from the same defect as sophisticated quantified probability assessments—both assume that if an infrastructure element (node or connection) is not managed, the system is not managed. One clear objective of recent network of networks modeling has been finding out which nodes and connections, when deleted, bring the network or sets of networks to collapse. Were only one more node to fail, the network would suddenly collapse completely, it is often argued.[4]

But "suddenly" is not all that frequent at the ICIS level. In fact, not failing suddenly is what we expect to find in *managed* interconnected systems, in which an infrastructure element can fail without the infrastructure as a whole failing or disrupting the normal operations of other infrastructures depending on that system. Infrastructures instantaneously failing one after another is not what actually happens in many so-called cascades, and we would not expect such near simultaneity from our framework of analysis.

Rapid infrastructure cascades can, of course, happen and were observed in New Orleans during and after Hurricane Katrina and, later, in northern Japan after the earthquake and tsunami of March 2011. Yet interinfrastructure cascades are less common than analysts suppose. Also a surprising feature of some of the worst disasters is a relatively rapid pace of recovery of service, such as in the 2004 Indian Ocean earthquake and tsunami. One reason for the latter, we argue, is the ability of control operators to fashion responses and recovery using interconnected control variables.

How can this happen? Cascade models by and large assume an unmanaged, near-immediate escalation in failure probabilities and consequences across interconnected systems. Yet individual infrastructures do not generally fail instantaneously (brownouts may precede blackouts, levees may seep long before failing), and the transition from normal operation to failure across systems can also take time. Discrete stages of disruption frequently occur when system performance can still be retrievable before the trajectory of failure becomes inevitable.

This means there is a granularity in both space and time between infrastructures in which reliability management can make a difference in the probability of failure of an individual infrastructure and failure across infrastructures. To put the point from the opposite direction, near misses and close calls demonstrate that operators have the time, albeit sometimes just in time, to prevent (significantly more) knock-on effects from initial disruptions or outright failures. This means that buying time for control operators as well as emergency responders can be decisive before system failure and even during it. We believe the greater granularity and time attenuation of interinfrastructural cascades are clearer when analysts and managers realize that the ICIS1 disaster scenario is not the only way critical infrastructure systems are interconnected for reliability and risk.

Infrastructure policy and formal risk management are regularly misunderstood, in other words, because they are often based on misleading models of how systems are managed. In fact, the conventional assumption is that infrastructures are not managed in failure, when the reality is quite different.

In many cases neither infrastructure control rooms nor their reliability contributions disappear during or after a large system failure. Their continued presence has major implications for recovery and for the establishment of a new normal in reliable operations after system failure. It is possible, we show, to evaluate rigorously the efficacy of control room operations in critical infrastructures before, during, and after a failure.

A further implication of our analysis is that as long as infrastructure regulation is equated with formal regulations and their enforcement, we will have a much too narrow understanding of how regulation functions to promote reliability in and across interconnected critical infrastructures. Infrastructure reliability is not just what regulators specify in way of requirements and procedures. It is also what the infrastructure operators and managers do that a regulator of record could never do on its own and that can even correct for errors made by regulators when seeking to ensure the safe and continuous provision of the critical service.

Regulatory reliability itself, we see later, is a significant variable in infrastructure reliability and risk. Too often, accident investigations of infrastructure failures stop at the discovery of human, design, or mechanical error without taking into account the interconnected infrastructure systems in which these elements are located, a stopping point especially worrisome because the very same regulators and policy makers profess that interinfrastructural vulnerabilities and choke points are what increasingly preoccupy them.

The upshot is that the regulators and risk analysts make a huge mistake when missing or dismissing the management dimension that produces reliability in and across infrastructures. It is a major error to conflate or otherwise ignore the differences among ICIS1 through ICIS6 perspectives. While much time and many resources have been allocated to analyzing those ICIS1 scenarios of cascading failure, this must not detract regulators and policy makers from spending far more time and effort on the other ICIS scenarios (including their hybrids) and what they mean for reliable critical infrastructures.

CHAPTER 3

HIGH RELIABILITY
IN CRITICAL
INFRASTRUCTURES

THE BEST-KNOWN BOOK ON THE RISK OF complex technical systems, *Normal Accidents*, written by Charles Perrow in 1984, introduced a vignette that has been modified and updated over the years into a major template for how large system failures emerge from smaller ones such as follows:

Imagine you start the day at home because you're having an important meeting downtown later that morning. Your partner has just left—without, however, having taken the coffee pot off the still-lit gas burner (an initial mistake). The pot's now unusable, but you need that morning fix and end up rifling through cupboards until finding the drip coffee pot. While you wait for the coffee to boil, you watch time tick away on that old cord wall clock. Once you've had the quick cup, you rush out the door to the car, only to realize you've left your cell phone, along with the car and house keys, inside (an additional mistake). Not to worry: you planned ahead for such contingencies by keeping a spare house key hidden outside. But then you remember that you gave that key to a friend, who has yet to return it (a failed redundant pathway). It's getting late, and you can't call anyone, but then there's always the backup of your neighbor's car! Since he doesn't drive much, you can ask him to let you use the hybrid this once. Alas, he tells you that the car's battery isn't working right, and it'll only be fixed later in the day (failed backup system). Well, you sigh, at least there's the bus. But the neighbor has just heard the TV report that bus drivers are on strike (an unavailable work-around). He lets you use his phone to call a taxi, but none are to be had because everyone else is getting a cab now. Nothing available from the ride-share programs either. At this point, you give up and call in saying you can't make the meeting. As a result, those at the meeting think you are unreliable when it matters most (worse ramifications can also follow).

Everyone reading this book has had such experiences or knows of them, and it is a compelling story because we all can imagine how small incidents in large systems accumulate and converge inadvertently in disastrous unreliability.

It seems to us, however, that the vignette highlights another equally important story: even when you had that bad day, the stove burner worked, water came out of the kitchen tap, the electric clock told the time, the neighbor's phone functioned when needed, and the road network was still used, albeit for a different traffic load that morning. Which is to ask: While infrastructures can and do fail because of the concatenation of error and incident and for want of investment, why do so many of them still work as reliably as they do? The answer to this question leads to an even better question: When infrastructure services are operating reliably, in what ways could the using public know—to the same degree that you learned how important the spare key was—just how close to the edge and limits of reliability the provision of these core services really are? This chapter explores at length how we would begin to answer these questions.

IN SOCIETIES SO THOROUGHLY reliant on critical infrastructures for economic productivity and well-being, it is not surprising that debates about them focus on investment. More money is needed for their maintenance and repair, more money is needed for better design, and far more money is required for those "smart" twenty-first-century technologies (smart phones, smart meters, and smart grids, among others).

What *is* surprising is the presumption that the added investment in technology, design, and replacement enhances if not ensures highly reliable infrastructure services. Far too many of these calls for investment miss the fact that management is then required to handle the reconfigured infrastructures and the new surprises never imagined or designed for. Active management of critical infrastructures has always been a necessity, given the abundant evidence that defects continue to be inadvertently baked into large sociotechnical systems at their design and construction stages (Turner 1978; Reason 1990; Bea 2006). When infrastructures end up depending on each other, as they do now, the assumption—build the twenty-first-century infrastructure and of course it will be managed—looks to be the sure road to more vulnerability and surprise and, thus *not* surprisingly, to far greater inefficiencies.[1]

Yet why would anyone be interested in how critical infrastructure operations are actually managed day to day? After all, the promise of innovation, design, and technology is to eliminate the shortcomings and risks of real-time operations.[2] An engineer once told us that the control room operators he was meant to support were "Neanderthals," the prevailing view being that operators are the past, not the future. We live in that interconnected world requiring visionary design and cutting-edge entrepreneurship, one decidedly not requiring any more functionaries intent on retaining antiquated jobs with prehistoric equipment. Why, then, focus on *current-day* infrastructure management in any more depth?

Our answer is that operators are responsible in practice (and often in accountability) for the high reliability management of our critical infrastructures, a high reliability mandated by law and regulation, public and political demand, and organizational mission. No technology or innovation is free of defect when it comes to real-time operations, and high reliability managers take real-time risks that follow very, very seriously. Who, looking at the evidence, can really expect risky contingencies to be eliminated by formal design and high-level strategy? And if these risks can't be managed now, how can we expect them to be managed later on?

The priority given to real-time risk management was evident in every control room we studied. One infrastructure, the Coast Guard's command center on Yerba Buena Island in San Francisco Bay, has its own formal, real-time risk assessment protocol for its search and rescue operations. "Everywhere there are risks, and you have to manage them," said one utility specialist with operations and emergency response experience. Operators may commit errors, but just as certainly infrastructure operators prevent all manner of errors, accidents, and failures that would have happened had the operators not been there to anticipate, correct, or mitigate them. This happens day in and day out across the world, saving many lives and vast sums of money. Indeed, when consulted—consultation is less frequent than one might suppose[3]—control operators do work to mitigate errors in the strategy and high-level design so prized by engineers and policy makers.

But high reliability management of a critical infrastructure is more than crisis prevention. It's both risk management and protection of the reliability managers who manage the risks. This chapter summarizes the rudiments of high reliability management in the critical infrastructures we have examined. We start with a discussion of a precluded-events standard for high reliability and then tracing its implications for managing operator precursor zones, maintaining reliability bandwidths, and avoiding unstudied conditions.

Nothing in what follows should leave the reader with any impression that high reliability always works, or can be established for all settings, or once established in a given setting is self-sustaining or persists indefinitely. In fact, by the end of this book, we will have demonstrated that alternative standards for infrastructure reliability are often evident in interconnected settings. Ensuring the safe and continuous provision of a critical service during the most difficult times requires a great deal of hard work, skill, and vigilance on the part of infrastructure operators; there is no recipe in any of this. We have observed the reliability they add to their technical systems in ways that even some of their superiors, and particularly external designers, regulators, and policy makers, do not understand or sufficiently appreciate.

THE PRECLUDED-EVENTS STANDARD
FOR HIGH RELIABILITY

The cornerstone for the pursuit of high reliability in organizations managing hazardous technical systems (such as nuclear reactors or air traffic control) is public dread of the hazards (Schulman 2004). This dread is both a constraint and a support. It constrains because careful and often-hostile media and regulatory scrutiny attend the operation of the hazardous systems and any errors made in their operation. It supports reliability in organizations because it can protect them from pressures of unregulated market competition or high-risk policy making and can also justify major budgetary expenditures to keep their operations safe.

The existence of a certain class of events—so awful they must never happen—has been crucial to the establishment and furtherance of high reliability in society's critical infrastructures (Roe and Schulman 2008). Significantly for our analysis, the logic of must-never-happen events can be extended to avoiding operational conditions that could be precursors to a dreaded event and that, as a matter of priority, operators also seek to avoid. Avoiding precursor events is, in this logic, a key way to prevent the precluded must-never-happen events. Without this set of precluded and avoided events, it would be very difficult for infrastructure operators to determine with clarity what are acceptable or unacceptable risks in real time. On the basis of this analysis, what are or are not acceptable risks follows from having adopted the precluded-events standard for high reliability management (a major reason why "reliability" precedes "risk" in this book's title).

The examples are many. Those managing California's state and federal water projects operate so as to avoid having to shut down the project pumps unexpectedly. "Never stop exports," one control operator for the federal Central Valley Project put it; a senior SWP staff person told us, "I don't want to hear, 'Shut down the pumps.'" The U.S. Bureau of Reclamation (USBR) manages in order to avoid overtopping of its major reservoirs.[4] "The last thing you want is to overtop a dam," said an official.[5] East Bay Municipal Utility District (EBMUD) manages its major water aqueduct to avoid anything that would crack or otherwise break the pipeline structure. "Whatever you do, don't shut down a[n EBMUD] pipe during a flood," we were told. Water utilities aim to avoid having their systems bled out, because with no water left in the pipes it is very difficult to find pipe breaks.

The Contra Costa Water District is managed to avoid contamination of its water supply with giardia or cryptosporidium and to keep its reservoirs from falling below fire-control supplies. The California Department of Forestry and Fire Protection (Cal Fire)—"You expect us to be there and do it," one official said—manages so as to avoid endangering firefighters. The Port of Stockton manages in order to avoid major accidents, such as those involving tankers with anhydrous ammonia, and to maintain its reputation for reliable service. "We have to make things work here, or we won't have customers," a senior port manager told us. "Our customers are very important, and it's important to be on time" is the way a Union Pacific manager put the railroad's priority. Those managing California's electricity transmission grid do so to avoid a major real-time imbalance between load and generation and, ultimately, a collapse of connectivity between generators and transmission lines, a condition known as "islanding," which would cause widespread blackouts. The Coast Guard's VTS manages so as to avoid collisions and allisions of vessels or grounding a vessel, and to do that it must avoid loss of direct communications with the vessels in their regulated navigation area.

We argue that the seriousness with which precluded and avoided events are treated in infrastructures does not come about just because they are authorized and mandated in legislation, regulations, or a mission statement. They are treated very seriously because they establish and reinforce the culture and motivation of operators in the control rooms of infrastructures that have such control centers. Before turning to the special features of control rooms, note the potential for conflict at the ICIS level of different precluded events. Precluding events in one system may introduce uncertainty or ambiguity in other infrastructures. Precluding overtopping of major reservoirs has led to, we were told, unscheduled releases of water that threatened downstream levees. We return to conflicting precluded- and other-event standards in subsequent chapters.

SPECIAL PROPERTIES OF INFRASTRUCTURE
CONTROL ROOMS

What did not become clear to us until we studied control rooms in inter-infrastructural settings was just how special an organizational phenomenon control rooms are. Infrastructure control rooms—and again not all critical infrastructures, as officially classified, have such control centers—are one of the few organizational frameworks that have evolved to promote high reliability in the management of complex sociotechnical systems over time and in real time. They are found in diverse settings, such as air traffic control, power plants, electrical grids, large water systems, rail networks, telecommunications networks, and nuclear missile and air defense command operations. While water differs from electricity and both differ from telecommunications or air traffic control, control rooms in different infrastructures share the same aim:

managing a critical service reliably, now. Reliability is not a contested concept for these operators and managers. Control rooms are the only place, we have found, where "water reliability," "electricity reliability," "telecom reliability," along with their counterparts in other infrastructures, have very real and consensual meaning, priority, and urgency—no matter how different the respective regulatory standards and mechanisms.

Yet infrastructure control rooms are under-researched in the organizational literature, and this is doubly true for the control room–to–control room relationships discussed in this book. A good deal has been written about control rooms in terms of their physical design and technology, and they have been analyzed from the standpoint of human factors research (Noyes and Bransby 2002; Stanton et al. 2009; Ivergard and Hunt 2008). But organizational analyses are few (Klein 1999; Perrin 2005; Sanne 2000; Woods and Hollnagel 2006; Roe and Schulman 2008; Mohammad, Johansen, and Almklov 2014).

Control rooms have important properties that distinguish them from many of the organizations described in contemporary organization theory and management. The control rooms discussed in this book have at least six properties of special significance when it comes to reliability and risk management in the infrastructures they operate, which we briefly outline here.

1. Centrality in relation to multiple networked units. Control rooms are not themselves centralized but have centrality in communication and coordination responsibilities. They often have legal authority over network participants, but the authority is grounded in the functional design and mandates of the large sociotechnical system in question.

These networked elements are frequently geographically dispersed (often part of separate organizations) and are brought into a functional interrelationship by control room personnel who are situated to monitor and coordinate their actions to produce a mutually desired output. Control room personnel are centrally placed to interpret, integrate, and propagate information, instructions, and risks in ways necessary to achieve reliable real-time operation well beyond the limits of foresight in any initial design and technology.

2. Control as a networked process. Control operators often do not run their systems directly by throwing switches or turning valves. Instead they offer instructions, frequently oral or otherwise communicated, to others who do throw switches, turn valves, or steer. These people are typically located some distance away from the source of the instructions. Even when a control operator pushes buttons or taps a keyboard, it is likely to be control at a distance—through electronic instructions or relay switches.

The control in a control room is complex coordination—operators take small, highly influential actions over short time intervals that cause larger actions to take place over a longer time. In this way, the potential for error is managed but always with recognition that even small energies can release much larger ones.

The networked relationship among component units is a defining feature of infrastructures. Even though control room centrality may give logical pre-eminence to its operators' instructions, participants within the networks must trust this logic and be willing to follow often-shifting instructions (and with them, shifting risks). At one point, a CAISO transmission grid operator told us in our earlier round of research, "We're not really the CAISO control area, we're the CAISO request area" (Roe and Schulman 2008, 242). A senior VTS official interviewed for this book noted similar contingent authority in the Coast Guard's control room. If VTS observes a sudden loss of vessel propulsion, its control operators defer to the shipboard pilot and offer assistance if needed: "You try to give them [ship captains and pilots] a directive without it sounding like one. . . . We direct for outcomes, not process, because we can't see what they see [at water level]."

3. Team organization with overlapping functions. Control rooms are team efforts. Role specialization among members is generally less discrete than that found in conventionalized bureaucratic settings. If the control room is organized by function—for example, generation dispatchers as distinct from transmission dispatchers in an electric grid control room or primary- versus secondary-side operators in a nuclear power plant control room—the close-coordination requirements for components of the infrastructure lead to overlapping attention during operation and disturbances. If the organization base is jurisdictional, as in the sector organization of air traffic control, the overlap occurs around the handoff of traffic from one sector to another. But during peak-load periods or with an airliner in trouble, overlapping attention becomes essential.

This is not the case just in air traffic centers. An experienced supervisor in the Coast Guard command center confirmed that "too much concentration of issues at one desk will lead to others automatically sharing the load," and a senior VTS manager stressed the need for sharing of both attention and experience: "That's why the cumulative experience in the VTS is so important. There's great benefit in having somebody really experienced in a different sector sitting next to you." We observed overlapping attention in all the control rooms we studied.

Most control operators work in shifts. We often heard that shifts differ in their behavior, a reflection of the character of team interaction of members. This in turn is a function of the distinctive personalities of the operators in the shift. Positions and roles in control rooms are not affectively neutral, as bureaucratic ideals of conventional organizations might have it. They are more personalized and a product of differentiated experiences and careers worked over different settings and times.

At the same time, however, roles have a collective rather than individual orientation. The team relations involve crosscutting communication during peak periods or disruption or crisis. The team collectively embodies the skill-based knowledge of control room operations. Control operators in nuclear power plants and electric grid centers, among others, formulate a set of action scenarios, each an if-then algorithm to cover responses to past issues. A VTS official told us that VTS control room traffic management had a great deal "to do with the what-if game, especially . . . do[ing] a what-if based on what's actually happening elsewhere." These what-if scenarios, once formulated, are held in mental inventory, available for recall to the conscious "workspace" of problem solving (Reason 1990) and as "schema" to guide decisions (Klein 1999).

Because no single individual in a shift is able to recall every pertinent scenario, the team forms a collective repository of memory. The return of a member to a team or shift after being away brings with it a gap in information and situational awareness: "You've had the crisis du jour [under way], so when [the dispatcher] comes back from vacation, here's a new crisis and [he or she] won't know what they're talking about," an infrastructure manager said, underscoring a widespread observation that there can be "definite problems during the periods of relieving operators or shift changes."

In addition, control room teams assemble a wide distribution of analytic and experience-based approaches that promote high reliability management. When asked whether different VTS traffic managers had different styles, one answered, "Definitely. Some are more risk averse; some are less."[6] We also found different types of dispatchers in our earlier research (Roe and Schulman 2008). The point here is that the constellation of types allows the shift crew to enhance its coverage and management of risks across several cognitive fronts: from critical analysis to experiential-based practices to rule-following orientations. What might look like an operator breaking a formal rule under exceptional conditions, for example, can instead be a case of that operator having learned through prior experience with others when not to follow the rule in order to ensure real-time reliability.

4. Near self-sufficiency of motivation. We also found that control room operators in shifts, along with their immediate support staff, frequently approach a self-sufficiency in their motivation for reliable performance. Better than others in the infrastructure, they understand how the system operates, the major risks incurred, and what must be done to keep the system as a working system.

To that end, control room operators are knitted together in the multiple logics of functional requirements to meet their various technical, legal, regulatory, and mission mandates for reliability. Their commitment to reliability is tied closely to their identity as control operators working with others on the shift and in support of them.[7] Their task overlap works against the development of frames of reference or modes of behavior that draw them outside their shared domain of competence. This form of motivational near self-sufficiency is important, especially so when infrastructure operations are disrupted or worse, as may happen in the context of ICISs.[8]

5. Coordination through a small set of control variables grounded in a clear, consensus-based causal model of how the infrastructure system operates.[9] Management of control variables is the process variance that converts an infrastructure's inputs into reliable outputs. Since control variables and the conditions under which they are managed are extremely important, we introduce them here and discuss them in detail later.

The design logic and the reliability mandates relevant to a large sociotechnical system are based on a causal model or models that identify essential control variables—a relatively small set of variables for which immediate action can be taken and whose changes in value are central to processes that manage the safe and continuous provision of service at the system level. Control operators in the SWP regulate pumps and floodgates to control the flow rates of water into and out of reservoirs and across dams. In like fashion, electric transmission grid controllers focus on directing generation amounts in relation to changes in load. They can also direct flow along alternative transmission lines and exert control over voltage and frequency. The infrastructures we have studied could not have stable outputs in terms of their services without these processes, and core to the effectiveness of the processes are control variables.

Control variables allow operators to leverage much larger adjustments from a limited set of relatively small changes. A key feature of the control variables is that they are actionable in real time. No extended planning or approval process is required. The most critical judgments and actions reflecting the full skills of operators are brought to bear in real time, and process variance is managed in ways that transform highly varied inputs into the output of stable service provision at that time. This means that when there are problems in ensuring coordination through control variables, it is almost always an issue for the control room.

6. Low-friction control variables. While other organizations have control variables, the role the variables have in control rooms differs from their role conventionally. In contrast to the stable control variables in most organizations (particularly their policies, rules, and procedures), which impose relatively persisting behavioral constraints, operators in control rooms can manage their control variables quite rapidly and flexibly—one instruction can quickly undo another. "Once [control operators] get the change in the allotment and a new plan, it's pretty much a change that can be done rapidly," a senior SWP control manager told us about unscheduled changes in daily water schedules. In conventional organizations, many policies, rules, and procedures are far more "sticky"—in fact their persistence is an important feature for the control of a conventional organization's behavior.

Air traffic controllers also must be able to order a rapid series of adjustments in airspeed, direction, and altitude of planes in their sectors. Generation dispatchers order increases or decreases in electricity generation among operating plants, order reserve generators on- or off-line, or make adjustments in response to sudden frequency changes across transmission lines and reroute power to avoid line congestion. Dynamic risks could not be managed without flexible, low-friction control variables. Not unexpectedly then, the potential loss of flexibility via new procedures can become a focus of control room attention. "Most of the calls are about clarifying procedures," said a control room manager about those less frequent occasions when dispatchers contact him when he is off-site. We return to procedure clarification and other means to increase options and flexibility in our later discussion of the operators' comfort zone.

The ability to make changes readily in control variables requires a reciprocal willingness in network participants to accept these instructional changes and act on them. Here too, control requires trust among network participants, trust that the control variable changes called for reflect a larger picture and a system logic that they may not see. Control in this way requires the ability of both control operators and participants to adjust rapidly in real time and a willingness of others to forgo rigidifying those adjustment behaviors.

IN THIS ANALYSIS, risks are not just shared through the physical connections in a networked system; they are shared through trust among operators in real time. The challenges are palpable, and never more so than when seeking to manage control variables across infrastructures. Both within and across infrastructures a great deal of control room management consists of learning what are and are not acceptable risks in real time. "One guy has been here for years, and he is still learning new things, mainly because operational parameters have to be adjusted as conditions change," a control operator told us, and this must also be said for others.

Current risk assessments of infrastructure vulnerabilities find it a fairly straightforward matter to show how vulnerability is related to a host of external factors, such as changing politics and regulation, poor policy making, volatile markets, and fickle shifts in society and culture. Such factors have been critical, but they by no means provide an adequate picture of how infrastructures change. These conventional explanations have missed the unique organizational properties just discussed that control rooms represent for design and practice. Change any one of the six interrelated control room features internally and that has direct knock-on effects for reliability management. Unusually high rates of turnover and attrition in control room operators because of promotions or retirements have immediate consequences for shift composition, crew interactions, and team situational awareness. Infrastructures as large sociotechnical systems are dynamic internal environments requiring very skilled professionals in their control rooms, even during their ostensibly slow times.

CONTROL ROOM SKILLS AND RELIABILITY PROFESSIONALS

So critical is the role of control room operators, managers, and support staff to the high reliability management of critical infrastructures that we have in prior writing termed them "reliability professionals" (Roe and Schulman 2008, 6). They are professionals, not through formal academic training and higher-degree programs, but typically through special cognitive skills as well as long careers and deep experience that have exposed them to the many facets of the large sociotechnical systems being managed for high reliability.

Referring to port operations, a senior manager told us, "It's its own discipline, this industry. You can graduate from the [nearby] Maritime Academy, but you need to have years of experience. . . . No one person has it in his head; we all do. It's part of being in this industry; you just get to know how things are interconnected, and you do a lot of collaboration." These professionals, we continue to find, are likely to be positioned in and around the control rooms or operations centers, as teams or networks of operators, shift supervisors, department heads, or technical specialists, to bridge the higher-level arenas of design and strategy with the lower-level of field operations and maintenance. This bridging function is connected with their special cognitive orientation to the work of the infrastructure. We illustrate this with Figure 3.1, which we developed in our earlier research (Roe and Schulman 2008) and then modified to fit the ICIS framework of this book.

Cognitively, the quest for reliability in a critical infrastructure occurs along two dimensions: (1) the character of knowledge brought to bear on efforts to render an operation or system reliable and (2) the focus of attention or scope of these reliability efforts. The knowledge base can range from formal, or representational, knowledge, in which key activities are understood through abstract principles and deductive models based on these principles,

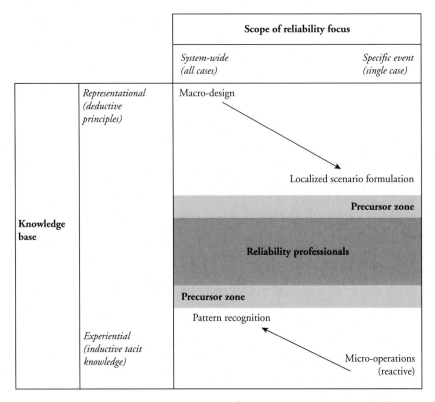

FIGURE 3.1   Reliability space for reliability professionals. *Source:* Roe and Schulman 2008, 71.

to experience, based on informal induction (pattern recognition) or tacit understanding.

At the same time, the scope of attention ranges from a purview that embraces reliability as a stream of predictable system outputs, encompassing many variables and elements, to a case-by-case focus in which each case is viewed as an event with its own distinct properties or characteristics. As for the latter, "there are hundreds of hydro units out there, and each one has its own issues," a grid planner told us.

Toward the extreme of both scope and principles is the macro-design approach to reliability. Here formal deductive principles are applied to understanding critical processes. It is inappropriate under this approach to operate beyond design analysis, and this analysis is meant to cover an entire critical system, including every important performance condition. Design in this sense is more than analysis; it is a major control instrument for system behavior. This approach dominates operations in nuclear power plants, where operating outside analysis is a major regulatory violation (Schulman 1993). At the other cognitive extreme is continually reactive behavior in the face of real-time shocks and surprises at the micro-operations level. Here reliability resides in the reaction time of system operators working at the event level rather than the anticipation of every eventuality by system designers. The focus of crisis managers and emergency responders may be exemplary in this regard.

The macro and micro extremes at either corner are, however, insufficient to ensure high reliability. Designers cannot foresee everything, and some degree of design error is inevitable. On the other side, case-by-case reactions may give an operator too specific and idiographic a perspective, losing sight of the forest for the trees. Experience in micro-operations can become a trained incapacity, undermining system reliability when operators are not aware of the wider ramifications of their actions.

What is the best strategy then, when the aim is high reliability? Attempting a direct connection across the reliability space from left top macro corner to right bottom micro corner is unlikely to be successful. A great deal of research confirms that attempts to impose large-scale formal designs directly onto an individual case—to anticipate, deduce, and determine the behavior of each instance from system-wide principles alone—are very risky (Perrow [1984] 1999; Majone 1978; Turner 1978). From the other side, reactive operations by the individual hardly constitute a template for scaling up to the system level.

Instead of corner-to-corner movements, Figure 3.1 indicates that reliability is enhanced when *shifts in scope are accompanied by shifts in the knowledge base.* This is the pivotal strategy for reliability professionals in critical infrastructures. It means that the dominance in conventional risk assessment and management of ICIS1 disaster scenarios, in which fully stressed and unmanaged infrastructures fail over into interinfrastructural cascades, actually *ignores* the knowledge and scope necessary to understand and manage risk in interconnected infrastructures. This is one reason why formal-risk analysts usually do not function as reliability professionals.[10] A key difference between their perspective and the multiple perspectives on ICISs (ICIS1 through ICIS6, described in Chapter 2) is that each successive frame adds different types of knowledge while shifting the scope of analysis of how infrastructure reliability can be managed.

Given the limitations of the extremes in the reliability space, it is important for reliability that operations take place in positions closer to a cognitive center that moves away (1) from "firefighting" reactions in a single case to pattern recognition across cases and (2) from system-wide designs to scenario formulation for action contingent on local situations and conditions. These skills in recognizing patterns outside formal designs and in formulating scenarios, often in real-time, set reliability professionals apart from many other professionals.

We know from research that reliability is enhanced when managers, technical personnel, and operators apply designs less globally and relax their commitment to principles that fully determine system operations. This happens when they embrace a wider range of contingencies in their application of design principles and customize scenarios to fit the case at hand. "Every case has its own response; it's not like we can say something covers every instance," a utility grid manager told us. From the other direction, reliability is enhanced when operations shift away from real-time firefighting and quick fixes toward the recognition of patterns and trends across cases in the system or even across systems and the imputed consequences of these for reliability.

We find the domain of reliability professionals in the middle ground. Control room operators and support personnel are reliability professionals because they have the distinctive knowledge base that keeps complex infrastructures reliable. They are neither big-picture system designers nor exclusively reactive field workers. They excel in discovering patterns and trends and in formulating scenarios and protocols to cover contingencies.[11] In doing so, they translate recognized patterns and contingent scenarios into reliable service provision. "We're translators [between ships and tugboats]," said a VTS operator. "I see myself as a translator [between CAISO and other decision makers]," a senior CAISO official told us. When it comes to the patterns and scenarios to be translated, what a Cal Fire official wanted most from those who staff command centers was "time in the field, lots of experience, and lots of different experience, plus good communications skills." A senior county emergency manager said that what sets apart seasoned emergency responders from others is that they can say, "I've seen this before." Thus, when a control operator says, as one did to us, "I've not seen this before," this was a call for experienced support. "There are a great many engineering and human-factors elements that come into play in each vessel transit," a retired Coast Guard specialist with an interest in high reliability management wrote us, "and the importance of experience cannot be overestimated in managing the slate of control measures that might be put in place to ensure a safe transit."[12]

This middle ground is not easy to claim in operational practice and if secured not guaranteed to persist, even when senior executives of the organization insist they too take reliability seriously. Organization designers and regulators may fully embrace both the technical and the legal logic of procedures, demand that all actions be taken following formal rules, and punish all deviation from these rules (Schulman 2013). Operators may consequently be given specific orders for specific actions in individual cases, orders that ignore the larger risks for such actions. In these instances organizations discount the expertise and special skills of reliability professionals in their cognitive space. However, this middle ground of reliability professionals is where system-wide designs and case-specific problems must be reconciled and where action on new cases must be transformed into a unique knowledge base for reliability management. In this sense the domain of the reliability professional is a crucible for the continual generation of new knowledge covering the reliable operation of a complex sociotechnical system, a core part of which is *knowledge about risks that follow from the standards of reliability being managed to.*

Let's stay with Figure 3.1 a moment longer, as it highlights four features of that link between reliability and the knowledge of risks just mentioned:

1. Translating unique knowledge. Since reliability professionals have wide experiential knowledge about operations that no one else in the large sociotechnical system has, it isn't surprising they find it difficult to explain to outsiders just what they are doing by way of managing from the middle. Nor is it surprising when the skills in pattern recognition and scenario formulation developed in one infrastructure are not transferable to other infrastructures. "Once I was talking to a [ship] pilot, and we were thinking of bringing pilots into the control room, but he said right off that he would not necessarily be a good VTS control operator. His point was that pilots aren't trained to be watching other pilots [as traffic managers do here]," a senior VTS manager said.

Operator knowledge of risks is not easily distilled into definitions or formulae. This is why these professionals resist efforts to render hard-to-translate knowledge into a well-demarcated set of macro-design principles or micro-operations checklists—though operators do update procedures and protocols in light of gained knowledge, as Coast Guard informants underscored. As we show later, the shared background of experience and operating assumptions provides another foundation from which risks are managed—particularly latent risks in interconnectivity.

2. Networked professionals. Where you see one reliability professional, you see more of them. It always bears repeating that high reliability management of critical infrastructures is so complex that no one professional could do all that needs to be done in the moment in which it needs to be done. Individuals on their own have cognitive limits and a bounded rationality that must be adjusted for with the help of teamwork.[13] High reliability management requires a team of professionals to have situational awareness, which is one reason why infrastructures are networked around control rooms. "We're an extension of the bridge team on the ship and can look way out farther than they can see," is the way a control room operator for the VTS put it.

For good reasons then, the *lack* of networked situational awareness is taken by many to be a major challenge to high reliability management.[14] One major finding of what has become known as the Great Blackout of 2011 (the September 2011 blackout of major parts of the U.S. Southwest, including parts of California) was the lack of real-time situational awareness among electricity transmission operators in the region, including the Arizona Public Service and CAISO (FERC and NERC 2012). If as we argue, situational awareness for high reliability management depends on networked professionals, then the issue of leadership and accountability in infrastructures becomes more complicated than many think, a point we return to in Chapter 10.

When high reliability demands require interorganizational coordination, reliability professionals often use informal networks of communication across the organizations. "I try to work the informal connections," a port manager told us. "Because of my permitting work with the regional water quality control board, I hope they can feel pretty confident about what we do here with respect to use of dredging material." "I have people call me . . . and ask me how confident I am in the forecast," a senior meteorologist told us. "They want personal verification about how confident we are in our forecasts. I know these people, and they know me. . . . Informal interpersonal communication is very important."

3. Identifying a precursor zone. Figure 3.1's precursor zone is best thought of as that set of system conditions to be avoided, particularly those that challenge the cognitive abilities of operators and their support staff. The precursor zone is where the skills of operators to recognize patterns and formulate scenarios are substantially challenged, as these skills are no longer matched to the intensified or novel conditions and tasks they now face. This is where operators may no longer be clear on what activities could lead to disruption or failure. As we argue earlier, high reliability management depends on a clear, shared identification of what constitutes precursor conditions, widespread acceptance of the need to protect operations from entering this zone, and if entered, support for actionable strategies to vacate it as soon as possible.

A precursor zone is not defined solely by objective technical criteria. It includes conditions deemed unacceptable for high reliability management by reliability professionals, who will work extremely hard to get out of them as soon as they can. We discuss the comfort zone of control room operators in Chapter 5.

4. Beyond risk into unstudied conditions. When operators are pushed out of their precursor zone into conditions altogether unfamiliar or unstudied, then system reliability confronts a huge hazard. Infrastructure operators being pushed into or beyond the precursor zone happens with a major disaster, but here too professionals know the great hazard of having to work outside the domain of competence.

Just what is that hazard of being in the precursor zone, at the limits of one's skills in pattern recognition and scenario formulation? When reliability professionals are pushed into and out beyond their precursor zone into unstudied conditions, they are pushed into areas for which risk cannot even be calculated, either as probabilities of failure (which depends on their skills in pattern recognition) or as consequences of failure in a worst-case scenario (which depends on their skills in scenario formulation).

Many worse-case interinfrastructural failures identified in our research have this aspect of being at the edge of or beyond the known. A Coast Guard emergency specialist started with this example: "Let's say a passenger ship has to come into a berth down in a [Bay Area] port because it was diverted from somewhere else. That's two thousand people who now need to get out of a city they haven't intended to visit, and that impacts airplanes and buses and other transportation. And then no ship that size would want to leave empty, so where are they going to get their passengers?" In a world where failure connects infrastructures in unpredictable ways, the risk of failure not only becomes extremely difficult to compute, but all manner of danger lurks in that incalculability.

SURPRISE, REQUISITE VARIETY, AND IMPLICATIONS
FOR CONTROL ROOM SKILL SETS

Because of component complexity and variety in large networked socio-technical systems and the variety of external factors that affect them (weather, fire, earthquake, or failure in other infrastructures), control room operators are inescapably confronted with unusual, varied, and surprising challenges and risks in their operations. "Sailboats do their own thing—they follow the wind," a VTS traffic manager told us after an incident involving one. "Any day is a crap shoot; it could be an earthquake," one Delta island specialist told us—or "a beaver," immediately added another. "We had snakes and cows on the plat-form during the 1970s flood, and no one planned for that problem!" a natural gas expert told us with respect to his company's major Delta gas facilities. "It rained in June. I mean, it rained in June!" an experienced but still surprised water control dispatcher told us. "Our [weather forecast] model, like others, is very good but not good for extreme conditions," a CAISO specialist said. "One degree off is one thousand megawatts, so three degrees, it's three thou-sand megawatts, which means a lot of additional generation will be needed." It is not unexpected, then, that such large systems require their own kind of reliability management and that their risk management is geared to meeting their formal reliability mandates.

In single self-contained high reliability organizations, low output variance in operations (the high reliability) is maintained by controlling inputs. Guns, gates, and guards have stabilized the physical environment of nuclear power plants. The plants are treated as baseload generators, so they are not subject to meeting fluctuating electricity demand. Nuclear power operating regulations affecting all plants are meant to protect plants and their owner utilities from highly competitive market pressures. Low and controlled input variance, then, allows low output variance to occur by means of low process variance—that is, rules, procedures, routines, strategies, and anticipatory planning.

But in the intense, dynamic, and networked settings faced by the control rooms that we have been researching for a decade and more, it is far harder to control inputs. "Surprises I expect," a Coast Guard watch supervisor in the VTS told us. "Murphy is always waiting out there," a PG&E electric grid manager said. Fires or weather at a distance can confront water and electricity control rooms with unpredictable outages and disruption. Demand for power can fluctuate dramatically throughout the day, building to peak-load periods and dropping off swiftly as night approaches and businesses close. Water utilities have their own demand curves and are affected by demand fluctuations affecting the electric grid they depend on. With high input fluctuation comes a greater managerial challenge to both the grid and water supply in producing low output variance. Operational reliability under these conditions lies in transforming the high input variance into the low output variance through higher *process* variance. This includes customizing some responses to input conditions by improvising and inventing options. By adding to their options variety, operators manage to keep system operations within de jure and de facto bandwidths for safe and continuous service provision (Roe et al. 2005).

"Most of the time the parameters [we work within] are wide enough that if we see an issue, we can meet the issue within the parameters," one control operator said. The Army Corps of Engineers and the USBR ensure that water levels in major Delta reservoirs do not exceed their regulated flood management reserve space, the SWP has maximum and minimum levels for pumping into its water collection reservoirs, and CAISO manages the Area Control Error (generation and load imbalances) of its transmission grid within parameters prescribed by regulators. The operations center for the Contra Costa Water District has time-of-use restrictions imposed by PG&E on its electricity use for pumping, just as the SWP runs its pumping schedules so as to sell its electricity during on-peak hours.

In summary, transforming high input variance into low output variance requires high process variance via flexibility in operator strategies and options across bandwidths—a "requisite variety" of responses, in other words, to match the variety of input conditions.[15] The pursuit of requisite variety to buffer the consequences of surprise leads to the distinctive cognitive approach of control room operators. When the unexpected happens and operators breach the bandwidths, they are pushed into their precursor zone or beyond; the key then is to have options and resources for bouncing back within the bandwidths (i.e., to move back from the precursor zone). This ability to bounce back we call *precursor resilience*, and we return to it in the next chapter.[16]

When operating in their unique domain of competence, control operators can increase their process variance by relying on a set of complementary performance modes within and across which they can operate depending on conditions affecting their infrastructure. These range from anticipatory exploration of options (just in case) when operations are routine and many control strategies and options are available, to a real-time (just in time) improvisation of options and strategies (i.e., adding to requisite variety) when task conditions are unstable. Operators may have to operate temporarily in a high-risk mode (just for now) when system instability is high and options are few and may also be able, in emergencies when options have dwindled, to impose onto network participants a single emergency scenario (just this way) in order to stabilize a situation. These alternative but interrelated performance modes are part of an overall requisite variety of responses needed to match the full range of input that variance operators can encounter in their systems. Yet as we see later, each performance mode has its own risks, and the challenge in control rooms is to manage the risks as conditions and options change— often in surprising ways.

Finally, since different infrastructures respond to different conditions with differing options, requisite variety across infrastructures has had to be high as well. We have been struck by the diversity of skills, outlooks, and units when infrastructures are considered within a multi-ICIS context as sketched in Chapter 2. What for some appears to be a source of vulnerability arising out of interconnectivity—the system of systems or network of networks, it is often said, is no stronger than its weakest infrastructure—turns out on closer inspection to potentially contain more options at the cross-systems level. When an infrastructure fails, others depending on it find ways to work around that failure, though again there are no guarantees.

OPERATIONAL REDESIGN AS THE EVOLUTIONARY
ADVANTAGE OF CONTROL ROOMS FOR
RELIABILITY MANAGEMENT

Control room operators do learn. Operators confronted by surprise add to or discard from their repertoire of recognized patterns and formulated scenarios. This is what gives them their evolutionary advantage: learning in ways that do not risk the survival of the systems they must operate and manage reliably (see Rochlin 1993).

The control room advantage lies in the ability to operationally redesign inevitably incomplete design and technology. Many defects, no matter how thorough the prior troubleshooting, become visible only in real-time operations—and then only as surprises—and it is in real time that high reliability management must reduce the risks arising out of such flaws. This means that new designs and technologies have to be redesigned during actual operations, or operators face the risks of (sub)system disruption or, worse, outright failure. In this way, high reliability is about operational knowledge catching up with the limitations of macro-design and micro-experience and in the process redefining for the future what that experience and design should be all about.

Many control operators term operational redesigns "work-arounds," which are typically disparaged by macro-designers, and work-arounds vary considerably. In a good many cases, work-arounds are necessary to ensure that control operators are comfortable with software and the givens of hardware. Also, work-arounds that started out as temporary become in some cases more or less permanent as formal patches to ill-designed software and hardware.

But even here, there are patches and then there are patches. What one worker on the Deepwater Horizon drilling rig told investigators holds generally: "We can only work around so much" (Urbina 2010, A1). Allowable work-arounds are at times limited to specified material or options available, such as on a minimum equipment list for commercial airline flights. But work-arounds are not the only example of operational redesigns. Resetting the de facto or de jure bandwidths for reliability management is also important when operator experience across a wide range of cases demonstrates that the margins for real-time adjustments can be changed. Under crisis conditions, for example, grid dispatchers may allow a transmission line to operate temporarily at or slightly above recommended capacity limits when they know from prior experience that these brief excursions have been successfully handled. Reset bandwidths can be as positive a reliability innovation as new software and technology that have been operationally redesigned. This holds, however, only when innovations are derived from or consonant with operator experience and not imposed from outside control rooms for reasons that may undermine reliability, such as a conventionalized reducing excess capacity to cut costs. When reliability of control operations ceases to be the norm and becomes instead the *problem* economists and risk analysts must solve, critical infrastructures are at added risk.

The evolutionary advantage of control operators as operational redesigners reflects the control room's unique organizational niche. Infrastructure control rooms occupy a central institutional location in which conflicting values or hard issues are often balanced (see, e.g., Steenhuisen 2009). Many conventional organizations try to reconcile conflicting values, such as reliability and efficiency, by policy that locks in a trade-off across time and multiple cases. But control rooms can adjust these balances to real time and to specific cases and still not lose track of reliability mandates or precluded and precursor events across the cases.

MULTIPLE MODES FOR RELIABILITY: NORMAL, DISRUPTED, FAILED, RECOVERED, AND NEW NORMAL STATES FOR INFRASTRUCTURES

So far, most of our analysis of infrastructure reliability has focused on what we now know to be a narrow concept of reliability—operational reliability within a single infrastructure at any one time. It is necessary to expand this frame and recognize that reliability in critical infrastructures has different meaning across different conditions or states and also at the enlarged scale and scope of interconnected infrastructures.[17]

While formal risk methodologies typically assume that infrastructures have only two states that matter, normal and failed, reliability is operationally important for six different states when it comes to managing empirical risks: *normal operations, disruption* with or without *restoration, failure, recovery,* and the establishment of a *new normal.* Obviously operating reliability is directed toward maintaining operations continuously. But in highly dynamic networked systems this may not be possible and alternative states occur: *disruption*, which we define as a temporary and often partial loss of function or service, generally not over twenty-four hours, or *failure*, the loss of function or service, associated with the destruction of structures, equipment, or other assets and lasting considerably longer than twenty-four hours. The state of disrupted service is transient and can lead to two follow-on states: *restoration* that can lead back to normal operation or disruption that can fall over into failure. Failure, given its association with the destruction of assets, can be protracted and may be terminated only by *recovery* and a *new normal*.

What does reliability mean for these additional infrastructure states? In disruption, reliability is associated with the speed and surety of restoration to normal operation and the decreased likelihood that disruption will decay or flip into failure. In disruption, the services—not the infrastructures—disappear, and control operator reliability during disrupted service can be directed to containing lags, lapses, and errors that would delay restoration.

In failure, significant parts of infrastructure itself (but not its control room operators) can disappear, such as the loss of bridges, dams, substations, or major transmission lines. Reliability here means the speed and surety of reconstructing both physical systems and their interconnectivity. Control operators may need to formulate entirely new strategies to aid this recovery process. Recovery reliability can also mean that the recovered (new normal) operations in the infrastructure are at least as reliable, if not upgraded in reliability, than before failure—though this challenge enters the purview of higher-level organizational executives, political leaders, and policy makers.

But considering reliability in larger scale and scope also leads us now to consider a system perspective beyond that of a single infrastructure. Recovery especially, as we see now, is always an interinfrastructural process.

THE SPECIAL RELIABILITY OF INTERINFRASTRUCTURAL RECOVERY

From our perspective, recovery has special features within the different states of infrastructure operations that bear on how we should understand reliability from an ICIS perspective. For one thing, the precluded-event reliability standard of normal operations is moot once failure has occurred involving multiple infrastructures. The reliability challenge now must be directed toward coordinating, under failure, a variety of very diverse activities across many bureaucracies, including special emergency response organizations (often called incident command centers) that are mobilized at federal, state, local, and organizational levels within the United States. Recovery poses its own organizational and cognitive challenges for policy makers, political leaders, regulators, and control operators. The brief case study below—the 2004 Jones Tract levee breach and recovery, which at the time of writing was the last major levee disaster in the California Delta (California Department of Water Resources 2009b)—provides a graphic illustration.

Interinfrastructural Recovery: The Jones Tract Disaster

In early June 2004 a levee breach occurred on a levee, called the Upper Jones Tract, in the southern region of the California Delta. As flooding began, state, federal, and local agencies mobilized multiple emergency resources. The incident was officially closed about a month later and by the end of the year an estimated 150,000 acre-feet of water had been removed from Jones Tract Island and farmland adjacent to the levee. The costs incurred by the state for fighting the flood, repairing the levee, and pumping out were estimated by the DWR to be approximately $30 million. General estimates of claims of loss filed with the federal government were approximately $60 million (Suddeth, Mount, and Lund 2008). Lawsuits, filed against various state agencies and private parties, continue at the time of this writing, with some details related to the recovery remaining outside the public domain.

The Jones Tract levee breach and flooding involved multiple critical infrastructures in the failure and recovery stages. These infrastructures included adjacent levees, State Highway 4 (threatened by the flood), the BNSF railroad line and trestle (disrupted service and assets threatened by floodwaters), the Mokelumne aqueduct (part of the EBMUD water supply), state reservoirs and water systems (threatened by potential saltwater intrusion), and a major fuel transmission line running through the flooded area (owned by Kinder Morgan). Actual recovery involved many state agencies and private firms; a few of the more prominent participants included the U.S. Army Corps of Engineers, USBR, DWR, California Department of Transportation (Caltrans), the Central Valley Flood Protection Board, two reclamation districts (legal units responsible for managing and maintaining individual levees or sections of levees), the Port of Stockton, Dutra Group (a private company that supplied and shipped fill materials), and Ford Construction Company (which did the island dewatering under DWR contract).

A good deal of the literature and discussion on this levee failure has focused on determination of its causes—it was an unusual sunny-day event that occurred shortly after a levee inspection—and on the cost and difficulties involved in actual recovery. There are substantial differences of opinion on all this, on and off the record.

Relevant to our recovery reliability perspective, the Jones Tract recovery has been retrospectively characterized by two engineers working with DWR to oversee that exercise as being "about as good as it could be but also about as good as it needed to be." The first part of their conclusion is based on factors such as the speed of response, follow-through, and the effectiveness of the recovery measures that were implemented. The second part is based on the Jones Tract breach being characterized by some distinctly lucky features: the flow rate of the floodwater was relatively stable and predictable, the inundation occurred in sparsely populated areas, and weather conditions were not altogether problematic. True, major problems were encountered in the recovery,[18] but had a similar breach occurred in winter, with fewer resources, a slower response, and more unpredictable water flows and closer to a highly populated area, the outcome might well have been far less satisfactory.

ICIS Recovery to What Standard?

A conclusion that the Jones Tract levee recovery was simultaneously "as good as it needed to be" and also "as good as it could be" is important if the assertion is taken as an evaluative standard with which to assess how reliable future recovery is to be, given a new levee breach. If so—and we are speculating in the face of little prevailing consensus—the 2004 recovery could be a metric of a good-enough standard of recovery reliability when it comes to this type of levee failure. This recovery reliability standard would allow evaluators—including policy makers and regulators—to distinguish and compare both improvements to and departures from that standard when assessing future recoveries. In likewise fashion, the existence of such a standard beforehand enables a *prospective* assessment of recovery reliability once a new new normal

has been established (we return to the importance of the prospective orientation to reliability and risk in Chapter 5).

One prospective reliability standard therefore is this: given another similar
levee failure with interinfrastructural implications, could the 2004 Jones Tract
recovery be replicated? Would it be improved on, or has a serious deteriora-
tion of the capacity ("resilience" as we see later) to react speedily, flexibly, or
otherwise effectively taken place under the new (post-2004) normal? In other
words, a reference standard, like the Jones Tract event, would enable policy
makers, regulators, operators, and analysts to assess not only recovery response
prospectively but also recovery efforts comparatively as they are under way
and after a new normal had been achieved. In this way, a reference point on
which to base a standard of good-enough recovery capability could clarify
prospectively how different ICIS configurations might affect the likelihood of
overlapping versus competing reliability requirements for critical infrastructure system (CIS) recovery. This is a first step toward formulating a clear ICIS
recovery reliability perspective. (We return to a more detailed analysis of ICIS
reliability standards in Chapters 10 and 11.)

We must note, however, a sobering finding at this point: a number of informants in both individual infrastructures and emergency response organizations report that subsequent declines in resource availability (e.g., barges
and related material) and the skill base and experience of key personnel and
increases in regulatory and policy constraints make replication of the Jones
Tract recovery unlikely. One observer said, "People were willing to make
commitments of resources and incur large financial obligations as needed, in
advance of formal decisions by higher ups [during the Jones Tract incident].
This wouldn't happen today." Cost accounting processes now in place and
formal approvals required before undertaking an actual response, it has been
argued, constrain what were earlier more flexible resource commitments that
maximized timely actions. "Had it [Jones Tract breach] happened with today's
protocols, it would have been a catastrophe," asserted an informed observer. If
so, then in terms of the multiple states of infrastructure operations described
earlier, many professionals in the state's emergency response infrastructure *are
already in disrupted operations or worse,* outside their domain of competence
and in unstudied conditions, although many political leaders and the public
do not yet perceive the crisis, or they refuse to acknowledge it.

RELIABILITY SPACE FROM THE
INTERINFRASTRUCTURE PERSPECTIVE?

If Jones Tract illustrates the challenge of failure and recovery—both conditions can put reliability professionals outside their reliability domains and lock them into an intense ICIS setting—then what constitutes a shared ICIS reliability space for control rooms operating within their own domains of competence during normal or disrupted operations? This is an increasingly crucial question.

Start with the recognition that the reliability focus of control operators described above and summarized in Figure 3.1 has evolved in the context of single infrastructures. The figure describes a focus of attention for control operators confined to issues worth worrying about in relation to their own infrastructures and tasks. But in real-time operations operators often do not have the time or the information to extend the coverage of their reliability management to the operation of other infrastructures.

As an example, a major electrical transmission line passes over Sherman Island in the California Delta at the confluence of the Sacramento and San Joaquin Rivers (also at that point are the deepwater shipping channels to the ports of Sacramento and Stockton). As discussed in Chapter 2, the island, which is below water level, is protected by levees, and a levee breach anywhere could lead to flood conditions that render that stretch of line inaccessible to maintenance crews. A major storm that caused the flooding could knock out the line directly as well. We asked a dispatcher at CAISO if he ever worried about this line and threats to its operation. His response was instructive: "Well, it's either there or it isn't. If it isn't, we'll find a way to work around it."

At the same time, the operations manager of the nearby Contra Costa Water District noted that "our reliability concerns are really focused on the impacts of our failures on our clients," a good number being other infrastructures. Here the district's focus is on those infrastructures but mainly from the district's output side. Utility concern with the operations of the infrastructures that provide inputs into the district's operations is less evident—often because as a reliability strategy individual infrastructures have attempted to buffer their operations from perturbations in the external reliability they depend on, at least in the short run. To that end, they have backup generators, stockpiles of critical supplies, and redundant sources for needed materials, if only for short-term work-arounds. This asymmetrical focus in an ICIS setting on the output side of critical service production and provision is a very important strategy in an ICIS reliability space.

But this output-to-input interconnection is only one piece of the inter-infrastructural reliability space during normal or disrupted operations. Shared control variables, we argue, are just as instrumental, if not more so, in creating a shared reliability space. Reliability professionals pay attention to overlapping or shared control variables, and so too must we. They recognize and connect similar patterns, and they formulate compatible scenarios for action. This overlapping reliability space requires communication and coordination between control rooms. How this happens and the challenges posed by it we fully analyze in Chapter 5. But first we analyze the modes of interconnectivity possible for a system of infrastructures.

CHAPTER 4

A FRAMEWORK FOR ICIS RELIABILITY MANAGEMENT

To UNDERSTAND RELIABILITY MANAGEMENT within the context of multiple but different ICISs requires answers to a variety of questions raised by the preceding chapters:

- Different infrastructures have conflicting precluded- or avoided-event standards (emergency releases of water to prevent overtopping of a dam may lead to overtopping of levees downstream). How can reliability as an ICIS property be realized in such circumstances?

- How can reliability be secured across infrastructures when some, like a levee system, do not have control rooms to ensure real-time reliability?

- What happens when interinfrastructural connectivity results in one or more control rooms being pushed into precursor or unstudied conditions?

- What happens when control variables are jointly shared but are managed by one infrastructure in ways unknown to other infrastructures interconnected with it?

- What happens when knowledge requirements of an infrastructure's domain of competence are so intensive and demanding that its control operators can't realistically know the other infrastructures they are connected to with the same depth as they know their own systems? Does this mean that there must be a control room of control rooms to address interconnectivity issues related to reliability across systems?

These questions all have to be taken seriously in order to understand both the reliability and the risks of modern interconnected infrastructures. Unfortunately, current discussions about interconnected infrastructures fail even to address them. Instead these infrastructures are nearly always generalized as tightly coupled, complexly interactive infrastructures on their way to cascading failure (Graham 2009; Schewe 2006). Arguments and scenarios are framed around technical systems so complex that when fully stressed they can no longer be managed and spiral out of control. Consider three examples of this popular perspective:

The problems of too much interconnectivity present enormous challenges both for organizations and for society at large. Our most advanced systems and infrastructures have become so complex that they are hard to manage effectively. . . . Our technological networks are so pervasive, and we use them so intensely, that we have good reason to worry that data about ourselves and our families might float out of our sight and our control. (Palfrey and Gasser 2012, 2)

Technology tightly links the operations of big banks and markets. Hedge funds and equity funds, securitized products—even equity markets—are more and more international by nature. Only the most draconian and destructive regulatory measures could stop this interconnectedness. . . . The greatest structural challenge facing the financial system is how to deal with the widespread impression—many would say conviction—that important institutions, such as the large international banks, are deemed "too large" or "too interconnected" to fail. (Volcker 2011, 74–75)

Any number of events that once would have been manageable now will have catastrophic effects. Complex systems like the markets, transportation, and the Internet seem stable, but their complexity makes them inherently fragile. . . . Accurate GPS has been available to civilians for less than 20 years. When it fails, commuters will only be inconvenienced, but most air and water transport will stop. The Internet was designed to survive all manner of attacks, but our reckless dependency on it is nonetheless astounding. When it fails, factories will stop, power stations will shut down, air and train travel will stop, hospitals and schools will be paralyzed, and most commerce will cease. What will happen when people cannot buy groceries? Social chaos is a pallid phrase for the likely scenarios. (Nesse 2013)

The sample is easily enlarged, but the common theme is that our large sociotechnical systems are on course to failure—unless, say the critics, new designs, innovative technologies, or far better regulation are introduced. We have no choice but to innovate or evaporate. The status quo is untenable, and everyone knows this.

Well, not quite everyone. You can imagine how simplistic and uninformed such calls for change sound when presented to reliability professionals who *are* managing large sociotechnical systems with technologies that can *never* be fully designed for the level of reliability demanded, technologies that in turn would be fully stressed to failure were it not for their active and vigilant management. This is true even while the systems are more complex than the critics can comprehend.

More complex than critics and designers comprehend? And yet the systems are managed, many to high levels of reliability. How is this possible? In answer, we offer a framework for understanding and assessing complex interconnections among infrastructures and the challenges they pose to reliability professionals and their skills and strategies in system operations. Our framework has two parts: This chapter details an approach to understanding the interconnectivity across systems; the next chapter extends the analysis specifically to risk management and reliability space at the ICIS level.

THE DESIGN-MANAGEMENT CONTINUUM
FOR INFRASTRUCTURE OPERATIONS

It is helpful to start by thinking of design and management as a continuum formed around two contrasting approaches to the promotion of reliable infrastructure operations. At one end, it is assumed that operations are and should be constrained and determined fully by logics of design; at the other end, it is assumed that management can substitute or compensate for design logics that are never fully fit for purpose when it comes to ensuring reliable operations and the management of risks in large sociotechnical systems.

In the first approach design and technology largely determine how the system is operated, where managerial options and discretion have deliberately been minimized. (Think of the engineer, quoted in Chapter 3, who said he was out to design systems that are so foolproof that even a damned fool couldn't screw them up.) That design and attendant technology can and should impose their own logics on operations and management is a point we have heard in many forms. A Union Pacific manager said of a major elevated routing element in his facility, "The hump is what governs: you can only go so fast with only so much over it" when it comes to rail traffic through the yard.

At the continuum's other end is the case of managers having wide discretion to modify or operationally redesign a system in operation. As we were told at CAISO, "Different shift managers, depending on their personality, drive the system differently." Operators are able to do so because they too have a reliability logic that emerges through routines, procedures, work-arounds, and decisions that have already been taken. A port manager told us, "Remember: once you do one thing, other things have to happen; a decision causes others to happen."

We have observed this gradient between design-driven and management-driven operations of infrastructures, with formidable implications for their cross-infrastructure interconnectivity and risk management. The approach taken to risk assessment and management varies accordingly as different configurations of interconnectivity are involved at different points along the continuum between "we operate as the system demands" and "this is the system we have to manage."

Suffice it to say, most infrastructures we have studied with control rooms and reliability professionals fall toward the management end of the continuum rather than the design end: they have to be made reliable *beyond design*. Some large sociotechnical systems, such as CAISO when we studied it earlier, have technology, hardware, and software so complex and at times novel that major technical problems arise and have to be worked around. In such cases, the only way the infrastructure operates reliably is that its operators remain vigilant to prevent technical failures from arising or correct for them once they do arise.

One telling feature of management-driven infrastructures is the use of resources for reliability that are distinct from the formal design and even the formal organization of the infrastructure. Pilots of tankers watch for levee instability and loss of structural integrity on the water side of the deepwater shipping channels they pass through (high water levels mean they also watch for clearance levels with respect to highway bridges under which they pass). Delta island residents drive levee roads and thereby provide an extra pair of eyes for problems emerging on the water- or landside of the levees. Monitoring changes in the physical condition of the levee road is said to be a good measure of what is happening on the levee below—for example, a widening dip or cracking in the road may mean the levee is shifting. Residents watch the levee because they cannot rely on design alone to ensure reliable (safe and continuous) operations.

Wherever an infrastructure may be along this design-management continuum, its mission and legal and regulatory requirements are in place to ensure reliable provision of the critical services, notwithstanding how interconnected they are. The logics of design may determine management, or management may have to compensate regularly for inevitably incomplete designs, immature technologies, and unpredictable contingencies. Our argument is that shifts can occur in an infrastructure's placement on the continuum because of changes in interconnectivity between itself and other infrastructures. To see how, we must first lay out what interinfrastructural connectivity looks like from the operational perspective of the infrastructure control rooms where reliability management occurs.

AN OPERATIONAL PERSPECTIVE ON INTERINFRASTRUCTURE CONNECTIVITY

Why do we start with management across infrastructures rather than with their physical or technical components as is common in much of the engineering and technology literature today? We do so because most large critical infrastructures we study have control centers monitoring interconnected inputs and outputs in real time. As we have seen, this requires active management of infrastructure operations, including interconnected risks involved in that operation arising from the standards being managed to. Equally important, focusing on interinfrastructure connectivity directs our attention to where the crises and disasters are often best understood or first appreciated—in the control rooms that come to depend on one another before, during, and after a crisis. Our focus on interconnectivity enables us to identify more clearly the wider nature of risk assessment and management at the interinfrastructural level including the *system* nature of resilience, robustness, and sustainability at the ICIS level.

From a management perspective, think of an interconnection between infrastructures as an interaction between them. Two rudimentary distinctions from the literature are important. To begin, interactions can be dependent or interdependent (Nieuwenhuijs, Luiijf, and Klaver 2008). A dependent interaction is unidirectional, or one way, in which a change in one critical infrastructure system (e.g., in operating conditions) leads to a change in another infrastructure, which in turn can lead to a change in a third infrastructure and so on:

$$\Delta CIS_1 \rightarrow \Delta CIS_2 \rightarrow \Delta CIS_n$$

An interdependent interaction, in contrast, is bidirectional, or reciprocal, in which a subsequent change in one infrastructure feeds back into the infrastructure whose initial change had affected it:

$$CIS_1 \rightarrow \Delta CIS_2 \rightarrow \Delta CIS_1$$

The differences between dependent and interdependent interactions explain why the first "I" in ICIS does not denote "interdependent." Conflation of "interconnected" with "interdependent" would imply erroneously that we exclude from our analysis dependent, unidirectional interactions across critical infrastructures, whereas in fact, the latter are by far the most frequent (see, e.g., van Eeten et al. 2011).[1]

A second set of interaction distinctions is as important. Dependent and interdependent interactions can be spatial, functional, or both. As Rae Zimmerman puts it,

Spatial dependency refers to the proximity of one infrastructure to another as the major relationship between the two systems. Functional dependency refers to a situation where one type of infrastructure is necessary for the operation of another, such as electricity being required to operate the pumps of a water treatment plant. (2004, 4059)

Spatial and functional can intersect, as when a levee breaches, taking out the electricity transmission pylon behind the levee, which in turn leads to a power line failure beyond. In such ways, the spatial and functional interconnections may be unidirectional (indicating a dependency), reciprocal (indicating an interdependency), or in combination. The levee breach can destroy the telecommunications dish behind the levee structure but not vice versa. On the other hand, the destruction of that dish could bring down local telecom service, making it difficult to recover from that breach or prevent another. These types of interactions are an important part of what distinguishes the different system models of critical infrastructures.

MODELS OF CRITICAL INFRASTRUCTURE SYSTEMS

Single-CIS Model

Chapter 3 introduces the six states of an infrastructure that are key to system reliability: normal operations, disruption, restoration, failure, recovery, and the new normal of operations. These operating states can be represented by a set of stylized concentric circles, moving from "normal operations" as the outer ring to the inner ring of "new normal" operations for a single critical infrastructure system, CIS_1, as if it were operating entirely on its own (Figure 4.1).

Consider the single-CIS model carefully (our example is the CAISO electricity transmission grid). First, it shows the two-sided nature of the loss of service. Failure is having lost normal operations with infrastructure damage *and* not having yet recovered operations or established new-normal operating conditions. Note also that if operations have failed, the only possible future state is to recover those operations. In contrast, when operations are disrupted, the infrastructure can assume two additional states: it can restore operations directly back to normal or it can lapse into failure, requiring eventual recovery (where possible). Once again, all risk calculations based solely on two states—normal and failed operations—mean analysts are likely to misperceive the full range of performance possibilities, a substantial shortcoming of conventional event- and fault-tree risk analyses. As we show, disruption (the temporary loss of service) and service restoration are of major importance in assessing and managing risk at the ICIS level.

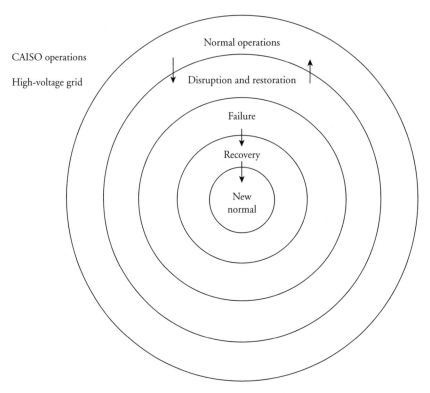

FIGURE 4.1   The infrastructure states: a single-CIS model.

Recovery is altogether more significant than "recovering operations" can convey, since recovery entails repairing the infrastructure itself and is a much more intensive and extensive exercise than restoring normal operations after a disruption. (Our terminology of "restoration from disruption" and "recovery from failure" is not standardized usage for all infrastructures. For example, recovery of the electric grid after having islanded is commonly called "restoration of the grid.") In our framework, "recovery" means establishing new conditions for the reintroduction of normal operations. Since recovery is not automatic, it proceeds by management strategies that necessitate an important role for the respective control rooms.

Recognizing that the system in failure differs from the system in normal operations is essential and also that an old normal and a new normal may well differ. To assume that infrastructure failure is all about the failure of normal operations misses that normal operations frequently tell us very little about the state of infrastructure management and operations in other stages, including most significantly the conditional probability of another failure when infrastructure recovery is under way. A control operator saying of normal operations, "Every day is different," and an emergency responder saying, "Every event is different," are not saying the same thing, if only because control operators we studied consider the probability of failure to recover to be far greater at times than the Pf during normal operations.

Two-CIS Model

We move now to a two-CIS model, in which CIS_1 and CIS_2 in Figure 4.2 constitute an ICIS made up for illustrative purposes of the CAISO control room operations and the Banks pumping station, a key one for the California SWP. As drawn, CIS_1 depends on normal operations of CIS_2 and vice versa. CAISO provides electric power to the pumping station, and the pumps move water that later provides hydropower back to the grid, so this is an interdependent system. Normal operations may range from a narrow zone of contact between CIS_1 and CIS_2 to a wider zone of overlapping contact (as illustrated in Figure 4.3, later in the chapter).[2]

The two-CIS model allows us to take up the central case of two infrastructures that share or have some interconnected control variables and consider

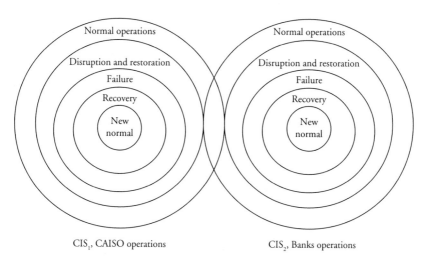

FIGURE 4.2   Overlapping cycle stages for a two-CIS model.

the implications for intrasystem and intersystem states of operations. Control variables, those actionable features of an infrastructure (e.g., voltage and frequency for an electrical grid, water-release schedules for a dam or reservoirs), are managed so as to alter larger system behavior. As we saw in the preceding chapter, control variables are part of an infrastructure's process variance, used to transform inputs to the infrastructure into outputs for use by other systems. For example, the SWP uses its pumped water flows to generate electricity as an output to the CAISO transmission grid. Pumped water flows are managed according to on-peak and off-peak electricity schedules, in which the SWP treats the scheduling of water flows as a control variable that can be adjusted to meet, among other things, requirements for electricity output by the CAISO. CAISO in turn provides electricity to operate a major part of the SWP, including pumping for water flows. Because of this relationship, an unscheduled outage in electricity generation, whether occurring in the SWP or on the CAISO grid, can disrupt SWP or CAISO management and operations processes (for specifics, see Chapter 8).

Our research found many examples of overlapping and closely linked control variables. Consider the backfire, an important tool of firefighters. A backfire is set in the path of an oncoming wildfire to deprive the primary fire of fuel by the time it reaches the site of the backfire. An important tool of the SWP has been regulation of the rate and timing of pumping at the Banks station, so as to mitigate effects on endangered fish around those pumps during their spawning season. However, when backfires are set too near the electricity transmission lines (since the right-of-way under high-voltage transmission lines can be more accessible to firefighters) or when the operation of those SWP pumps is changed under court order for protection of an endangered species (thereby potentially altering generation and load for the electricity grid), the control processes of the respective systems become operationally interconnected. Backfires next to transmission lines threaten the stability of those lines, yet not to backfire there may compromise firefighting; altered operation of the pumps can mean keeping the lights on or not during high-load times. In both cases the processes of converting inputs into outputs of the respective infrastructures are interconnected.

Linked control variables are clearly a major reliability and risk issue when one infrastructure managing its control variable (managing for reliability) does not know or cannot know that the other infrastructure is also managing the same or a closely linked variable—a risk that arises from managing this way. Although the SWP electricity generation is prescheduled with CAISO, from time to time CAISO changes the preschedules in ways that the SWP operators do not fully understand or, for market reasons, cannot know. This has knock-on effects for SWP pumping, since the preschedules determine important pumping periods. This phenomenon of interconnected control variables is the foundation for our operational definition of interinfrastructural interconnectivity:

Definition 1: Infrastructures are interconnected not only when the output of one is the input of another. They are interconnected when shared or overlapping control variables are being comanaged, whether formally or not.

Other Key Definitions

The first definition of ICIS interconnectivity puts us in the position to define how such properties as resilience and sustainability become system-wide properties. First imagine that operations have been disrupted in CIS_1 but not in CIS_2 (Figure 4.3).

As drawn, disruptions in CIS_1 (the CAISO grid) do not disrupt CIS_2 normal operations (SWP pumping with backup reserve generators); that is, the

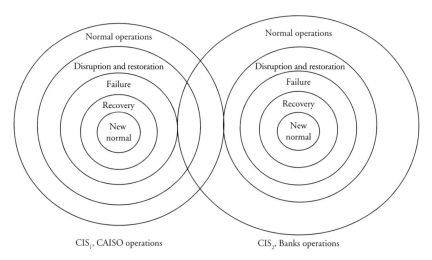

FIGURE 4.3 CIS_1 in disrupted operations while CIS_2 in normal operations.

CIS$_2$ concentric circle for normal operations overlaps CIS$_1$ disruptions. That their input, output, or control variables may be interconnected does not appear to be affecting CIS$_2$ (Banks station) in the same manner as it does CIS$_1$ (CAISO). This leads to our second definition:

Definition 2: Operations in an infrastructure are robust *with respect to disruptions, failure, or recovery in another infrastructure when the former continues normal operations in the face the latter. The normal operations may well depend on the* precursor resilience *of that infrastructure in managing its reliable operations following surprising or unexpected input conditions arising from the other infrastructure.*

In this view, CIS$_2$ is *robust* with respect to CIS$_1$, when CIS$_2$ can reliably manage its normal operations despite surprises or shocks introduced by CIS$_1$. CIS$_2$ absorbs or bounces back from CIS$_1$-induced perturbations in ways that do not disrupt safe and continuous provision of CIS$_2$ services. In the terms of reliability management, an infrastructure's process variance (the ability of its control operators to move across different performance modes as conditions change) is *robust* with respect to its low or stable output variance (its control operators are able to maintain stable services in spite of the perturbations of the infrastructure to which it is connected).

It may be that a disruption in CIS$_1$ operations does disrupt CIS$_2$ operations but only temporarily before CIS$_2$ restores its normal operations. This leads to a third definition:

Definition 3: Operations in an infrastructure are restoration resilient *with respect to disruptions or failure in another infrastructure when the first infrastructure is readily able to restore normal operations after its own disruption from the disruption or even failure in the other.*

CIS$_2$ is *restoration resilient* with respect to CIS$_1$ when CIS$_2$ absorbs or bounces back from CIS$_1$ surprises or shocks that have interrupted CIS$_2$ normal operations and led to a temporary loss in CIS$_2$ service. An infrastructure's process variance is *resilient* with respect to other infrastructures when the ability of its control operators to move across different performance modes is sufficient to return infrastructure operations to their normal levels of low or stable output variance, despite conditions in the other infrastructure.

Definitions 2 and 3 both treat resilience as a property of an individual infrastructure, in this case CIS_2, conditional on the operating state of another infrastructure, CIS_1. The interaction, however, can be reciprocal; that is, interdependent as defined earlier. This is especially evident in recovery, for which we offer the following definition:

Definition 4: CIS_1 and CIS_2 are recovery resilient *when both CIS_1 and CIS_2 can coordinate the replacement of their respective control variables and assets.*

Here resilience is intensely interorganizational. In the earlier terminology, the infrastructures involved have sufficient options and resources for necessary cross-infrastructure coordination. This interorganizational prerequisite is captured in the statement one reclamation district representative made to us: "No reclamation district has the ability to recover from a catastrophic event without help," by which he meant not just money but direct assistance from other agencies and departments.

In summary, whether a risk manager within a reliability setting is analyzing robustness or resilience or the conditions under which a given infrastructure displays one rather than another, that risk assessment and management focuses on the ability of control operators to reliably manage control variables even when interconnected to other CISs. This understanding of robustness and resilience as system properties differs considerably from a simple focus on robust or resilient infrastructure elements, be they separate structures or facilities. Our argument is that to assume that elements are suitable proxies for system robustness and resilience is to commit the major analytic error of confusing the design end with the management end of the design-management continuum.

A better understanding of an infrastructure's *sustainability* within an ICIS framework is also now possible. Sustainability is a subset of robustness or resilience that operates across all infrastructure stages:

Definition 5: Operations in an infrastructure are sustainable *with respect to disruptions or failures in one or more connected infrastructures when the former can maintain normal operations in the face of any changes in the latter's operations.*

By definition, then, *sustainability* is the overall persistence of normal operations in a CIS relative to all stages in the loss of normal operations in one or more additional CISs, even if they have interconnected control variables throughout. Sustainability's appeal to an infrastructure is that buffering against unwanted impacts on its own control variables not only preserves or adds options but also reduces or ensures lower system volatility (more on that below).[3]

To be clear, Figures 4.2 and 4.3 describe two among many empirical configurations of interconnectivity. The addition of other infrastructures to expand on the two-CIS model opens possibilities for many more arrangements, not least of which involve third-party mediation and coordination, in which a CIS_3 coordinates operations for more resilient or robust operations in CIS_1 or CIS_2.

DIMENSIONS OF INTERCONNECTIVITY

A major finding in our research is the multitude of interconnectivity configurations that critical infrastructures in the Sacramento–San Joaquin Delta take on. We found no one dominant form or relationship for how one infrastructure is connected to another; actual interconnections are configured through many different permutations, at a single point in time or over time, and from one position in the design-management continuum to another. Specific types of interconnectivity that exist within normal operations shift when one or more of the systems moves along the range of operational conditions to different states, such as a disruption or failure. The shift points in interconnectivity are exceedingly important to appreciate, as they represent the transformation of latent interconnections (i.e., not part of normal operations) into manifest ones.

The observed diversity in actual and latent linkages among infrastructures stands in marked contrast to analytic models of and prescriptions for interconnectivity found in handbooks for engineering, systems modeling, and organization theory. From a reliability management perspective, however, this diversity can constitute a requisite variety useful to the work of reliability professionals, no matter how difficult they are to model in formal network analyses.[4] To better appreciate this diverse interconnectivity, we offer four analytic dimensions of interinfrastructural interconnectivity, the first three of which determine the fourth:

- *Directionality* of causality. As mentioned, this can be *unidirectional* (a one directional dependency from one CIS to another), $CIS_1 \rightarrow CIS_2$, or *bidirectional* (mutual causal interdependency between two or more infrastructures), $\text{CIS}_1 \leftrightarrow \text{CIS}_2$. In this way, directionality is the differentiating characteristic between dependency and interdependency.

- *Probabilistic* or *deterministic* influence. Interconnections can be *probabilistic*, in which disruption or failure in one increases Pf in another ($\text{Cf}_{\text{CIS}_1} \rightarrow \uparrow \text{Pf}_{\text{CIS}_2}$, such as a power outage and telecommunications failure), or *deterministic*, in which failure in one leads invariably to failure in another ($\text{Cf}_{\text{CIS}_1} \rightarrow \text{Cf}_{\text{CIS}_2}$, as when the collapse of a bridge takes out the gas or power lines that run across it).[5]

- *Complexity* of configurations of interconnectivity. When there are mixes in directionality or probabilistic-deterministic interconnections within a configuration of multiple infrastructures, that configuration is more complex.

- *Manageability* of the interconnections for the infrastructures involved. Differences in directionality, influence, and complexity of interinfrastructural interconnections impose key knowledge requirements for infrastructure managers and can affect system volatility *and* options to manage that volatility. In the terminology of high reliability management, interconnections can make operating environments more or less volatile for their managers; interconnections can also lead to more or fewer options with which to manage that volatility. For example, a deterministic relationship in which one infrastructure failure necessarily leads to another (the collapsing bridge that takes out the telecommunications cable fastened to it) is one that reduces the manageability of interconnections. In contrast, a probabilistic interconnection between two infrastructures for which substitutes or otherwise alternative options exist is more manageable (for example, when congestion along one roadway in a road network does not foreclose firefighters using alternatives, be those other roadways in the network or other transportation means, such as helicopter).

The central position we give to the manageability of interconnections among infrastructures should be clear. Suppose a new engineering analysis shows that one section of a Delta island's surrounding levee structure has a considerably higher Pf than its other sections. The island's reclamation board has to decide if this new information demands action (in relation to the associated Cf, for example), what priority should be given to it over and above other requirements, and to which state or federal levee maintenance, improvement, or capital development program it should apply for funding.[6] These programs are themselves embedded with other infrastructures having their own budget constraints and claims on funding.

In terms of the manageability of this vulnerability (and all else being equal), immediate action cannot be expected on this island's levee problem. If the island in question is Sherman Island, the manageability challenge changes considerably given the importance of that specific island to the SWP (again, in terms of its Cf). Remedial action on a levee stretch that a reclamation district's budget cannot handle may well be manageable for a larger infrastructure system, even though it too is constrained by its budget. From the perspective of the SWP, a levee section with a higher Pf than originally thought may be the kind of problem it can address because it is on Sherman Island and not somewhere else.

To summarize, differences along the four dimensions pose a wide range of variation in interinfrastructural connectivity, whether expressed in current operations or waiting to be expressed under alternative conditions. Importantly, a manifest configuration of interconnectivity has associated with it latent counterconfigurations of interconnectivity that can—under stress, disruption, or failure—become manifest.

LATENT AND MANIFEST INTERCONNECTIVITY
CONFIGURATIONS

To illustrate how latent and manifest configurations work, four of the more important configurations we have observed in our research are examined here (following Thompson 1967 and LaPorte 1975).

1. Sequential (or serial) interconnectivity. A unidirectional interconnection (a dependency) exists between two or more infrastructures (see Figure 4.4). A Delta island road below the adjacent levee's water level depends on pumping facilities to prevent flooding out during the rains. The pumps in turn may depend on electricity grids to function.

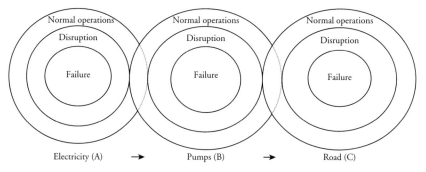

FIGURE 4.4   Sequential interconnectivity.

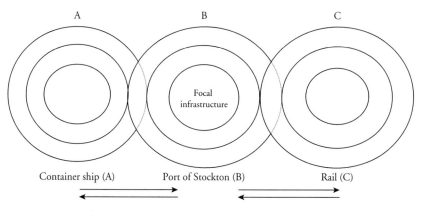

FIGURE 4.5   Mediated interconnectivity.

2. Mediated interconnectivity. One infrastructure is interconnected to another through the operations of a third or focal infrastructure (see Figure 4.5). Deepwater tankers passing into San Francisco Bay bring imports to the intermediating Port of Stockton and the intermodal railroad for onward distribution beyond Stockton. The port also enables goods from the railroad to be loaded onto ships bound for export markets overseas. Under normal operations the port mediates a bidirectional connection between incoming vessels and outgoing trains or trucks. Further, during times of disrupted schedules, port officials arrange mutual schedules for inward ship arrivals and outward rail or truck departures, factoring in the availability of its own off-loading and storage capabilities.

3. Pooled interconnectivity. Multiple infrastructures are connected *indirectly* through their shared use of a collective resource (in this case a focal infrastructure). The focal infrastructure manages a common resource, but unlike the mediated relationship, the users may not specifically identify one another: they are connected indirectly through their common use of the pool resource.

For example, the Coast Guard VTS manages San Francisco Bay naviga- tion areas for a variety of vessels, some of which are unaware of others; CAISO manages the high-voltage grid for many different generators and distribution utilities. In these cases, the navigation areas and transmission grid are common resources that one infrastructure manages for other users or infrastructures. For CAISO, this pooled relationship affords it, as the focal infrastructure, multiple grid management options and buffers the grid from the failure of any one electricity supplier or medium-capacity transmission line, as illus- trated in Figure 4.6.

4. Reciprocal interconnectivity. A fourth configuration of interconnectivity is reciprocal interdependency, in which multiple infrastructures are or can be interconnected directly with one another via bidirectional interdependencies across the infrastructures. Shared communication networks such as supervisory control and data acquisition (SCADA) systems or the California Environmental

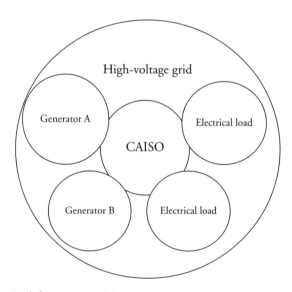

FIGURE 4.6   Pooled interconnectivity.

Data Exchange Network, to which many infrastructures both contribute their own and use others' information, are examples of this type of interdependency.

INITIAL IMPLICATIONS OF INTERCONNECTIVITY CONFIGURATIONS

At least six implications of these diverse types of interconnectivity are important when it comes to risk assessment and management within the multiple infrastructure settings studied:

1. *Deterministic unidirectional sequential* interconnections basically put disruption and failure beyond the reach of real-time management. This relationship is the assumed causal framework for interinfrastructural failure cascades (noting again that actual cascades can be more probabilistic and granular in time and across space). Mindful of this risky interconnectivity, upstream infrastructures can undertake extra investment to reduce their Pf. This deterministic interinfrastructural relationship exists primarily where spatial overlaps exist between infrastructures—where they physically share the same site or location as in ICIS1 scenarios. We have seen, however, that spatial overlap often involves *elements* of infrastructures and does not fully determine the failure mode of the larger infrastructures as systems.

2. More commonly present are *probabilistic unidirectional sequential* connections that allow downstream infrastructures to anticipate and strategically buffer the connected probabilities. For example, the downstream infrastructures ensure the availability of redundant or substitutable capacities to activate if the upstream infrastructure is disrupted or fails (e.g., the availability of backup generators for the provision of electric power during electricity disruptions). This probabilistic connection also allows time and positive slack for managers to assess and even invent new options to make their operations robust or resilient to upstream failure.

3. *Bidirectional probabilistic* relationships allow and motivate each infrastructure to coordinate with its paired member. These relationships may well exist where the two infrastructures have interconnected control variables. The operational reliability mandates of the infrastructures, however, could be quite different and complicate the development of shared strategy

(e.g., in operational terms flood control infrastructures prefer an emptier dam but hydropower generators prefer a fuller one).

4. *Mediated* interconnections, because each infrastructure can identify the other participants, provide a clearer context within which to coordinate actions and strategies. In fact, the focal infrastructure undertaking the mediating can be well situated to facilitate the coordination. However, in the event of disruption or failure of the focal infrastructure, such as a longshoremen's strike or major storm at the Port of Stockton, both infrastructures, railroads and ships, may be vulnerable to schedule interruptions no matter how motivated they are to coordinate locally.

5. *Pooled* interdependencies can, under some conditions, disperse risk among multiple players if they are providing substitutable services or resources (as in the availability of reserve generation for emergency use by CAISO in its management of the transmission grid). But under other conditions (the loss of generation reserves), the pool relationship can be at risk to the level of its least reliable participant. If the infrastructure managing the common resource is disrupted or fails, a pooled interrelationship can convert to a reciprocal interdependency requiring mutual coordination among multiple players. Again, when the Coast Guard VTS has been disrupted or worse, vessel pilots and others onboard the separate vessels are expected to mutually adjust their passage through the navigation areas.[7]

6. But *reciprocal* interdependency can impose high information costs and communication burdens among multiple participants when they directly coordinate their activities. In this configuration, the possibility of error and the risk of misjudgment (a significantly greater risk in just-in-time performance conditions) are high. Misjudgment and errors are especially likely since the players have lost the capabilities the managing focal infrastructure had for seeing a bigger picture and maintaining situational awareness.

SHIFT POINTS IN INTERCONNECTIVITY CONFIGURATIONS

As just noted, the sequential, mediated, pooled, or reciprocal arrangements are considerably altered when infrastructures are stressed during normal operations, actually disrupted, or have failed entirely. If this happens, shift points in interconnectivity occur: what was latent becomes manifest by way of inter-connection. For instance, during conditions in which load is high and electric-ity generation reserves are limited, the pooled grid relationship just discussed can become one of reciprocal interdependency. Multiple infrastructures that had been indirectly connected through a common resource being managed for them now become directly interconnected because of problems affecting the focal infrastructure as manager. Under very tight load conditions, the loss of one electricity generator can trip the transmission grid into forced inter-ruptions of power or blackouts. The balance of the grid can in effect become hostage to the least reliable generator.

Similarly, maritime vessels in the San Francisco Bay navigate their way though a crowded waterway by means of a pooled traffic control connectiv-ity with the VTS as the focal organization. In the rare conditions when VTS loses its communication or radar capacity, vessels have to operate under a re-ciprocal interconnectivity of pilot to pilot, a form of self-organization under which they would work out directly among themselves their rights-of-way among clusters of proximate vessels. Under pooled interconnectivity these interdependencies were latent; they become manifest in a reciprocal intercon-nection. The interconnectivity under stress or in failure has become different in directionality and influence.

To summarize, shift points in our framework denote that latent linkages have become manifest, and with the shifts come changes in the suite of prob-abilities for disruption, restoration, failure, and recovery (thus shift points can be thresholds for interconnectivity transitions). We've just seen how unidirec-tional dependencies can become bidirectional interdependencies, as when levee seepage occurs and roads and levees become functionally intertwined in fight-ing the flooding and repairing damage. Other things remaining constant (and they often don't), this interlocking means that the Pf for either infrastructure ascends to the highest single-failure probability. In some cases, the shifts are less a movement of a specific Pf along a given distribution of Pfs than a move-ment of an entire distribution of Pfs; that is, a new set of failure consequences (Cfs) and associated probabilities come into play for a time.

An illustration is helpful here. High reliability management can be con-sidered the best case in managing interconnectivity and establishing alterna-tive failure trajectories. This places it at the other extreme from the worst-case

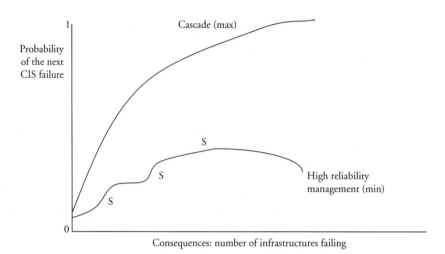

FIGURE 4.7   ICIS risk trajectories: maximum and minimum cases of ICIS risk.

cascade of rapidly escalating probabilities and deterministic consequences of the ICIS1 scenario. The range between worst- and best-case probability distributions is presented in Figure 4.7.

As drawn, the worst-case cascade trajectory is one without any intervening management (the systems involved are again assumed to be fully stressed and unmanaged at the point of failure). As each additional infrastructure fails, that increases the probability of the next failure, until all infrastructures in the ICIS have failed. In contrast, the lower trajectory reflects best-case high reliability management in the infrastructures. Here, strategies along the design end of the continuum buffer one infrastructure failure from another by means of backups, redundancy, and default protocols that decouple tight interconnectivities. But just as important, at the management end the increase in Pf in one infrastructure triggers management and operational strategies to reduce what would have been higher Pfs in others. This is core to the resilience defined earlier.[8]

In unmanageable situations, interconnections become tightly coupled and compounding; in high reliability management situations, strategies are deployed to shift the nature of the interconnectivities so as to reduce their potential for failure (these positive shift points are labeled "S" in Figure 4.7). The shift points emerge as managed interventions that introduce slope changes in the trajectory of Pf in an ICIS. Some shifts trigger latent-to-manifest interconnections so as to escalate follow-on Pfs. Other shifts can be managed, such as isolating a failed section of an electric transmission grid, working out a pilot-to-pilot reciprocal interconnectivity among ships or rescue teams when a pooled or mediated interconnection has failed, or reallocating flood fighters from other areas in a timely manner, thereby reducing the probability of follow-on failure among infrastructures that remain operating.

Higher-manageability shifts are positive with respect to the worst-case scenario. With lower-manageability shifts, the step function moves the management trajectory closer to the cascade trajectory. While higher-manageability shifts are positive with respect to avoiding an instantaneous cascade, this does not mean they represent the preferred strategies of the infrastructures. Return again to the example of a large vessel coming into the San Francisco Bay on its way to the Port of Stockton with shipments to be off-loaded onto rail cars for outward transportation. As we saw, the Coast Guard's preferred strategy is having redundant communications and monitoring systems to guide that vessel through the regulated navigation areas. If those systems fail, the pooled interdependence of the Coast Guard defaults to the reciprocal interdependencies involving vessel-to-vessel communication. Once the vessel reaches Stockton, the port's preferred strategy is the sequential, routinized process of assisting the vessel to dock, having union labor on-site to off-load, and having railcars waiting and ready to move on.

However, we also saw that in a disruption or emergency, the port defaults to a focal mediating role between ship, union labor, and rail transportation to coordinate schedules in nonroutine ways. Once cargo is reloaded onto rail, the preferred strategy, at least for Union Pacific, has been to route the respective shipments in sequence to their destinations. If something goes wrong, the default is for shipments to be rerouted through a variety of alternative sequences.[9] But none of this would be instantaneous: "We'd take about a week to work around a two-day shutdown of [a specific] port," a rail manager told us.

To reiterate, in these cases (Coast Guard, port, and rail) what had been latent configurations of interconnectivity become, under stressed, disrupted, or failed conditions, manifest configurations of interconnectivity. Reliability management must always be ahead of the risks when those risks themselves shift as a result of shifts in manifest and latent interconnectivity. Being prepared for the shift in working relationships is part of reliability and risk management. What changes are the directionality, influence, complexity, and most important, the manageability of the interconnections in the form of the default configurations. We underscore that the triggering of default configurations often means more work, attention, and preparation on the part of control operators than during normal operations.[10]

Nevertheless, these key shifts from latent to manifest are where both vulnerabilities *and* resilience in the constituent infrastructures are most visible.[11] One VTS operator said, after averting an incident, "I saved this"—and that save was as real in reliability management as the incident would have been had it happened.[12] "Our success is measured by what doesn't happen," another operator told us. "That's the yardstick for our work."

CONCLUSION: THE MANAGEMENT OF LATENT INTERCONNECTIVITY

If the preceding framework for ICIS reliability management is largely correct, a major part of the management challenge for pursuing reliability across infrastructures is the management of not just manifest interconnectivity but latent interconnectivity as well. There are many examples of the management of latency. Trying to manage water reliably in dry season or drought periods is something Californians and the water infrastructures have had to do in the past and remains a dormant template to be activated for management purposes under unusual conditions. We were told that if a major disaster were to lead to in-Delta flooding, saltwater intrusion, and the indefinite shutdown of the SWP Banks pumps, the state and federal response would be to act *as if* California had immediately entered dry conditions regardless of the timing of the disaster. The state would have to rely on what water was already available in existing south-of-Delta water reservoirs, canals, and storage facilities. Water rationing, for example, would impose command and control unidirectional relationships that overrule many and more common bidirectional coordination arrangements.

Formal and informal communication between infrastructures during normal operations is also the management of latent interconnectivity. In this regard, infrastructure control rooms may not appreciate all the good they do by keeping communication going and channels open. This includes the mundane: by copying e-mail to many recipients or calling all those on the list of an official or agreed-on rota, one is recognizing that systems are interconnected.

There is also the less mundane. Unusual communications may reflect concern that a given infrastructure does not disrupt the input side of other infrastructures that depend on it. In other cases, persistent real-time communications are the core of meeting reliability mandates, as in the Coast Guard's VTS. What happens, we asked a VTS watch supervisor, when you no longer can communicate with a vessel in your regulated navigation area? "I call the pilot's office and see if I can get the pilot's cell phone or call the Marine Exchange to see if there's a tugboat there I can communicate with. It might just be the pilot can't get to the radio. All of this, though, raises serious red flags for us, especially if [the vessel] is near a bridge." (Note again the importance to high reliability management of having a network of contactable professionals.) In fact, observing the VTS control room traffic managers over time leaves one with the distinct impression that a good deal of even routine communications—a continuous stream of receiving messages from vessels on one channel, having those repeated back for confirmation, and then broadcasting that to a wider audience on another channel—is itself a real-time enactment of the interinfrastructural system of vessels and waterways the VTS operators are coordinating.

Communications are central to the management of interconnectivity in *whatever* state of operations the infrastructure is in and thus to control room management of both reliability and risk. Not surprisingly, then, worries about telecommunications were the one interinfrastructural commonplace in our research. "Telecoms is a problem," an infrastructure manager told us. "We're dependent on [one provider] not just for phones but for data transfer. If telecoms went down, that would have a real effect on operations." A dispatcher in a different control room said, "I keep telling people I'm one phone call away from tragedy. If we lose telecommunications, it could mean a major loss of critical infrastructure." An operator in another control room said, "You asked me what would really screw things up: loss of telecommunications! We are dependent on real-time data." Still another infrastructure manager reported, "We're really dependent on microwave communications. . . . If we lost this [during a storm], that would be major." A senior departmental emergency manager said, "My greatest worry here is telecommunications [during a flood event jeopardizing their facility]." Loss of data transmission is an especially major interinfrastructural concern. PG&E, CAISO, and the Western Electricity Coordinating Council, for example, depend on shared data.[13] Thus, the all-too-familiar call by conventional organizations for more and better communications is by no means hackneyed when made by control operators. Here, the deficiencies in communications may represent a threatening erosion of team situational awareness and background support.

CHAPTER 5

A FRAMEWORK FOR ICIS RISK MANAGEMENT

H AVING ESTABLISHED THE DISTINCTION between latent and manifest interconnectivity and the challenges they can pose to managing reliably, we now extend the analysis directly to the management by control operators of associated risks across infrastructures that come with that management, the second piece in our overall ICIS framework.

In this chapter, we reexamine the reliability space within an interinfrastructural context centered on risk, itself both manifest and latent, by describing control operators' comfort zone. We also expand our earlier description of the performance modes of operators within this comfort zone and the operational risks associated with each mode. This ends in a discussion of factors related to what are or are not acceptable risks within operational settings interconnected to other infrastructures along with implications of what this means for such topics as innovation, coordination, and efficiency.

FOUR TYPES OF UNPREDICTABILITIES FOR
CONTROL ROOM OPERATORS

In Chapter 3, we examine control operators' reliability space (see Figure 3.1). Now consider this concept solely in terms of how operators manage probabilities and hazards, including those arising from interinfrastructural interconnectivity. To do so means shifting our focus to the kinds of unpredictabilities that operators differentiate. A useful typology for the ICIS setting comes from the work of researchers Andrew Stirling and David Gee (2002) and is summarized in Table 5.1.

Four types of unpredictabilities can be distinguished, a few of which are by this point familiar. In general terms, the first, *risk*, is knowing the probability and consequences of failure (Pf and Cf) of an event. You know the risk even though you may not be able to predict the exact timing of an occurrence and aftermath or the number of such occurrences. For example, the probability, more or less, of an earthquake of a given magnitude and the hazard (its consequences) posed by a quake of that magnitude might be known (e.g., roughly a 20 percent mean annual probability over fifty years of an earthquake of 7.0 or greater, which in turn has a range of other impacts associated with it, including loss of life and economic losses). Risk calculations can of course be less formal. "Right now we can predict [that] every year we'll have a hump in the channel [riverbed of sediment and debris from snowmelt or rains], and we know what to do; it happens frequently enough, and we've dealt with it before," a port manager told us.

Ignorance is not knowing both Pf and Cf; that is, what may be a hazard is not known, and thus nothing is known about its likelihood. "What surprises me?" said an experienced government hydrologist working with DWR's Flood Operations Center. "All those unique things that come out of nowhere!" For

TABLE 5.1   Four types of operational unpredictability

		Knowledge about outcome (Cf)	
		Specified or well defined	Unspecified or poorly defined
Knowledge about likelihood (Pf)	More empirical basis	Risk	Ambiguity
	Less or no empirical basis	Uncertainty	Ignorance

Source: Adapted from Stirling and Gee 2002, 524.

many, the suppressed panic arising when skills in pattern recognition and scenario formulation are too few or of little avail (as in the first hours after a major disaster or the first minutes of having lost real-time communications and data transmission) comes closest to capturing what it means to be in state of ignorance. The threat of having to operate in ignorance never goes away for the reliability professional: "There's always a fog of war" in unfolding events, we were told by a senior manager of the Coast Guard's command center.

Uncertainty is knowing the hazard (the consequences of a tsunami of a given magnitude is a defined hazard) but having little or no knowledge of its probability (it might have never happened in a particular coastal area before). In our typology, uncertainty is knowing the outcome of an event but not its likelihood. A government hydrologist told us, "What we can't really predict or forecast for are thunderstorms; we do not forecast them at all, since there are too many parameters determining where they will be and the amount of rainfall they bring." A great deal of what drives current Delta infrastructure research is uncertainty.

Last, *ambiguity* is having a good idea of the probability of an event happening but the outcome or consequence is ill-defined or poorly understood. "A flood here, for example, is more complex than an earthquake elsewhere," a long-time county emergency manager informed us. "In an earthquake you have buildings that collapse with people inside, and you know what you have to do. In a flood here, it is dynamic; you don't know where the breaches are going to go." For the California Delta, experts may have better agreement on the probability of levee breach than on what constitutes an official emergency after a breach, sufficient for the release of funds.[1]

The most important implication to be drawn in terms of the typology is that all too frequently infrastructure designers, high-level executives, policy makers, and regulators fall victim to errors of estimation and assume they are operating and calculating in the domain of risk when in fact they are working under uncertainty, ambiguity, or worse, outright ignorance. Risk assessment itself as a profession has been shown by recent events (be it Fukushima or the most recent financial meltdown) to be vulnerable to this misestimation and associated hubris.

For the purposes of this book, one important take-home message of the typology is so obvious it may be missed: when it comes to risk, those who decide on the basis of likelihoods are the same as those who decide on the basis of consequences. Less formally, the assumption is that when it comes to risk, those who know likelihoods know the consequences, and vice versa. Yet our research has identified many instances where knowledge of likelihoods and knowledge of outcomes is held or produced by quite different units, agencies, or organizations such that to know one does not automatically mean the other is known or understood by the same group. One agency does the official study on the chances of levee failure; another identifies the economic and human consequences of failure. The good news is that control rooms of critical infrastructures are the places where those managing the risks are frequently those who know the real-time probabilities of failure and the real-time consequences of that failure.[2] The bad news is that policies and decisions can increase infrastructure volatility and reduce operator resources to handle that volatility and thus also reduce operators' ability to manage risk.

The second striking feature of the typology from a management perspective is that unpredictability of ignorance. As shown in Table 5.1, the nature of ignorance is that it is unspecifiable—it is by definition a region of unstudied conditions. Unstudied conditions are famously those unknown unknowns, and they are in that uncharted space outside the domain of competence and an operator's precursor zone. One does not need to search far and wide to see why, from a reliability standpoint, this position is hugely consequential. Simply put, those in conditions that are outside their domain of reliability competence and pushed into unstudied conditions can believe anything they want and ignore anything they don't want to hear.

In a state of ignorance, learning is a very precarious possibility and includes many opportunities for misperception. Whatever else the domain of ignorance is, it isn't risk assessment and management. Since infrastructure operators in normal conditions operate under mandates to be reliable—safe and continuous provision of a critical service—they have to manage against ignorance by avoiding unstudied conditions during the real-time management of their large and critical systems.[3]

A third feature of the typology is also important: one immediate consequence of moving the analysis from only one infrastructure to that of interconnected infrastructures is to add new hazards without known probabilities (increased uncertainty) and at the same time lose understanding of the full consequences of other hazards with known probabilities (increased ambiguity). Furthermore, a risk management success at the ICIS level may well differ from success at the critical infrastructure system (CIS) level, as when flood-fighting personnel are sent to some priority sites and infrastructure clusters before others under rapidly changing conditions.

HOW OPERATORS AVOID IGNORANCE

How do reliability managers in infrastructure control rooms stay out of unstudied conditions? How do they manage against ignorance? One answer is that the professionals we study *avoid ignorance by engaging in trade-offs between ambiguity and uncertainty.*

The task for infrastructure managers is to manage in combinations of ambiguity and uncertainty they can live with. They manage these uncertainties and ambiguities in unequal degrees as a way of avoiding ignorance altogether. Greater uncertainty about likelihood can be compensated for by less ambiguity about consequences and vice versa. In this way they operate within their domain of competence, grounded in and bounded by their skills of pattern recognition and scenario formulation to prevent working in unstudied conditions. Operators we've talked with call this their "comfort zone," though as one CAISO control room supervisor hastened to add, "I'm always uncomfortable." "Comfort" here does not mean complacency. Surprises they expect, and in this sense their comfort zone must always be uncomfortable. Knocking on wood, a VTS traffic manager said, "Pretty quiet this morning—so far." For schematic purposes, we show the stylized comfort zone in Table 5.2.

High reliability management professionals we study practice vigilance to stay out of the area below the curved line and stay within the area above

TABLE 5.2 Inside and outside the high reliability management comfort zone

		Knowledge about outcome (Cf)	
		Specified or well defined	Unspecified or poorly defined
Knowledge about likelihood (Pf)	More empirical basis	Risk	Ambiguity
	Less or no empirical basis	Uncertainty	Ignorance

Source: Adapted from Stirling and Gee 2002, 524.

it—that comfort zone. To maintain this level of comfort they tolerate some ambiguity about outcomes, which is offset by having high confidence in probabilities. They tolerate some uncertainty about probabilities, for example, by having higher confidence that consequences are limited. Or they determine that they are comfortable with unknown effects of an event because it is offset by confidence in the low likelihood of that event—all within the context of team situational awareness.

In this way reliability professionals seek to avoid unknown unknowns by focusing on what uncertainty and ambiguity they can tolerate in their comfort zone as risk managers. Toleration of some uncertainty and some ambiguity along with avoidance of unstudied conditions characterize the real-time management of control rooms we have observed, not a simple reduction of uncertainty, as discussed more often in the literature on conventional organizations.

Operators accept this extended range of operation because they realize that it's better to pursue reliability under difficult circumstances and try to manage (some) ambiguity and uncertainty than to delude themselves and others that they are within the domain of calculated risk. Uncertainty is a form of latent risk because, although an outcome is known, its likelihood isn't. In this respect control operators have told us they manage against the *possible* not just the probable. Ambiguity is also latent risk because, although the probability of failure is known, its outcomes aren't as well known. Here they may try to compensate for unknown outcomes by trying to reduce probabilities as far as possible. One way is through clarification and elaboration of procedures. These procedures become part of their comfort zone that can and must be lived with because, under certain conditions, their clarification, when it comes to how procedures actually apply to a specific real-time event, may increase options, reduce volatility, or both.

The signal implication is that high reliability management in interconnected infrastructures can never be a process of reducing uncertainty and ambiguity to zero in the operators' comfort zone. No matter how good the managers and their technology, they cannot manage for reliability solely as managers of manifest risk. Latency is always ready to become manifest. (This is the sense operators use when telling us that accidents always come "hunting for them.") In effect, there is no stable resting point for reliability-achieving operators in critical infrastructures. New arrangements, including those involving new interconnectivity configurations, are always producing other scenarios to adapt to and use if required.[4]

A great deal of reliability management across infrastructures depends on how much of this management can be accommodated, if not proceduralized and clarified, within an interinfrastructural context. The Port of Stockton manages against ignorance by managing its on-site uncertainty and ambiguity through procedures, routines, and strategies that accommodate the demands and needs of those elsewhere in the supply chain. That way each day begins to look more like other days. In the words of a long-time senior port manager, "You've got to remember there's a lot of repetition in our work; after a while we've learned what to do and expect."[5]

Note that the line separating the comfort zone from what can't be lived with, just like the line separating the precursor zone of the domain of competence from unstudied conditions, is surprisingly bright but not permanently fixed. The actual management of risks, uncertainties, and ambiguities within the comfort zone can and does change over time. The operators we have talked with are always having to learn when it comes to being prepared for operationally redesigning defective equipment, software, or strategies. Another issue in the domain of competence of operators is the challenge of having to identify the uncertainties and ambiguities that professionals can and must tolerate to be situationally reliable with respect to one another. This requires that operators share a *background* from which to practice their skills in pattern recognition and scenario formulation.

To our knowledge, the concept of "Background," as used here, was first applied by a philosopher, John Searle, to assert that the exercise of any skill (he described skiing downhill) must involve nonconscious experience and abilities that are not themselves brought to the level of conscious decision making when exercising that skill (Searle 1983). In fact, a person deliberating consciously about everything that made for skillful skiing while going downhill would be a very poor skier. The *individual* tacit knowledge each professional demonstrates in quick response times under reactive operations in the reliability space is thus not the only tacit knowledge important for high reliability management. There is also that *shared* tacit knowledge held by professionals, developed over time and expressed in team situational awareness.

When we asked Searle what the best synonym for Background would be, he said immediately and without prompting, "comfort zone." In our framework, to move outside the shared comfort zone is to move toward unstudied conditions in ignorance or conditions of uncertainty and ambiguity that can't be lived with as comfortably. When doing so, there is no shared Background for acting on latent and manifest risks; there are no special skills or a shared confidence in decision making.

One feature of the Background deserves special note. The Background of shared, taken-for-granted knowledge enables operators to be especially sensitive to the *limits* of their knowledge and the problems of going beyond those limits to a precursor zone.[6] Consequently, that operators do not talk about some problems does not mean those problems do not exist. They don't need to be talked about because everyone on the floor knows them as difficult operating conditions. We have observed short-term consultants failing to understand that just because an operator doesn't offer a specific response to the consultant's query, "What's the problem here?" doesn't mean there is not a host of real problems so obvious they need no explicit articulation.

HOW OPERATORS KNOW LATENT RISKS ARE SHIFTING INTO MANIFEST ONES

The shift from latent (inactive) risk to manifest (active) risk is indicated to operators in at least two ways, one obvious to the public, the other not. The first is when the infrastructure itself is disrupted or fails in terms of providing the critical service. Failure often comes with "major, major breaks in the system," one telecom manager put it, when a major earthquake, storm, or other event destroys physical structures. This is the crisis that the public sees almost immediately.

What is a crisis to the public may, nevertheless, be preceded by an internal crisis for the infrastructure operators. In this case, the shift from latent to manifest risks is indicated by the operators shifting their performance mode, because options or task volatilities have changed even before any major breaks or disruptions in the hardware or software of the infrastructure. Operators detect something unusual, that something does not fit in, is out of the ordinary, or is not consistent with the patterns or scenarios they typically see in the circumstances. "So if we see a ferry stop suddenly—it's not going along its track vector [on the screen]—we contact it to see what's up. . . . Overall, we look for what's normal and what we're seeing that isn't normal," a VTS traffic manager explained.

"Operators need to be trained to spot anomalies," we were told in different forms on many occasions, if only as part of their job in being skilled to think through what-if possibilities. "I know it [a water flow] is going to shut off in an hour; if it doesn't shut off then, I've got to figure out why. That's what I get paid for," a water system control operator put it. In cases in which the unusual occurs and conditions necessitate a shift in performance, so too do the dominant risks change. System volatility and operator options with which to respond change when what was inactive or unknown by way of latent risks is now seen in manifest ways.

Several examples help here to show how latent connections become manifest and the implications that follow. Separate watersheds and river systems in the San Joaquin basin can become more tightly interconnected during a major weather event, as when their uncontrolled inflows into the San Joaquin River threaten flooding in the basin. A USBR official put it this way: "Another issue you [have] got to think about in staging releases is that increasing the flow along one river affects what can flow on a connecting river." Otherwise, more water could be released than could be carried downstream without flooding: "If we followed the rules, we might have combined outflows [greater than] the river capacity. . . . [I]n an emergency, it is not possible to operate each reservoir in isolation; releases have to be coordinated." Such considerations mean that dam discharges into the watersheds, which are normally uncoordinated or only loosely so (we were told, "If it's their reservoir, it's their call"), have had to be comanaged as an interconnected control variable in real time to manage inflows into the San Joaquin River.

An earlier example occurred in Northern California, where uncoordinated outflows from two reservoirs, one on a major river and the other on another river, caused flooding during the rainy season at the point where outflows converged. Now, reservoir releases are coordinated so as to reduce downstream flooding. What had been loosely coupled systems became tightly coupled for managing the shared control variable, water flows. Risks can change, and if not managed, the resulting river system would end up vastly different from the system under prior conditions. What had been dormant features of the watershed—their interconnectivity in terms of coupling and interactions—became, under the storm event, manifest interconnections unavoidable for the purposes of risk management and emergency response.

FOUR PERFORMANCE MODES AND THEIR OPERATIONAL RISKS

Let's turn to what operators actually do when it comes to managing latent and manifest risks. As we discuss in Chapter 3, to manage changing risks, operators have to maneuver across different performance modes. This again provides the requisite variety necessary to cope with diverse conditions. But at the same time each performance mode also poses risks to operations as the task and resource conditions change (Table 5.3). Think here of volatility as being the degree of unpredictability or uncontrollability of the operators' task environment and option variety as being the degree to which different resources and strategies exist with which to respond effectively to the volatility faced.

Just-in-Case Performance

When options are high and volatility low, just-in-case performance dominates: reserves are large, excess capacity exists, and so do ample backups or fallbacks. Under normal conditions, a telecom system has many backup resources—reserve generation at its major land antenna sites, a variety of mobile switching centers and mobile antenna and relay units, including cells on wheels

TABLE 5.3   Four performance modes and major associated risks for high reliability management

		System volatility	
		High	*Low*
Options variety	*High*	Just-in-time performance: risk of misjudgment, with too many variables at play	Just-in-case performance: risk of inattention and complacency
	Low	Just-for-now performance: risk of losing options, with lack of maneuverability and cascading error	Just-this-way performance: risk of failure in complying with command and control requirements

Source: Roe and Schulman 2008, 48.

and cells on light trucks. So too we were told of backup pumping resources in the Delta if dewatering is required on an island; port and railroad officials told us they have backup generation just in case it's needed. A major risk would be operators or managers growing complacent because of this positive redundancy and not paying attention to potential changes in system volatility or options availability.[7] "One of the most challenging aspects of [our control] operations is to maintain attention to detail even when things slow down. . . . We can't be complacent," said a senior VTS support official.

Just-in-Time Performance

When options and volatility are both high, just-in-time performance dominates. What worked yesterday by way of reliable service provision may not work today at the same time and even under similar conditions. This performance mode demands real-time flexibility, or the ability to quickly develop and use differing options, resources, and strategies to meet the reliability requirements under highly volatile conditions. Here, alternative options are assembled or improvised as required and often at the last moment. The major risk in this flexibility that combines creativity and discretion is misjudgment under the pressures of time and having too many balls in the air. "A lot of variables need to be kept in mind," said the same VTS support person. "Plus, you need to keep attention on more than one location." According to a rail manager, "There's a lot of things going on at once—two or three conversations at once. You've got to handle pressure, think quickly on your feet; you got to know what's going on in the yard." A Coast Guard emergency specialist told us of the well-known view that the Coast Guard's motto, *Semper paratus* (always ready), should actually be *Semper gumby* (always flexible).

Just-for-Now Performance

Using resources can deplete options with which to respond in the next step or later on. When option variety is low but volatility remains high, just-for-now performance dominates. This is the most unstable performance mode of the four and the one operators and managers want most to avoid or exit from as soon as they can. Here the risk is tunneling into a course of action that leads to no further escape alternatives, or as one air traffic controller once put it, "You have to watch your mistakes play out in slow motion." Speaking of a major

Bay Area vessel collision and spill, a VTS support person noted, "The closer it [a large ship] got to the bridge, the more the options dwindled."

More, the few options remaining may be such that to use one risks *increasing* volatility elsewhere or later in the system. Such conditions may require operators and managers to go outside official channels or formal procedures to keep things reliable. For example, a grid dispatcher called a power plant manager to say, "Keep that generator online, just for now!" One long-time water system manager told us, "In an emergency [our partners] often know their facilities better than we do. . . . They may have flows or levels at variance from the scheduled [ones] because they know local conditions better than anyone else at that time." Another reliability professional told us, "You have to realize an emergency may require action that is at odds with regulation, so that you undertake your response and then have to document it and justify it after the fact to the regulators, point[ing] out in the process that you restored half the grid in undertaking your emergency action." Yet to take one from many examples, keeping equipment online because of an emergency when its maintenance is overdue has its own risks of pushing operators into a corner they can't get out of if that equipment also fails.

Just-This-Way Performance

When option variety is low and volatility must also be lowered, just-this-way performance can be introduced by some infrastructures. An emergency can be declared and command and control frameworks can be activated. The Coast Guard's captain of the port has broad command and control authority— for example, he or she can stop any vessel for inspection within the respective jurisdiction. When electricity load is high and generation reserves low, CAISO can declare a state of emergency and order both load shedding by utilities and specific generators to come online. A Cal Fire representative made it a point to stress the command and control powers Cal Fire had when it came to wild-fires in the state. The great risk here is that not everyone who needs to comply will comply. When the reliance is on close compliance, deviance can come as a very unwelcome surprise.

IN SUMMARY, the high reliability management we observed depends on the ability of the control operators to maneuver across performance modes—

and managing their differing respective risks—as conditions and options change.[8] Their task environment changes for reasons other than just that the weather is unpredictable or, if predictable, the consequences of that weather for the infrastructure are uncontrollable. Volatility may be high because control variables have become more correlated when most often they are less correlated. Unusual correlations are now added to the mix of unusual external conditions for high volatility.[9] All this, in turn, requires a risk appraisal far more sophisticated and sensitive than formal methods, if only because risks shift when conditions change.

SOME IMPLICATIONS OF ICIS RISK MANAGEMENT FRAMEWORK

Since they are already sophisticated risk appraisers in their own right (particularly when compared to formalistic, less operational risk assessors elsewhere in the same organization or in external regulatory organizations), the reliability professionals we study appraise novel policy, technology, and design proposals by asking: Does the proposed improvement increase options, reduce volatility, or enhance operator maneuverability to meet reliability requirements as and when performance conditions change? You would think that the burden of proof lies with the proponents of the improvement and that the operators would not have to prove that the proposal would undermine reliability or simply not work. This too is often not the case.

Operators have a prospective orientation to reliability ("We're no more reliable than the next error ahead") that renders the retrospective orientation of innovation proponents ("Well, it worked in the earlier tests") antithetical to their approach to high reliability.[10] The huge problem with relying on a retrospective orientation to reliability is the illusion it gives to what constitutes acceptable risk. What has been acceptable or successful in the past can give a false confidence about future reliability. The prospective orientation, in contrast, is sharply defined with respect to the standard of precluded events. Operators who see technical defects and policy or regulatory shortcomings lying in wait for them and who know they are no more reliable than the first failure ahead are understandably vigilant. "Unless you're running scared all the time, you're gone," as Bill Gates famously put it once—though this in itself is, as the operators we study insist, no guarantee of high reliability (quoted in Waters 2009, 9). No one should want improved risk assessment and management methods to unintentionally decrease prospective real-time risk management and assessment capabilities of operators charged with reliability management in an interconnected critical infrastructure setting.[11]

The difficulty we have observed is that some major innovations in critical infrastructures pushed control room operators into unstudied conditions and thus were antagonistic to ensuring high reliability of the system being managed in real time (see the case study in Chapter 9). Rather than increasing the options for managing reliably, some hardware and software innovations reduced them through rigid requirements or inflexible application. Rather than lessening the task volatility that operators faced, the innovations destabilized the task environment through unexpected failures; rather than enhancing the maneuverability of operators across different performance modes as conditions changed, they reduced it by limiting work-arounds or preventing a fallback to prior strategies of operation. These innovations actually undermined the precluded-events standard of reliability by pushing operators into precursor conditions.

This makes it all the more difficult for operators to exercise their evolutionary advantage in large sociotechnical systems: their ability to operationally redesign innovations in real time through work-arounds and improvisation. Many proponents of innovation do not understand that innovations in technology and regulation can both reduce options and increase volatility as if control rooms never existed or are otherwise perfectly malleable to whatever business or regulatory model has favor today (we return to the topic of regulation in Chapter 10). Suffice it to say that the designer's innovation[positive] can all too readily be the manager's innovation[negative].[12]

Most readers understand there are times when each of us is pushed into emergency conditions we've never been in before, and in the abstract, almost everyone can understand why pushing real-time operators into unstudied conditions can cause unimagined problems. Yet a project engineer might insist, "I'm always working in unstudied conditions on a project. I've got to make all manner of assumptions." Others ask, "How can a field or discipline grow if it doesn't move into unstudied conditions by innovating?" We respond to these points with our own insistence that there are better and worse practices for introducing innovations into project engineering and management of infrastructures.[13] The burden of finding those better practices rests with the innovators. After all, the focus here is on the domain of high reliability management under extremely consequential situations, and, yes, here innovation should *not* be undertaken if it pushes infrastructure operators into conditions of ignorance, reduces their options in the control room, increases their task volatility, or diminishes their performance mode maneuverability.

This means that innovators must also rely more on the operators' evolutionary advantage for operational redesign. Why? Because the components of risk management practice in large sociotechnical systems are necessarily multiple and dynamic, always. The probability of a single infrastructure failure (Pf_{CISI}) is only one part of the overall interconnected infrastructure systems in which society has a great stake. We have seen how the notion of Pf in normal operations has to be expanded to include Pf in the other stages of an infrastructure's cycle, including Pf during recovered operations. This is why a design assumption of static rather than dynamic Pf values obscures latent risks and can add to uncertainties and ambiguities. What one agency specialist in levees told us—"Our levee goal is to sustain levees statically, trusting that we are not going to have an earthquake near term"—cannot be a reassuring statement from a reliability standpoint even if there were no earthquake, ever.

We also now see why ICIS formulations, such as the probability that island roads will fail, given that island levees breach, can mislead risk assessment and management efforts, when the importance of those roads and levees is not framed for analysis within the context of their overall infrastructures and their reliability management. "What is the probability that the road network will fail, given that that stretch of island road fails?" and "What is the probability that the levee system will fail, given that those island levees fail?" are far more important questions to address when it comes to the ICIS level.

Yet this elemental realism is too complex for many risk methodologies. The event- and fault-tree analyses identified in Chapter 2 consider only risk made manifest, and such analysis conventionally requires the probabilities all add up to 1. But in a world in which latent as well as manifest risks enter the operators' calculus of management, the sum of all probabilities over many trajectories of disruption and failure could be *greater* than 1. In this sense the probabilities must be seen as dynamic and not static, as conventionally posed.

Control operators who treat probabilities as dynamic must also be expected to treat *possibilities* involving uncertainties and ambiguities (those latent risks) just as seriously.

Just as worrisome is that unrealistic limitation of conventional risk analysis to those two states, normal and failed, misses entirely why requisite variety is central to large sociotechnical systems: since surprises are inevitable, disruptions must be treated as a possible state of operations for which operators require resources to be resilient. When one control operator tells us that with the approach of summer, "we start banking water up in the [storage reservoir]," he is talking about managing really-existing possibilities of disruptions during higher demand times; he is not creating what some are wont to label wasteful excess capacity when it comes to optimizing water deliveries.

By this point, readers should also recognize that in the absence of demonstrably interconnected control variables and conditions that give rise to their comanagement, we would not expect interinfrastructural coordination just because infrastructure elements of CIS_1 and CIS_2 are spatially adjacent to each other. A stretch of levee may be right next to an oil refinery storage tank behind it, but there is no reason to believe that these elements will be comanaged at an ICIS level—unless that levee stretch and that refinery tank represent system choke points within their operations and risk management processes. In other words, we must always ask just how reasonable is it for infrastructures to come together to coordinate their respective activities in any case before us?

A legislative or regulatory requirement for critical infrastructures to coordinate because their service areas overlap or their facilities are near each other, in effect, insists that spatial trumps functional. It insists that the control variables of the infrastructures are, notwithstanding the actual conditions, everywhere interconnected via their adjacent individual elements, irrespective of their stage of operations or the robustness and resilience they manage so as to buffer themselves from the impact of negative interconnectivity. This assumption can, as has been seen, lead to less reliable management of individual systems because of reduced managerial options, thereby increasing risks for all involved.

To continue to insist that this spatially circumscribed overlap of multiple infrastructure elements should be managed, both operationally and for risk management, as its own ICIS choke point is to imply it must have its own high reliability management—that is, its own operations center for managing inputs and outputs and its own control variables for converting those inputs into outputs without regard to the effect this partitioned approach would have on the infrastructural operations and system risks in which the elements are located.

Thus, when it comes to ICIS risks, it is essential that the amount and degree of coordination already going on within and across interconnected infrastructures be noted. Coordination is, to repeat, a very central feature of an infrastructure's control room. As for infrastructure-to-infrastructure coordination, that too is going on—again, when interconnectivity matters functionally at the system level. We were told that the BNSF railroad had its own desk in Union Pacific's central Omaha control room, and the companies shared tracks under agreement.[14] CAISO's new control room, unlike the older one, has its own desk for real-time scheduling of renewable energy from multiple sources.[15] We've seen how staggered releases of water flows from different reservoirs north and south of the Delta are an example of more effective coordination between different operating units. The Coast Guard VTS and Union Pacific worked out an agreement that improved the timing of train traffic over the Union Pacific drawbridge and ships passing under the structure when it was elevated (prolonged stoppages for both shipping and rail traffic had been occurring). CAISO, we saw, sought to coordinate with Cal Fire about setting backfires in the access way under major transmission lines. The raison d'être of the California Utilities Emergency Association has been to ensure better coordination of water, electricity, and telecom utilities in times of infrastructure disruption and worse.

Of course, much remains to be done by way of coordination, as our informants themselves pointed out, and more opportunities could be exploited to mutual advantage of the infrastructures involved, especially when the same control variables—a drawbridge for shipping and rail traffic, tracks for two rail companies, water flows for ship traffic and hydropower—are shared by multiple interconnected infrastructures.

It is too easy to recommend more coordination when the reality is that managing reliably within a large sociotechnical system is a highly knowledge-intensive activity on the part of the control room. Its knowledge-intensive demands may well work against coordination with other infrastructures around anything else except when and where control variables are obviously interconnected. It's impossible for one control room to know the internal workings of the other infrastructures it depends on with the same degree of unique knowledge it has for its own infrastructure. We had the following interchange with a water control operator:

Authors: Do you see the following other infrastructures when you look at your screens: Levees?
Operator: No.
Authors: EBMUD [East Bay Municipal Utility District's Aqueduct]?
Operator: We have an intertie valve, but really I don't see anything else.
Authors: Railroads?
Operator: No.
Authors: Electricity?
Operator: No, just that we get it from PG&E. We don't have any knowledge of their systems. All I need to know is if they are wanting more or less water from our system.

This operator is not alone in such an orientation. "You don't hear about levees in the CAISO control room," one of its supervisors put it. "Not in a blue moon. They're total responsibility of DWR." A CAISO senior manager put it this way: "Levees and water are a limitation, like fuel is a limitation [to the transmission grid]. Either it's there or it isn't. If it isn't, then we have to find another way to get the transmission." Another experienced CAISO support person added, "Hopefully, they're building for $N - 2$," meaning that other infrastructures, he hoped, could be operated reliably even if they lost an important element.

This explains the importance of the asymmetry mentioned in Chapter 3—the infrastructure manager being more concerned about the effect of disruption or failure in his system on others that depended on it than about the effects of a disruption from other systems, like power, on his own. The point of reference here is again societal dread driving the precluded-event standard. In our earlier round of research at CAISO, we were reminded that "if the grid fails and there are blackouts, people die." If generalized to the ICIS level, this asymmetrical concern for an infrastructure's outputs over its inputs could have a positive effect for reliability across the infrastructures involved. Were this the case, each infrastructure connected to another would have its input reliability determined or ensured by the anterior infrastructure supplying it, and the shared ethos for each dispatcher would be, as one in the water utility said, "The users are my responsibility."

This, to be clear, is no easy task: "You have to realize many of the critical infrastructures still operate in their own silos," a senior state emergency manager emphasized, and legal and regulatory restrictions work against the sharing of knowledge and resources.[16] Nonetheless, the silos are a logical and practical outcome of the extremely dense and specialized expertise it takes to manage an infrastructure. The electricity side of a utility might not know what is going on in the gas side and vice versa—at least with the degree of depth each has for its own side—even though the systems are interoperable. In fact, the infrastructure managers we studied are reluctant to talk about operations outside the bounds of their competence with the kind of detail and attention they give to their own operations, including the exact nature of the vulnerabilities to which other infrastructures subject them.

This, we stress, *is not a unique finding.* This intense cognitive challenge has been highlighted in the important work of two psychologists, Daniel Kahneman and Gary Klein, who note, "Weather forecasters, engineers, and logistics specialists typically resist requests to make judgments about matters that fall outside their area of competence. People in professions marked by standard methods, clear feedback, and direct consequences for error appear to appreciate the boundaries of their expertise" (2009, 523).

In like fashion, the special features of control rooms discussed earlier entail operational requirements that are so intense as to render control rooms unicentric—they are focused on their own reliability concerns to the extent that the outside world becomes only a problem to be solved within the confines of control room perspectives on reliability. This is a sobering finding, and we defer until later whether there can be a system of systems, at least in the sense of a super control room of control rooms.

ON RELIABILITY AND EFFICIENCY

The ICIS context and the risks following from the mandates for reliability bring clarity to what has been a thoroughly misleading debate over reliability versus cost efficiency. Many economists and engineers insist that efficiency, specifically with respect to cost, should trump reliability, especially when the latter is conceived as fixed. For these economists and many engineers, the calculation should be reliability at a *given* cost, in which determining the cost precedes determining the level of reliability. Indeed, the adherence to an earlier reliability-at-any-cost standard in service pricing was one important reason for the deregulation of many integrated public utilities (for details, see Roe and Schulman 2008).

A contrary position is being argued here within the context of ICISs. As demonstrated repeatedly in this book, the mandate for high reliability, the precluded-events standard, determines what risks are to be managed, which in turn determine the costs of that high reliability management. Reliability precedes costs and accepted risks, not the other way around. The reliability mandated sets the initial conditions for calculating costs, including those associated with the risk management that follows from operating to the standards.

But none of what we discuss in this book has been reliability at any cost in the infrastructures we have studied. As an illustration, control operators may have paid for 103 megawatts, knowing the scheduled requirement was 100 megawatts; but operators would not pay for 200 megawatts on the rationale that 200 megawatts is even better than a just-in-case 103 megawatts. The operators we have observed recognize that cost effectiveness—given the standard of high reliability, what is the least cost to realize it—is a direct and immediate part of high reliability management.

Also, the focus of an infrastructure on ensuring reliability in its output, rather than solely its inputs, has onward implications for cost within an ICIS setting. The high process variance needed to transform inputs into stable outputs means a premium is placed on ensuring equifinality (multiple options) in achieving outputs when it comes to high reliability management. Where the economist or engineer sees excess capacity at the single-CIS level, control operators see equifinality and reliability of output at the ICIS level.

There is as well the more subtle issue of control variable costs at the CIS and ICIS levels, as in the case of control variables, like water flows, being used by multiple infrastructures in their reliability management. A favorite classroom example in economics is the coal-fired electricity generation plant whose price of electricity does not include (internalize) the costs of pollution from that plant. In like fashion, one infrastructure's management of its control variable, unbeknownst to other infrastructures that manage the same variable for their own control purposes, may cost (or in some cases benefit) the other infrastructures.

Note, however, the difference between examples: internalizing the costs of pollution in the price of electricity and internalizing the costs of sharing or managing the same control variable deploy different units and levels of analysis. One can well imagine how the full-cost pricing of electricity reflects pollution (a common enough practice in cap-and-trade and carbon pricing schemes) without coming anywhere near reflecting the far harder-to-measure costs of managing the shared control variable of hydropower, be it for that electricity or for a large-scale water system.

Obviously, the critical services provided by these infrastructures can be and are priced, and those prices imply tradeoffs, if only in terms of opportunity costs of the forgone alternative in using such resources. But the argument here is akin to that made in ecology, in which, while ecosystem services can be monetized, it is far more difficult to do so for the ecosystem processes that give rise to these services (see, e.g., Fischenich 2011, 45). "One area of confusion in the valuation of [ecosystem] services has been the difficulties faced in deciding on what should be valued—the ecosystem processes or the service. Actually, benefits are the end element of an ecosystem process-service-benefit chain and only these benefits enter into the domain of well-being that is likely to be analyzed" (Kumar et al. 2010, 1). So too and in similar fashion for the relationship between a reliable infrastructure and its critical services: The reliability is far harder to monetize than are the services that derive from it. (Indeed, the relationship between ecosystem and infrastructure is direct, as in the case of an infrastructure service that is actually based on an ecosystem service, such as water.[17])

At this juncture it is appropriate to ask: How does this approach to understanding interconnected critical infrastructures compare to other ICIS perspectives in circulation? How does our approach help in better understanding the risks in an increasingly interconnected society? What gaps are filled when compared to those frameworks favored by engineers, economists, and system modelers? We turn now to these questions.

CHAPTER 6

OUR FRAMEWORK
IN A COMPARATIVE
ANALYTIC PERSPECTIVE

THE ENDURING IRONY OF CRITICAL INFRA-
structure studies is that many who insist everyone keep
the analysis simple insist in the same breath that, when it comes to the cat's-
cradle of complex cross-infrastructure networks, everything is connected to
everything else. It would be unfair to reproduce the dense networks that have
been identified by infrastructure experts, with their intersecting nodes and
links and crisscross hatching of multidirectional connectivity (compare Min
et al. 2007; Min, Beyeler, and Brown 2006; Lifelines Council 2014, 24). The
irony deepens when we drill down into the densely drawn figures and find that
those nodes and links are not comprehensive enough. The effort to show all
plausible combinations or correlations of interconnections ends up still falling far short of reflecting even the major latent interconnections that become
manifest only under certain system conditions. "Incomprehensible but still not
comprehensive enough" scarcely seems the right aegis under which to develop
our understanding of interinfrastructural interconnectivity.

Current theory isn't in a position to help much: no overarching, generally
accepted framework exists in the peer-reviewed literature for demonstrating
how infrastructures are spatially or functionally interrelated at an ICIS level.

What instead exist are conceptualizations that range from toy models to those very complex ones. This dilemma raises a logically and empirically prior question: Why would anyone want to make an ICIS model more complex when, at least according to the evidence, not all the interconnections are equally important in practice?

PRIOR EMPIRICAL RESEARCH ON
INTERINFRASTRUCTURAL INTERCONNECTIONS

Two helpful empirical studies on cross-infrastructural interconnections are accessible to the public and researchers. Both underscore that fewer dependent and interdependent interactions are present than might be supposed.

The Zimmerman Study

The first empirical study was published by Rae Zimmerman in 2004: "Decision-Making and the Vulnerability of Interdependent Critical Infrastructure." Zimmerman compiled a purposive (nonrandom) database of failures and sequences of failures across major infrastructures that had been reported in a variety of venues for the period 1994–2004. Structures of interest included, among others, electric lines, fiber optic and telephone lines, gas lines and oil pipelines, sewers and water mains, street lights, and transportation elements (e.g., bridges, rail, roadways, tankers). The evidence appears to be primarily from the United States. The data were analyzed and organized in terms of what infrastructure failures caused failures in other infrastructures.

Briefly, water main failures caused more failures in other infrastructures than the reverse. In contrast, gas line failures were more likely to be caused by other infrastructure failures rather than to initiate failure elsewhere. Zimmerman also found that some combinations of failures were more pronounced than others:

Certain types of infrastructure were frequently linked with one another, whether they caused or were affected by infrastructure failures. This database showed that the most likely combinations, in decreasing order of the number of events were: gas lines and roads (16), water and gas lines (12) electric and water lines (10), and electric and gas lines (7). This may simply be a function of how frequently these facilities are co-located, or alternatively, may reflect unintended interactions that occur when these facilities are subject to external stress. (2004, 4062)

Zimmerman's last point about failure related to collocation of structures or external stress that affects all structures independently is especially noteworthy. Note also the importance of water, roads, gas, and electricity in the failure combinations.

TNO-DUT Study

The second study on interinfrastructural interconnectivity is more recent and ambitious. The Dutch research body TNO Defence, Security and Safety and the Delft University of Technology (DUT) compiled a database on infrastructure disruptions (Luiijf et al. 2008). That database was subsequently updated and the analysis expanded (van Eeten et al. 2011; see also Roe 2013 for a discussion of these data).

As of September 2008 (roughly about the same time our Delta research began), the TNO-DUT database encompassed 2,650 CIS disruptions in 164 nations, with 1,090 cascading outages. From these data the researchers identified a subset of nearly 1,750 CIS failure incidents in nearly thirty European nations in which an incident, when not independent and isolated, could have initiated a cascade in the critical infrastructure itself or with respect to another infrastructure.

The majority of incidents were found to be internal to an infrastructure. For the most part, disrupted critical infrastructures acted as if they were independent of each other rather than interdependent. The study notes, "Our analysis of the collected data shows that most cascades originate from only a limited number of critical sectors (energy, telecom) and that interdependencies occur far less often than most theoretical studies assume" (Luiijf et al. 2008).

In other words, there was a higher probability of an incident happening within an infrastructure than between infrastructures—though interinfrastructural incidents were more prevalent than a presumption of them being low-probability, high-consequence events would lead us to believe (Luiijf et al. 2010). In specific terms, when interinfrastructural disruptions occurred, more likely than not they involved electricity and telecommunications. Water supplies also appeared vulnerable at the ICIS level, according to both

TNO-DUT and Zimmerman databases.[1] So too in the California Delta. "Electricity, water, and natural gas—those, to my mind, are the most important," said a senior CAISO official with long experience in electricity transmission and its interconnections to other infrastructures in the state and beyond.

The TNO-DUT database highlights two considerations slighted or overlooked in infrastructure modeling of how everything is connected to everything else. First, "interconnected" does not equate solely with "interdependent." One major point made in the TNO-DUT study (Luiijf 2008) and by Eric Luiijf and his colleagues (2010) is that dependencies (*A* leads to *B*) are empirically far more prevalent than interdependencies (*A* leads to *B*, which leads back to *A*). Second, a major reason why intrainfrastructural incidents do not morph into interinfrastructural disruptions or failures is that individual infrastructures are managed by their operators to dampen active interconnectivity. Dependencies among infrastructures, write Luiijf and his colleagues (2010) in their analysis of the TNO-DUT database, "are anything but unmanaged." Michel van Eeten and his colleagues pick up that point in their later, detailed analysis of the data:

The cascades that we find point to dependencies that are anything but unmanaged. Very few organizations operating in [critical infrastructures] are unaware of their dependency on energy or telecommunication. Even the most rudimentary processes of risk assessment would bring these vulnerabilities to light. Organizations experience these dependencies with a clear regularity. In 25 per cent of all cases, an incident triggers another incident, that is, it brings to light a dependency. This relatively high frequency makes it unlikely that operators are unaware of this problem. Of course, mistakes still occur. There are many examples where backup power generators did initially manage to prevent a cascade, but they later failed because the organization was unable to organize the refuelling of the generators. In other words, these dependencies require persistent efforts to mitigate their impacts, but they are hardly "unmanaged." Again, the fact that energy and telecommunication trigger a significant number of cascades could reflect economic trade-offs, rather than unmanaged dependencies. (van Eeten et al. 2011, 396)

These considerations are highly consequential for modeling risk (as that product of the probability and consequences of infrastructure failure) in ICISs. The popular view is that an incident or failure in one critical infrastructure triggers consequences ($\mathrm{Cf_{CIS_1}}$), which in turn increases the probability of failure of another infrastructure ($\mathrm{Pf_{CIS_2}}$), and so on:

$$\text{E1: } \mathrm{Pf_{CIS_1}} \rightarrow \mathrm{Cf_{CIS_1}} \rightarrow \uparrow\mathrm{Pf_{CIS_2}} \rightarrow \ldots$$

The sequence E1 is that common mode failure dominant in present-day discussions on interinfrastructural cascades and core to Chapter 2's ICIS1. Yet as the TNO-DUT database helps illustrate, while E1 is evident in some cross-infrastructural interactions, more often than not disruptions in one critical infrastructure do *not* lead to incidents in others. This containment reflects in important respects the management of critical infrastructure dependencies so that the consequences of disruption in one infrastructure do not adversely affect the probability of failure in infrastructures depending on it. This is the high reliability management we have described.

The most empirically common relationship between interconnected critical infrastructures is not E1 but E2, in which the consequences of disruption and malfunction in one infrastructure do *not* cascade into the other infrastructures failing:[2]

$$\text{E2: } \mathrm{Pf_{CIS_1}} \rightarrow \mathrm{Cf_{CIS_1}} \boxtimes \uparrow\mathrm{Pf_{CIS_2}} \ldots$$

How E2 happens by way of management and what it tells us about preventing E1 is the aim of our ICIS framework. That management includes strategies of resilience and robustness, bandwidth management, requisite variety, and multiple performance modes to manage shifting risks, be they latent or manifest. Our framework allows us to draw out four implications of this empirical work to date on ICIS interactions.

FOUR IMPLICATIONS FOR OUR ANALYSIS
FROM PRIOR EMPIRICAL WORK

First, our analysis makes clear that not all empirical consequences triggered by disruption and failure are negative. Increased management options to prevent failure may become possible only when operations have been disrupted. Notably, California state emergency declarations free up possibilities for emergency responders to shift resources from one infrastructure to another. In fact, once time enters into the equation, the consequences of failure (Cf) in one CIS may actually *reduce* the Pf in other infrastructures if one takes a longer time horizon:

$$E_3: Pf_{CIS_1} \rightarrow Cf_{CIS_1} \rightarrow \downarrow Pf_{CIS_2}$$

Electrical blackouts on the grid led to more rapid installation of backup power sources by Silicon Valley firms to ensure an always-reliable supply of electricity for their servers. A burst water main forces the closure of a road but also brings forward road improvements that had been planned for later. Island flooding may be the way companies and others pick up the cost of replacing legacy equipment and facilities that were all but impossible to replace otherwise. The impact of compensating outcomes on reliability is highlighted in Chapter 11.

Second, our analysis makes clearer why cross-infrastructure cascades are empirically fewer and more granular than commonly understood. Conceptually, cascades are said to happen so fast as to be almost instantaneous. However, normal operations in an infrastructure by no means trip over into failure directly when subjected to a shock or perturbation. Frequently that intervening stage of disrupted operations (a temporary loss of service) can be restored back to normal operations, with or without later tripping into outright failure. This suggests first looking at cases in which operations were interrupted before failing.

The 2003 Northeast Blackout is commonly described as a cascade, but some participants saw it at the time as in no way escalating inevitably. To those insiders, it did not happen so fast that it could not have been managed or controlled. A similar line of argument has been made about the sequence of events leading up to the Deepwater Horizon explosion. Things did not happen instantaneously and the outcome could have been managed differently. In actual practice, many distinct configurations of interinfrastructural connectivity for normal and disrupted operations are more granular and differentiated in terms of time and scale at which management takes place before failure.

Third, while infrastructure management is critical empirically, the opposite is assumed to be the case methodologically. Since systems are managed, why then should we assume they are unmanaged for modeling or formal risk assessment purposes? Consider one of many such descriptions of network analysis and research under way:

In their analysis of connected networks, the researchers found a type of mathematical behavior that couldn't have been predicted from knowledge of single networks. When a node is removed from a single network, the failure tends to propagate gradually, the network coming apart bit by bit by bit. But removing nodes in a network of networks means the breakdown can occur abruptly. As nodes go offline, the system initially appears to be working properly. But all of a sudden, a threshold is reached. Lose one more node and—poof—the whole thing falls to pieces. "Even if one more node fails, the network collapses completely." (Quill 2012)

Not only are sudden events infrequent in the systems we have studied for reasons already outlined, a major finding in earlier versions of network analysis was that changing the configuration of the network actually *opens up* new opportunities for exchange and resources among network participants in some cases.[3] The assumption that infrastructure elements are deleted as if they were not empirically managed to prevent such deletion or that, once excised, the resulting network reconfiguration would not open new management options at the same time is, in our experience and research, highly unrealistic and not empirical.

The assumption that the best way to study interinfrastructure failure is to assume that no management (or utterly inadequate management) is occurring in systems that are fully loaded and stressed pervades current risk methodologies. To be clear, ample evidence exists—and we have observed this ourselves—that infrastructure managers do see increased risks and respond to them when infrastructure systems are run at full bore. As the director general of Eurocontrol, a European air traffic management agency, acknowledged, "When airspace is filled to capacity, 'there are going to be more opportunities for things to go wrong'" (Michaels and Pasztor 2008, B4).

Yet while systems sometimes do fail outright even before they operate at capacity, disrupted operations are more frequent and more frequently restored back to normal operations without triggering failure. Too much of the risk assessment with which we are familiar has narrowly centered on the probability and consequences of system failure when, in actual practice, control room management focuses on avoiding or managing disruptions. In addition to the many other reservations we raise with respect to conventional risk methods, the notion that Pf and Cf vary independently of each other is sorely tested in real-world situations—for instance, new designs and technology enable building larger dams with lower Pf but also entail higher losses (Cf) if these dams do fail (see, e.g., Egan 2007).

Another problem in risk analysis has been the validation of risk estimates and methods. One way engineers validate their estimates of failure probability for levees is to compare and adjust these in relation to levee sections that have been induced to fail under controlled conditions (Hamedifar 2012). This is a sounder methodology than that of producing otherwise unvalidated methods. But the assumption again is that what matters when it comes to failure is that the infrastructure is at the point of maximum stress in an unmanaged condition. But really-existing control rooms reduce levee stress by managing water flows adjacent to the levees. The entire point of control rooms is that they manage so as to maintain normal operations, mitigate disruptions, and prevent failure; that, after all, is why they have simulators and training programs.[4]

Fourth, just as it is impossible to describe all the ways the cat's-cradle of interconnectivity could—might, may, potentially, perhaps—go wrong across critical infrastructures, so too is it not possible to describe all the ways really-existing interconnections are going right. The thrust of our ICIS framework is that things can go right when it comes to interconnectivity.[5] To be a reliability professional is to manage the unplanned in ways that avoid unstudied conditions. As Bauke Steenhuisen put it for the UK and Netherlands rail traffic controllers he studied, "Fitting unplanned train movements into the flow of trains and tightly planned schedules" is what they do (2014, 3). In contrast, thinking within conventional organization theory assumes that, far more often, complexly interactive and tightly coupled critical infrastructures portend more negative than positive outcomes as a result of generating or confronting unplanned conditions.

For those in everyday infrastructure practice, it is considerably more difficult to dismiss or avoid the positive features of interconnectivity, including surprises that turn out to be positive. Engineers are correct to insist that notwithstanding the downsides of interconnectivity, normal operations of infrastructures critical for survival and well-being would not happen without interconnected reliable electricity and telecoms systems. We certainly see both positives and negatives of interinfrastructural connnectivity when we move from current models of interconnectivity to the infrastructure crossroads of the California Delta.

On the ground, do the pluses of interconnectivity outweigh its minuses? To answer that, we must appreciate that the positives and negatives of infrastructural interconnectivity can come in tandem or are difficult to parse in reliability management—which is exactly why there are *risks* that also have to be managed when it comes to interinfrastructural interconnectivity. Risks, it bears repeating, exist on all sides of infrastructure operation: "A ship that is doing nothing is dangerous just sitting there," a senior port manager told us. How that risk and other risks are being reliably managed or not is decisive when determining what outweighs what. This is patently the case when moving from management theories to practice in the face of contingencies.

THE VARIETY OF INTERINFRASTRUCTURAL INTERCONNECTIONS: EXAMPLES FROM DELTA RESEARCH

Consider a few of the many cases of positive and negative interconnectivity in the California Delta and what they mean for both infrastructure vulnerabilities and resources for control operators we have studied. Our samples have been chosen to mirror the diversity of connectivity sketched in the preceding chapters and reflect what is reported as going on elsewhere in cross-infrastructure settings in the United States and abroad.

The California Delta is repeatedly described as a system of systems, especially because of its levee system for flood management that protects and supports not just Delta islands but other infrastructures that pass through the region, including major highways, shipping channels, transmission lines, gas lines, water supplies, and other infrastructure elements (see, e.g., Delta Protection Commission 2012, 58, 66, 70, 89). Given the conception of the Delta as a system of interconnected systems, the risks of interconnected infrastructure failure are considered to be high. Particularly vulnerable as a starting point are the levee structures themselves. Long stretches of Delta levees do not meet federal standards, and those federal standards, if met, are for hundred-year storms, which many consider an inadequate standard for the future (e.g., in light of regional climate change).

The Pf and Cf of Delta levee breaches have been estimated to be high with respect to an earthquake, a major storm, or even a sunny-day event (as in the Jones Tract case described in Chapter 3). An engineering report that's part of California's Delta Risk Management Strategy calculated the probability of an earthquake greater than magnitude 6.7 occurring over thirty-five years at 62 percent (Healey, Dettinger, and Norgaard 2008, 111). Sherman Island is reckoned by the same report to have a greater than 7 percent mean annual probability of levee failure over twenty-five years because of earthquakes or other high-water and dry-weather events (URS 2007, 21). Another Delta Risk Management Strategy report (California Department of Water Resources 2009a, 12) estimates the total economic cost and impact of multiple levee failures after a major earthquake in the Delta to be in the tens of billions of dollars. One major-storm scenario, which considers an area much larger than the Delta, estimates losses in business interruption alone of over $325 billion, considerably more than currently calculated for Katrina or the loss of the World Trade Center (U.S. Geological Survey 2011, 138). These high estimates of risk have not been uniformly accepted or, when accepted, acted on by decision makers in ways many would prefer.

All that is the negative, which we return to later in the chapter; but where is the positive?

Samples of Positive Interconnectivity

Key informants at CAISO told us that the reliability of managing the state's transmission grid has improved through having multiple telecommunication vendors along with an increasingly reliable Internet. Some utilities run their lines along railroad corridors, thereby ensuring both easier access in time of trouble and a second pair of eyes on their own elements. PG&E, the Northern California gas and electric utility, added generation resources so as to mitigate reliance on a single Delta generation plant to better meet mandated water temperature limits for striped bass spawning near that generation.

Many organizations and infrastructures are interinfrastructural by mandate and operation. PG&E manages both electricity and gas infrastructures as interoperable systems: a minor electrical event can have implications for its gas infrastructure were that event to disturb backup gas pumps and generators.

Real-time knowledge of such interoperability has been, we were told, important in some transmission infrastructure hiring practices. The state of California manages water supply, levee flood protection, and electricity generation infrastructures under one organization, the Department of Water Resources (DWR). The Port of Stockton is an intermodal transportation hub for shipping, rail, and truck traffic. Union Pacific has its own electricity generators as a fallback in case of emergency. PG&E, DWR, and Union Pacific contract out some infrastructure requirements, such as helicopters, divers, and other services as and when needed.

The California Utilities Emergency Association is a major public-private partnership of water, energy, and telecommunications, whose executive staff have been housed in the California Governor's Office of Emergency Services (formerly California Emergency Management Agency) and whose role is to interconnect various utility resources and serve as a single point of contact in emergencies (on the importance of such partnerships, see NIAC 2009). Cal Fire necessarily works with other infrastructures during fire emergencies and under mutual aid agreements; the same applies to the Coast Guard's San Francisco command center, where search and rescue operations can involve a great many other agencies, including California Highway Patrol and Caltrans. The Coast Guard's VTS routinely manages both the waterways in its navigation areas and the ferry and vessel traffic in those waterways and regularly coordinates with vessels of other agencies—for example, the dredging and multipurpose command vessels of the Army Corps of Engineers stationed in its command area.

At the time of our research, the control facilities of the SWP, Flood Operations Center, and the federal Central Valley Project were collocated in the same building to encourage ease of communication and coordination (along with other important agencies, including a National Weather Service unit). A senior hydrologist with long experience and credibility had desks in the National Weather Service unit and the state's Flood Operations Center, alternating work between the two. The Coast Guard's VTS and command center for search and rescue operations are right next to each other for the same reason. Interinfrastructural connectivity can be established in ways other than collocation. A senior Port of Stockton manager was also affiliated with reclamation district boards whose levees are an important part of the port.[6]

In these cases (and there are more), infrastructural interconnections are explicitly more a resource than a source of vulnerability (i.e., collocation is positive, not negative as in the ICIS1 scenario). Surprises arising out of interconnectivity are by no means always negative either. A senior official with multiagency emergency response experience reminded us, "Sometimes the surprise is positive, you know. No matter the emergency, there always seems to be someone who rises to the occasion and makes things happen." Said another longtime state emergency manager, "In spite of everything, in spite of all these problems, you know we're going to respond." Such statements are not only about the continued presence of management but also about reactive micro-operations coping with what can't be managed or imagined beforehand.

Samples of Negative Interconnectivity

Cases of negative interconnectivity touched on earlier bear further mention here. Emergency releases from upstream dams and reservoirs to prevent overtopping were often mentioned as having potentially harmful effects downriver on levees, shipping, and population centers. CAISO, as we saw, complained of firefighters starting backfires near or under easier-to-access transmission line corridors. Storms have taken out electricity distribution lines, which are needed for pumps to dewater some flooded Delta islands. "When it comes to storms, the environment never helps us," a group of reclamation district discussants said. High winds can necessitate bridge closures and restrictions on ferry dockings—the only way to get to some Delta islands is by ferry—and stop vessel traffic on the shipping channels. Telecommunications field workers worry about getting to their facilities on unpaved roads during the storms, and although improvements in telecommunications have helped some infrastructure managers, others told us worrisome issues and uncertainties remain.

During heat waves, sections of sagging power lines over transportation lanes can reduce vehicle and vessel clearance. Environmental consequences arising from conflicting infrastructure requirements have posed a constant challenge and range from well-known concerns over water flows with respect to endangered or threatened Delta species and habitat to how shipping ballast can spread invasive species. "In the past, we could spill [ballast]," a water control room manager told us, "but now, with all the environmental regulations, if we spill water out, we go into reporting mode, someone is in trouble, we're probably having to write up a violation report. You don't want to do that, or you'll have the state in your business." Such environmentally related events often are interinfrastructural by nature: "We wanted [DWR] to pump more at night than during the day," a CAISO senior manager told us, "but they said they were mandated to regulate their pumping so it wouldn't disturb the fish." A USBR staff member in the Central Valley Project told us of the multiple standards to which the federal water had to be managed "with a different standard controlling each day; today it is the outflow number."[7]

No single interconnection is negative or positive in all circumstances, and one does not necessarily net out the other. High-temperature days cause problems for the electric distribution system (e.g., increased use of air conditioning in offices) but are good days for the natural gas system, as gas demand for heat falls on those days. An earthquake damages the electric grid but also reduces load requirements immediately afterward during initial recovery. All sides of the risk must be managed.

If you asked the informed public in the San Francisco Bay–California Delta what their worst-case scenario for the region was, they'd probably say a major earthquake or storm. If pressed, a few might insist that their next-worst crisis is the one we are already in: the stalemate resulting from the multitude of conflicting organizations, stakeholders, and institutions claiming some control over or stake in the Bay-Delta, including its infrastructure crossroads (Hanemann and Dyckman 2009).

However, our focus on managed systems—managed by infrastructure operators for *both* positive and negative interconnectivity with other infrastructures—sets the context for understanding why and how infrastructure operators, when asked for their worst-case challenges, often describe triggering events from other infrastructures. Different scenarios frequently entail different infrastructures. The EBMUD aqueduct failing beneath a deepwater shipping channel means coordinating with the Coast Guard; pipes from the same aqueduct failing under a different river may mean coordinating directly with DWR. Rather than being scenarios about unmanaged systems failing one after another, operator scenarios are typically about how abrupt changes or malfunctions in one infrastructure pose quite specific management challenges to the infrastructure in question.[8] Remember, the empirical evidence is that the challenges are, by and large, met in many infrastructures—though again high reliability management can assume no iron guarantees here.

In high reliability management terms, operators undertake scenario formulation from within their domain of competence. Some worst-case scenarios that have happened are illustrative. An untethered barge hits a bridge pylon—and that activates the Coast Guard because the waterway is involved and Caltrans because it is responsible for the bridge. Other agencies become involved, and the interaction of different infrastructures and agencies complicates quickly. As another example, a vessel on a deepwater shipping channel to Stockton hit a section of levee protecting Bradford Island (Bradford, like Sherman Island, is in the western Delta). Levee damage was reported by another vessel operator the next day. The county sheriff's office and Coast Guard was notified, and an incident command center established. At one point, the incident command center thought the island should be evacuated (some one hundred residences were said to be on Bradford). It was also reported to us that an evacuation order would have had to be issued by the county sheriff, which we were told was not done. The Coast Guard controlled navigation on the river channel and established a minimum-wake zone to facilitate barge movement for levee repair. By the start of the next week the event had played itself out with the levee being attended to and the minimum-wake zone suspended.

Key informants at the Port of Stockton set out major-impact scenarios of what would happen—regionally, statewide, and beyond—if goods shipped into and out of the port for surrounding agricultural production were disrupted. A VTS manager told us of the Bay Area response to a Sumatra earthquake and tsunami, "We stopped all cargo transfers [and] cranes, and ferry companies suspended activity." A senior CAISO manager told us his worry involved generation infrastructures: "The worst-case scenario is when you miss your peak of high [electricity] load because you don't have the capacity, as you've had to curtail due to low water levels," meaning that curtailment of hydropower generation is problematic because it is exceptionally useful in high-tempo situations.

When it comes to negative scenarios involving multiple infrastructures, a bottleneck for Bay-Delta navigation has been the elevated rail bridge crossing Carquinez Strait, we were told. In another case, a DWR emergency response manager reported, "Look what's happening in the drought when it comes to wildland fires. By drawing water for firefighting from the groundwater, like in San Diego, groundwater levels are going down, and we're losing capability to ship and transfer it. What's going to happen if the drought continues?" For PG&E managers at their Vacaville electricity control facility, "it would really be bad if something happened to the COI [California-Oregon Intertie, a strategic transmission line]—if we had a storm when the COI was already derated or worse and then we lost the COI in the storm." With respect to providers of telephone landlines and ethernet fiber communications, a telecommunications manager working in the Delta saw his unit's dependency on them to be a key vulnerability: "If they lose these land linkages, the cell phone operation goes down." And in case anyone doubts that many interinfrastructural worst-case scenarios involve life and death stakes, consider the example a senior CAISO manager gave us. "In 2006 we issued announcements to conserve electricity, including setting your thermostat up to 80. But when some older people or others did it, they put their lives at risk, so the last week we modified our statement: conserve electricity if this does not put you at risk."

The list of worst-case scenarios is easily expanded, but the point remains: what is going on in actual infrastructure management and scenario formulation is about as far away as one can imagine from the modeler's assumption that a system's links and nodes can be deleted or excised, as if up to that point their being managed counted for naught and after that point those left being managed count for naught as well.

SYSTEM IN FAILURE VERSUS SYSTEM IN NORMAL OPERATIONS

The term "vulnerability" recurs in the preceding discussion, and once "vulnerability" is touched on in the study of critical infrastructures, predictions of system failure are never far away. This holds for many system-of-system models as well as in the perception of experts and decision makers who rely on them. Vulnerability is the first step in those crisis scenarios in which large engineered systems, such as those for financial services, nuclear power, and oil or natural gas exploration, have interconnections so complex that vulnerabilities are not recognized until systems fail. But up to and after presenting shifting interconnections, *the systems studied here are still managed*. Yes, a Coast Guard specialist in emergency management stressed, "All the possible interconnections can't be imagined." But the corollary can be just as true: "It takes only once for something like this to happen, and you don't forget it," a VTS supervisor told us. Once something happens, no matter how unforeseen, what then matters for reliability professionals is that it could happen again, whatever the formal probabilities. When it comes to control room operators, scenario possibilities are just as real as scenario probabilities.

When we turn to actual system failure, we confront a paradox: for a topic so conspicuously discussed, system failure is curiously underconceptualized when the point of departure is the managed system. Return to the observation made at several points in this book: major managed systems are so complex that when they fail, they look nothing like they did during their normal operations. This was evident in Hurricane Katrina, the global financial meltdown, Deepwater Horizon, and Fukushima; this too will be seen in the Delta if catastrophe happens there.

In the view of a research scientist and engineer with experience on deepwater platforms, "The blowout on the [Deepwater Horizon] rig and the apparent failure of the blowout preventer was 'beyond the realm of expectation,' most likely a combination of unimaginable human and mechanical error" (quoted in Rosenthal 2010). "If we fail, we fail miserably" is how an experienced port manager described the difference between normal and failed operations.[9] In reality, the only formally designed and managed system for the specific context of a catastrophic interinfrastructural failure may be the emergency management and response infrastructure.

Note that the system in failure includes not only the incomprehensibly complex but also the immediate loss of knowledge about the infrastructure. Under normal or disrupted conditions, repair workers can see water leaking from broken underground water mains, but when the water system has bled out because of the inability to make repairs on these mains, the system in failure becomes more difficult to bound, understand, diagnose, and fix—that is, to know and comprehend. Unlike a crisis in the control room that the public may never see, system failure is a fundamental discontinuity in the whole cycle of infrastructure operations witnessed by all concerned.

To be clear, "the system" in the phrase "the system in failure," might never have existed before the failure but exists now and afterward for purposes of recovery. On Sherman Island the levee road is needed to repair the electricity distribution lines, which are in turn connected to pumps for dewatering. Each is not conventionally thought of in its own right as "the levee roads system," "the distribution line system," or "the pumping system." Yet if the river floods and overtops the levee, taking out with it the levee road, distribution lines, and pumps, the sequence of river flood–levee overtopping–road failure–collapse of distribution lines–dewatering pumps now inoperable becomes its own collective system in failure. While this latently interconnected system was not manifest before failure, it can become strategic in recovery of the broader levee protection system, electricity distribution system, and regional road system in which these infrastructure elements have failed. Moreover, control rooms where they exist do not disappear when their technical systems fail. "You may have to stop all nonessential operations—that's what an emergency is about," a long-time utility specialist with grid management experience said. Even when the system in failure differs from the system in normal operations, control operators continue working.

MULTIPLE DIMENSIONS IN TIME AND SCALE FOR INTERCONNECTIVITY AND RISK

The preceding factors underline that interconnectivity and associated risks change over time and scale. This vital point is one we spend the remainder of this chapter and the entirety of the next chapter clarifying. Here we focus primarily on how the issues look from inside an infrastructure; Chapter 7 casts this infrastructure focus within an explicit ICIS setting.

We stay with our case study and start with time. Normal operations of the Contra Costa Water District revolve around eight-hour shifts, but managing the actual water flows and treatment involves thinking in terms of twelve to twenty-four hours, spanning what lies ahead and what has already happened: "Many things you set in motion won't be completed until the next shift," one operator noted. The twenty-four-hour look back is required for system-wide pattern recognition, while the eight-hour-ahead perspective is necessary for scenario formulation. So too elsewhere. "Our operators must look one to two hours ahead, their supervisors twelve to twenty-four hours, and me five hours to ten years," a senior manager of the Coast Guard's VTS told us. For a senior port manager, "The Coast Guard is ninety-six hours out, only concerned when the vessel is ninety-six hours from the port."

The head of the Coast Guard's command center reported that his "job is also to keep continuity over shifts, maintain continuity through the watches." A port manager said, "Reliability means that I know in March that I need to dredge in August and how long it's going to take them to process our requests so that dredging starts when we have our [regulated dredging] window." Yet "our dredging window is getting smaller and smaller," another port manager told us. "It takes months to get our storage to maximum, which is what we want in the summer months," an EBMUD manager told us. "That's why breaking a pipe is so bad from our perspective. It takes six months to get our storage at capacity, so any major break would have major implications." *How much time does this buy us?* is a major question asked of any response intervention in a disruption or worse.

With time comes scale. In normal operations, water delivery from initial intake to final distribution takes time to flow across space. In an emergency, planning water releases from reservoirs means that infrastructure managers take into account the volume and rate of water flow. For instance, it may take days for the water pulse, or plug, to reach the saltwater intrusion zone after a western Delta levee breach—though, as we were warned by an informed source, "all this depends on getting the staging of releases right."

Rerouting shipping and train traffic takes time, and delays affect customers across regions. "We're a business, we have to make it work; we can't allow the system to break down," a senior port manager reported. But if port operations do fail, the effects can ramify across the country, disrupting rail schedules for months, and across the world, disrupting, for example, rice markets in Asia. Similar considerations were mentioned by Union Pacific representatives. In a time-critical, multiple-scale context, both control operators and emergency responders speak of having to watch mistakes propagate: "We have to watch our mistakes play out over time. A minor error in a ten-hour transit during the first half hour can result in a very nasty situation," said a VTS manager. This means that "we have to see an event though different lenses—the mission area, scope of responsibility, current and future time," an experienced supervisor in the Coast Guard command center told us. All the lenses have to be in the room.

The combination of time, scale, and risk is evident in a number of cases: Coast Guard search and rescue professionals informed us that the longer the mission, the greater the risk typically. At CAISO we were told, "If we don't pick load up in a couple of days [after a grid emergency], then you know it really is bad." When it comes to recovery, about the only thing our key informants reiterated is that it can be a lengthy process—precisely because scale and risks necessarily vary along the way. "Remember: recovery can take a long time, and in that time technology can change as well, so you won't be recovering to what you had before anyway," a senior state emergency manager informed us. With time and scale come the expectations and decisions for managing reliability, and thus risks, in infrastructures. This was nicely put by one control operator: "Take a look at this system breathing in and breathing out; keep the whole picture in mind, and have a set of expectations. You pay a lot of attention, but you've already decided what the system is doing, so when it's doing it, things are going smooth. When it doesn't meet your expectations, then things aren't."

When it comes to time, scale, and risk, it is also essential to recognize that the Delta as an infrastructure crossroads has been built up over time and space as an artifact of many individual infrastructure-related decisions on their own, a number of which were made in light of what other infrastructures had been doing nearby. With roads came people; with more people came more roads, water supplies, and other structures. This means not only that infrastructures change with respect to each other over time and scale; what may have been a redundant element in one infrastructure can at a later point become unique because of those evolving spatial and functional interconnections.[10] What was once a bypass road might evolve into a major thoroughfare for shopping and residence. There are also infrastructures that have had the time, like Union Pacific over more than a century, to build up their knowledge base for all kinds of risks, conditions, and emergencies and across a very large scale. "We have tons of experience with different scenarios," a rail manager told us. So too for the U.S. Coast Guard: "Different regions have their different disasters. Here it is earthquakes; elsewhere it is flooding or winter storms. In the Coast Guard, people get a lot of experience across these different regions and their different disasters during their careers."

In light of this evidence, four points need to be highlighted that have not been sufficiently stressed by other ICIS approaches about *managed* interinfrastructure operations that vary with time, scale, and risk. First, normal operations of infrastructures can be very poor predictors of what their reliability operations look like in failure and recovery; but the reverse is also true. It is difficult to imagine that even the proverbial Martian, visiting our planet for the first time during the Deepwater Horizon disaster, could reconstruct what its various participants—the Coast Guard, BP, others—were doing "normally" before the incident. To put the point differently, learning is in no way a necessarily additive process across divergent conditions.

Second, one must not, however, assume normal and failed operations are two different universes. They aren't completely decoupled from each other. It's worth remembering that normal operation is a state in which accidents and failure are waiting to happen—and with varied and changing risks—because incidents would happen had not reliability professionals prevented them from occurring. If it weren't for the persistent threat of failure, high reliability would not be the better-case management standard for key infrastructures. Were management not active but itself only waiting to happen (i.e., triggered only by the accident having occurred), then you would not have high reliability management; you'd instead have some version of emergency response.

Third, when time and scale interact, context becomes everything for infrastructure reliability and risk management. A major storm at 4:00 a.m. triggers a set of interconnections different from what it would during the traffic commute hours later. The same storm hitting the Oakland and Stockton ports triggers different scenarios if only because Stockton manages ships directly, while the Oakland port has different terminals with their own vessel management. A major storm that is a fifty-year storm rather than, say, a ten-year storm will affect staff—control operators and emergency responders—who show up for work differently. "If we had a fifty-year storm, I'd be at home protecting my family," one infrastructure manager told us (and others admitted much the same).

An earthquake triggers interconnectivity differently than a major storm forecasted five days in advance. If either hits a major dam or reservoir, each structure could fail in a distinctive way with differing consequences, if only because each impounds a different watershed and has its own capacity features.

This means that emergency responders, let alone control room operators, may not know what resources are required for response until disruption or failure or recovery reveals the manifest interconnectivity and resilience required.

Fourth, mistakes, glitches, and defects are likely going on that *no one* recognizes, even in managed systems. The complexity, transaction speeds, or lack of transparency of the technical systems may be so great that nobody sees or notices the mistake in real time or manages the consequences. Think of the problem of slow oil seepage into underground structures[11] or undetected (undetectable) accidents in computerized voting. Society may already be tolerating malfunctions that neither we (outside the infrastructure) nor they (its insiders) are managing because no one is aware of them now or planning for them in the next steps ahead. Ultimately, this is concerning because many macro-designers of systems and policy do not realize that unstudied conditions arise directly out of system designs and technology that must somehow be managed by system operators as the last line of defense. This is even more challenging within an ICIS framework, especially when it comes to the intertwined issues of time, scale, and risk, as we see in the next chapter.

CHAPTER 7

THE FULL CYCLE OF
INFRASTRUCTURE
OPERATIONS

T HIS CHAPTER CONSOLIDATES CHAPTER 6'S
empirical descriptions of the interaction of time, scale, and risk into our ICIS framework. Doing so enables a deeper probe into the types and nature of operations an infrastructure undertakes under its reliability mandates within settings interconnected with other infrastructures across their respective states of operation. Our organizing mechanism for this deeper probe is the infrastructure's full cycle of operations.

Figure 7.1 introduces an idealized version of a single infrastructure's entire operational cycle, covering all system states from the perspective of its control operators and other reliability professionals (including their support staff). Return to the critical infrastructure as an entire system, be it water supply, electricity grid, or deepwater port, over its different operational states. Beginning from the left side of Figure 7.1, this infrastructure's control operators typically maintain operations within (de facto and de jure) bandwidths of reliable system and performance conditions. Notice that "normal" does not—cannot, as we have seen—mean "invariant": adjustments are to be expected within bandwidths to enable adaptation to a stream of contingencies and unpredictabilities. As one water control operator put it, "Every day is a new adventure. No day is

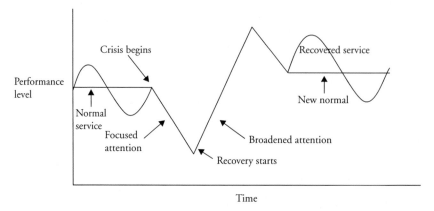

FIGURE 7.1   Whole cycle of service provision for a critical infrastructure.
Source: Adapted from Bales 1953, 116.

the same as before. If things go wrong, it won't happen the same way twice. We're always busy, always learning, because we get new equipment or procedures." And this statement reflects the views of many with whom we talked.

Control operators enter a crisis condition when they confront or anticipate conditions that threaten their cognitive skill to understand a situation in terms of recognizing patterns and to respond to a situation in terms of formulating action scenarios that they then translate into strategies of action. A crisis could begin with loss of communications or some other requirement for the management of their control variables. The crisis starts for control operators when they are pushed to operate at the edge of or beyond their domain of competence, where skills and task requirements are matched.

As we have underscored, this team situational awareness of the crisis might not correspond to an actual disruption or catastrophic loss of service; it may well precede it. The time period for the crisis from the perspective of the operators may be advanced in every phase over public perceptions and even the perceptions of organizational or political leaders. The latter may see the crisis only at the point of loss of service. But by the time that stage is reached, control room operators could be on the road to restoration or even beginning recovery. From its first cognitive challenges, a crisis gets the full attention of the control room. "Granted, emergencies aren't our normal business; 90 percent of our job isn't emergencies," a VTS manager told us, "but we do have to be prepared for them. When emergencies do happen, they supersede normal operations until the emergency is over."

The crisis begins a period of intense and focused attention on recognizing what's actually happening: discovering a pattern or patterns and assessing action scenarios. This activity can restore disrupted service, and if it does, constitutes the restoration resilience defined earlier. If failure occurred, the recovery takes a different form of problem-solving activity on the part of control room operators. The focus shifts from narrowing attention on understanding the particular character of the failure to expanding the scope of factors attended to, *including related infrastructures*, in pursuit of recovery strategy. Recovery necessarily involves many outside organizations and personnel whose actions have to be carefully coordinated if it is to be successful. During this period there are likely to be two contrasting perspectives: the attention of the public to the interruption of service and the reliability professionals' enhanced attention to developing and weighing recovery options.

Since recovery of infrastructure performance entails concentrated, extraordinary, and time-consuming problem-solving activity on the part of operators and emergency responders *across* infrastructures, nothing guarantees recovery. Remember, the probability of failure can frequently be higher in recovery than in normal operations. Trying to rebuild electrical grid connections after the islanding of generators, switching stations, and transmission lines has been described as a lot like trying to build a house of cards. The first slip can send you back to zero. "We're good at [emergency] response in California, but we're not good at recovery," a long-time security manager told us. "The big question in recovery," according to a senior state emergency manager, "is how fast can you bring up minimum service to high-risk areas and populations?" "On-demand systems, with just-in-time production, are difficult to wind down but [take] even longer to wind up again [after a disaster]," a Coast Guard emergency specialist said.

In nominal terms, the whole cycle of infrastructure operations ends *after* recovery, when control operators are at a new normal, with scenarios and patterns added to their management repertoire, along with new facilities and equipment as well as with any new regulatory or policy constraints. The "new" in the "new normal" could be above the old normal's performance effectiveness. But it could also be below. Untried equipment, hasty reorganizations, or new regulatory constraints imposed from a public-accountability more than a reliability perspective may leave control operators and other reliability professionals with far fewer options and more unstudied conditions than they confronted before the crisis. In either case the new normal may go unnoticed by the public with the recovery of service, just as the public may never have noticed the first crisis stage in control operations preceding the disruption or loss of service.

The whole cycle described above entails varying risks and sets of risks. As we have described, even normal operations pose a set of multiple risks, if only when high reliability management requires that operators be able to maneuver across different performance modes. But risks do not stop there, since, under mandates for reliability, the whole cycle of states must cover far more than normal operations. There are also those stage-specific risks of keen interest to the system's reliability professionals, including (1) the risk of disrupted services given crisis conditions in control room management before any actual service disruption, (2) the risk of failed services if disrupted infrastructure services are not restored, (3) the risk of failure in recovering services given the difficulty and complexity of recovery operations, and (4) the fresh risks of a new normal in infrastructure services postrecovery (e.g., is the infrastructure now more resilient or brittle?). To be clear, nothing in the cycle sequence implies the system lumbers from stage to stage or that the interconnections during each stage remain static. The system could fail straight from normal operations and never move into disruption or out to recovery.

The whole cycle returns us to those time and scale limitations associated with site and regional analyses of interinfrastructure reliability and the associated risks. Focus first on scale. With regard to our research area, the cycle's spatial scale is decidedly *not* the California Delta, legally defined or regionally understood. Rather it is the scale at which each infrastructure is managed and operated for purposes of reliability as a system property. Now add time to scale. If a major storm is forecast to move into the Delta, the inland ports will reroute tanker traffic elsewhere, outside the San Francisco Bay Area, to ensure the deepwater shipping channels are not blocked. Union Pacific has several alternative ways to reroute rail traffic and its timing, should it be disrupted in or around the Delta. Now add the interconnectivity: the same infrastructure element—for example, Union Pacific's elevated bridge that crosses Carquinez Strait (around which Union Pacific told us it would reroute train traffic if that bridge became inoperable)—could become a major choke point to shipping traffic up and down the deepwater channels, in the view of the Coast Guard's

VTS and command center, depending on the level at and manner in which the bridge failed. On the positive side, the strengthening of Delta levees near or adjacent to the EBMUD aqueduct serves as flood management for other infrastructure elements close by as well. Linking respective control variables means the scale and timing of operations shift together.

AN EXAMPLE OF THE WHOLE CYCLE'S TWO DIMENSIONS

To further understand the interaction of time and scale across infrastructures, we turn to an example of how the whole cycle frames operations over time and at any point in time in terms of our ICIS framework explicitly.

Figure 7.1 has two major dimensions, the horizontal dimension of different states of operation discussed above and the vertical dimension (performance effectiveness), which we detail below. Return first to the horizontal dimension. In natural language when people talk about "recovery" of critical services, they can mean four kinds of resilience (reading from left to right in Figure 7.1): the control room adjusting back to within their bandwidths so as to continue normal operations; restoration from disrupted operations back to normal operations; emergency response immediately after system failure; and the recovery of the system to a new normal. Each, we have seen, has its own key features: (1) normal operations are not invariant, and real-time adjustments back to within the bandwidths of operation are periodically required; (2) restoration reminds us that many disrupted infrastructure operations are managed so as not to trigger failure; (3) failure and emergency response occur together frequently, since life-threatening consequences are involved; and (4) full-service recovery after failure is so intensive (with its own high probabilities of failure) that "recovery effort during failure" may itself be the new normal for an indefinite period of time.

Among the important implications of this over-time perspective on infrastructure operations is this: resilience is not a stage of the whole cycle but rather a property differently configured at different stages. It is not a static feature or an on-off property but occurs along the stages as precursor resilience, restoration resilience, and recovery resilience—in short, resilience is not reducible to "emergency response and recovery" only or even primarily. A control room that is effective in precursor resilience may or may not be more effective in restoration resilience, and a control room effective in both may not be particularly effective in recovery resilience. After one CAISO recovery simulation exercise, several officials conceded that they did not think the organization was well prepared for recovery management.[1] Certainly, interconnectivity shifts, as discussed in Chapter 4, have a significant impact on resilience.

An example of the cycle's vertical point-in-time dimension is the 2010 San Bruno, California, gas explosion that killed eight people and involved a natural gas pipeline of PG&E. (Although the city falls outside our research focus on the California Delta, the explosion was within the PG&E gas system, important transmission assets of which do cross the Delta.) Major San Bruno investigations have understandably zoomed down to root-cause analyses of what happened to the specific stretch of San Bruno pipeline that failed.

Our ICIS framework would require accident evaluations by investigators to zoom up and zoom across *at the same time* as zooming down. In zooming up, we would want to know what happened to the PG&E natural gas system as a whole during and after the event. In the same moment, we would want to know what happened to other ICISs as a result of the explosion, either directly (e.g., what happened to the road network in and around San Bruno as a result of the explosion) or indirectly (e.g., what disruptions or worse were caused by the explosion in other infrastructures dependent on PG&E gas lines, not least of which is the PG&E electricity system).

But the analysis needs to go further since precursor, restoration, and recovery resilience, as measures of performance effectiveness, may themselves be interrelated. Ideally, the analysts would also zoom down, up, and across other examples for the same company in which earlier gas line operations were disrupted but restored without an explosion having occurred. The company's precursor and restoration resilience may have earlier prevented explosions or worse disasters or ones that would have otherwise affected other infrastructures more severely. This is important knowledge to have in hand when the impulse is to change regulation in light of any single failure.

From the ICIS risk perspective, it is not sufficient to undertake a root-cause analysis (zooming down) of an explosion and then institute company reforms on the basis of that analysis alone without having assessed (1) what prior accidents were prevented under the pre-explosion profiles of precursor and restoration resilience; (2) how post-explosion reforms will affect those resilience

profiles, negatively or positively; and (3) how post-explosion reforms will affect other related infrastructures. Yes, of course, this is complex analysis and
investigation; but how else is risk to be managed under the existing reliability
mandates and within the interconnectivity for that reliability?

We emphasize that the point-in-time zooming down, up, and across is an
activity that holds elsewhere along the whole cycle and not just after recovery.
Consider the design end of the design-management continuum. As we saw, a
macro-designer who believes in the sufficiency of system design in ensuring
reliability is also likely to believe that failure in system reliability must be designed out. Those of us who understand design is permanently incomplete (that
is why reliability requires management beyond design all along the continuum)
are not surprised that explanations of system failure, just like any root-cause
analysis, are necessarily incomplete as well. Part of that incompleteness arises
because infrastructure design has in our experience rarely been done within
an explicit ICIS framework.

As demonstrated in Chapter 9's case study, the designers of a new hardware
and software system for dispatching power in the California electrical grid did
not zoom down, up, and across in terms of drawing out the implications of their
major system redesign. This incompleteness of design from an ICIS perspective also helps explain why the knowledge requirements of control operations
must be so intensive. Control operators, in contrast to accident investigators,
formal risk evaluators, and system designers, must manage reliably *precisely
because real-time operations are those times when it is not cognitively possible to
zoom down, up, and across all the interconnections.* Operators look to signature
events rather than for full connectivity and causality. For a parallel, fuller
ICIS appraisal over time and across scale, we must look to system planning
and support staff and not just postaccident investigators.[2]

OTHER CONSIDERATIONS AND IMPLICATIONS OF ICIS
TIME AND SCALE FOR INFRASTRUCTURE RISK

The entire cycle embeds in other concrete ways scale and time in the analysis of multiple-risk operations and facilities within and across infrastructures.[3]
We were told that PG&E, if receiving a five-day forecast of a fifty-year storm,
would move relief resources and assets in advance of that storm. Any such

calculus of risk assessment and management must in turn depend on the specific scenario: Is the storm in winter or spring? If in spring, a set of additional issues arise for PG&E than would if it were during another season in terms of where to move assets. In such ways, the operational area of an infrastructure, at least to its control operators and support staff, is not the same thing as a planning region for Delta policy makers or the "impact shed" for state economists assessing the consequences of infrastructure failure over space and time. Obviously, the same scenario, like that fifty-year storm, would affect infrastructures other than PG&E and thereby be of importance to PG&E real-time operations.

Note that the impact area for operators can extend well beyond the area of operations and is important in their risk calculations of Cf. The Port of Stockton has its official boundaries, but unscheduled stoppage at the port has, as seen earlier, knock-on effects beyond the port site. The stoppage has considerable downstream and upstream impacts on shipments from the port out to other areas of the United States and for shipments being transported from the port to overseas. These downstream and upstream implications define the port's de facto area of impact, and managers of the port are well aware of the scale of this impact. The problem with focusing on the port, solely as a legally defined site or in terms of the impact consequences, is that the focus misses what is actually being managed, let alone what the port facilities have been redesigned for over time, as an operating infrastructure within a longer linked supply chain.

The infrastructure as operated and managed has a material presence for control operators and by implication for any ICIS. When we asked real-time operators of water supplies what they saw as the system they were operating, they were quick to describe it in terms of rivers and watersheds, dams, reservoirs, canals, pipes, pumps, and other physical structures and facilities that connected in discrete and palpable ways for them. They were also quick to explain how assets had multiple purposes; for example, pipes and canals are sources of water storage as well as of conveyance (just as natural gas pipelines function also as storage). An experienced USBR hydrologist told us, "I can see how we can get water from Friant [Dam], for example, to Southern California or elsewhere—how we can divert it or get it to a site from different ways. I've got the layout in my head, and I know where the water changes direction and where the terrain is steep."

An experienced dispatcher in the control center of a water utility saw clearly in her head the intakes into the canal, raw water coming in and flowing down; raw water users along the way, with water ending up in the reservoir outside her building and then moving to the treatment side of the house; and so on out to other customers. Electricity and railroad dispatchers told us that when they look at schematic diagrams of rail or transmission lines, they see the trains on the track, terrain under and around the lines, and the switching stations between line segments. In these mental models, risks are everywhere along the way. Once again we are back to that feature of California infrastructures—just how *dispersed* they are as physical systems to be managed (and comanaged when shared control variables are involved). Electricity load and generation are often separated by long distances or not distributed uniformly; the natural gas backbone transmission system of PG&E runs from the north to the south of the state; huge amounts of water move from the north to the state's south across multiple uses; major highways carry commuters from their homes to their work and back, often at long distances; and Coast Guard assets are spread still farther afield. Someone asked to focus attention on the risks said to arise because of the collocation of elements in these different systems must understand just how dispersed these systems are for the purposes of being managed reliably and the risks that can be managed that way.

APPLYING OUR PERSPECTIVE ON INTERINFRASTRUCTURAL INTERCONNECTIVITY

By now readers should better appreciate why the dominant assumption about interconnected critical infrastructures—the view that when elements of major infrastructures are spatially adjacent their collocation poses a critical vulnerability—can be so misleading. That assumption cannot be asserted a priori; it depends on whether the control variables and other managerial resources of the infrastructure systems in which these elements have a role are empirically affected by that collocation. This is such an important point and brings together so much of the preceding analysis on time, scale, and risk across infrastructures that we illustrate it by way of a concluding example to this chapter.

As explained in Chapter 2, the Delta's Sherman Island is considered a choke point for the very reason that it continues to be the physical locus of major infrastructural elements that pass below, on, and over it. The intersection of infrastructures entails, in this view, far greater chances of a common mode failure: the more infrastructures, the more one going wrong affects the others close by. This is why one senior emergency manager thought of choke points as "the first point of failure"—but then revealingly added, "The first point of failure depends on a lot of variables."

To understand those variables, return to the specifics of ICIS1 perspective. In this view, Sherman Island is a cluster of infrastructural interconnectivity that grows column-like from below ground, through the surface of the island, and well into the airshed above. The column rises from an earthquake fault and where segments of major gas lines are buried; up through and around the island bearing aging levees, a stretch of State Highway 160, and telecoms equipment, all next to deepwater shipping channels to Sacramento and Stockton; and up into the airshed, where major transmission lines cross and emissions are regulated. From this ICIS1 perspective, it's fairly easy to show how an earthquake renders these infrastructures interconnected through compounded impacts (Figure 7.2). Once one visualizes a choke point as a spatially circumscribed cluster of infrastructure elements, the next step is to suppose different events triggering different disruption or failure scenarios involving different infrastructure elements. Kick the barrel of interconnectivity one way, and it's KABOOM! Kick the barrel of interconnectivity another way, and it's CRRAASH!

All manner of scenarios are imaginable, if one takes the elements in the Sherman Island cylinder to be latently interconnected, each waiting to be manifested differently by differing disasters. Each different scenario would for risk assessment and management purposes be cast as its own set of conditional probabilities—for example, the probability that the island pumps fail, given that their electric distribution lines fail; the probability that those distribution lines fail, given the levee breach; the probability that the levee breaches, given an earthquake but not a major storm; and so on.

No wonder policy makers think the island is a major physical choke point, as indeed we did at the start of our research. No wonder such supposed

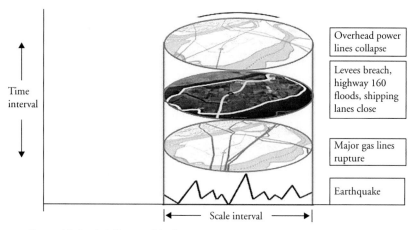

Overhead power lines collapse

Levees breach, highway 160 floods, shipping lanes close

Major gas lines rupture

Earthquake

Time interval

Scale interval

Geographical scale is Sherman Island

FIGURE 7.2   A cylinder of spatially connected infrastructure elements on Sherman Island.

choke points extend outward: analysts have only to widen the cylinder's circumference to include elements of the Pacific Flyway protecting migratory birds to the west or the railroads and major water facilities to the south (e.g., EBMUD's aqueduct or the federal Central Valley Project and SWP pumps). By extension, the legal Delta itself could be seen as its own choke point, given its description as the state's infrastructure crossroads. Whatever the circumference, though, the urgency for the policy maker supposedly remains: threaten the choke point, and the potential Cf are dire.

But serious policy and management problems fester in the cylinder conception of infrastructural interconnectivity, and our framework illuminates why. The cylinder does not adequately reflect time, it conflates the actual scales at which infrastructure operations and management take place, it focuses on too narrow a set of interconnections and treats them as vulnerabilities to the exclusion of interconnections as resources, and it misses how other factors work to mitigate those vulnerabilities. In short, the cylinder approach focuses on almost everything *except* the way control rooms manage their larger infrastructures via their control variables.

Our framework highlights that to analyze the interaction of infrastructure elements on their own when it comes to infrastructure risks is to miss or dismiss that elements within the cylinder have been designed, operated, or managed so as to reduce system-wide risks from the perspective of the respective infra-structures within which those elements fall. When it comes to interconnected risks of infrastructural failure, it may be that each infrastructure in this ICIS cylinder can maintain a safe and continuous provision of its services within its system, even if a storm breaches the levee, washes away the telecom tower, and snaps the power line above. The function over time of any element within its infrastructure has to be considered, not just the spatial collocation of the elements at a point in time. There is, in short, *no substitute for knowing how each of the systems is actually managed and operated.*[4]

This means that element-to-element interactions (e.g., the Sherman Island levee breaches and washes out the stretch of highway 160 that crosses the island) have to be placed squarely within their *managed* infrastructures—respectively, the Delta's levee protection infrastructure and the region's road infrastructure—before the conditional probabilities of interest at the ICIS level can be assessed. Probability assessments must contain the relevant managerial variables. The conditional probability that the island's stretch of highway 160 fails given the island levee breaches is, in other words, not *the* dispositive ICIS unit or level of analysis when it comes to infrastructure-centered reliability management. Rather, the probability of the Delta's levee protection system failing given that the Sherman Island levees breach and the probability that the region's road infrastructure fails given that the Sherman Island levees or the Delta levee protection infrastructure fail are the more important conditional probabilities to be assessed and managed. To phrase the conditional probability this way is to compel the reliability and risk analyst to ask an important empirical ques-tion: To what extent is there a Delta levee protection system or regional road system that is managed via its system's control variables?

For example, when it comes to levee flood fighting during a major storm, flooding of any given island may be allowed so that scarce flood-fighting assets can be used to protect other levees having a higher priority or being more ac-cessible to those assets. In some cases, flooding an island may *reduce* the prob-ability of adjacent islands failing, and prioritizing flood fighting elsewhere may be a sign of the resilience of the flood protection system as a system. It may be that flood-fighting resources, such as limited barges and stone (different in-frastructures may be in competition for the same assets) are sent to Sherman and not to other lesser priorities. (Government personnel we interviewed found it difficult to imagine a levee breach on Sherman Island without a remedial response.) What this means is that flood fighting, against the backdrop of all Delta islands and levees, cannot be and is not in practice determined solely for Sherman Island levees. Flood fighting functions as a control variable in the state's levee protection system, such that flood fighting spatially on one Delta island rather than on another still functions as *system-wide* flood fighting.

Such functional considerations illuminate the chief empirical limitation of the cylinder approach: What do you do when a critic argues that important infrastructure elements fall *just outside* the spatial perimeter drawn for the cluster of infrastructures? In our discussions with a utility, concern was expressed about its major facility lying a little outside the official Delta, which would have major consequences in a disruption. When we asked other engineers about treating Sherman Island as an interinfrastructural choke point, they recommended looking slightly beyond the island proper. We were told that a "greater Sherman Island cluster of infrastructures" should include not just the island but also the area to the south of it. That region includes not only Sherman Island roads and gas and transmission lines but also BNSF rail track, the Antioch Bridge, a stretch of highway 4, the Antioch and Pittsburg generators, other major transmission lines, the EBMUD aqueduct, cell phone towers, and more. When infrastructure proximity is the criterion of interconnectivity, we quickly move to the Delta as its own regional—state? national? Pacific Rim?—choke point. Quickly then, we are back to the notion that everything is connected to everything else, whereas *empirically* that is *not* the case when it comes to managing infrastructures as systems. To reiterate, some infrastructures—and it is up to analysts to know which ones—are more loosely than tightly coupled to others and are managed to be so with respect to both latent and manifest interconnectivity of their control variables.

Because of the importance of control variables in ICIS reliability and risk management, we turn in Chapter 8 to a case study to illustrate their interconnected relationship in practice. Chapter 9 details a case study illustrating the role of technological innovation in ICIS reliability and risk—the introduction of new market and technology software into CAISO. Both control variables and technological innovations have great positive but also disruptive potential when it comes to the safe and continuous provision of critical services.

CHAPTER 8

MANAGING INTERCONNECTED CONTROL VARIABLES

A Case of Electricity and Water

C ONTROL VARIABLES, AS DEFINED EARLIER, are specific and actionable parameters that infrastructure operators use to affect and adjust the overall state of their respective systems, often in real time. This is one very important way control rooms manage to transform high input variance into low or stable output variance. Yet interinfrastructural connectivity means that the respective control variables can themselves be interconnected. How one infrastructure manages its process variance may affect how another infrastructure manages its processes for transforming inputs into reliable outputs.

Since control variables are an essential feature of the ICIS framework, we devote this chapter to a fuller discussion of how they function and their potential impacts on interinfrastructure reliability management. A case study and empirical analysis are offered for a specific set of control variables connecting two major infrastructures, concluding with their implications for resilience within these interconnected systems.

To begin, return to the distinction between interconnected *elements* of two or more infrastructures and the interconnection of the infrastructures themselves. Consider the illustration below (Figure 8.1). On the left side are

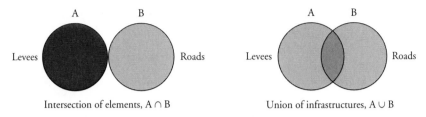

FIGURE 8.1   Sherman Island intersecting infrastructure elements compared to union of infrastructure operations.

elements of two infrastructures, levees and roads, that share the same location on Sherman Island. Their functions (and risks) intersect in that the loss of a levee takes out island roads and the loss of roads affects flood fighting and repair operations necessary to recover island levees. Here the intersection consists of a common spatial location and dependency with respect to failure. But the intersection of these elements that the Sherman Island Reclamation District sees does not constitute the interconnected infrastructures that DWR and Caltrans operate and manage (flood management and road transportation as larger systems).

The interconnection on the right, in contrast, shows the *union* of two infrastructures over a common set of points. Here the multiple Delta levees are connected with the regional road system running through Sherman Island. The union becomes a *system of systems* and includes not only the common properties of A and B but also other elements of each infrastructure not themselves spatially collocated or (inter)dependent. The union includes managerial mechanisms, including infrastructure control variables (in this case those for DWR and Caltrans) applied to their reliable operation. What those management mechanisms are is an empirical question.

Once we consider interconnected infrastructures in a bigger picture than that of intersecting elements, we can more properly analyze the relationship of control variables and their role in the management of the interconnected risks and resilience discussed in the preceding chapters. The control variables of two or more infrastructures can be *shared*, as when they are the same variable used by each infrastructure. For example, the raising and lowering of a drawbridge is a variable for both ship traffic flow through a shipping channel and railroad traffic above it; adjusting a large pump by the SWP is both a water flow control variable for the SWP and a load (electricity) control variable for CAISO.

Two or more control variables may be *conjoined directly* when they are dependent or interdependent with one another (i.e., the state of one affects the state of another—such as the firefighters' backfire near or under the transmission right-of-way that leads to overheating or grounding of the transmission lines). Or two or more control variables can *be conjoined indirectly*—that is, they may be separate variables, but both are affected by a third, or both may be necessary in combination for a common outcome (as when both ship and road traffic controls become necessary for levee flood fighting).

Given the importance of managed control variables to our understanding of interinfrastructural interconnectivity, an extended example is provided here of how the intersection of shared control variables operates on the ground for two infrastructures and what this says about infrastructure resilience. Suffice it to say, such intersections provide opportunities, not just vulnerabilities: shared control variables allow operators to apply a coordinated management strategy to prevent or contain disruption or failure in interconnected systems, a capability we identify as types of resilience.

It's useful to pause and acknowledge we are discussing an interconnectivity that differs from classic production functions, in which the output of one infrastructure is the input of another. In the case study, electricity from the CAISO transmission grid is an input used to run the pumps of the SWP so as to produce water flows to the south. But electricity and water flows are more than inputs and outputs. The rate, amount, and periodicity of these flows are shared ways the control rooms regulate and ensure the high reliability of their respective infrastructures as managed systems. Our case study examines the interconnectivity between water flows at the SWP's pumps near Tracy (the Harvey O. Banks Pumping Plant) and electricity flows from CAISO's transmission grid to power those pumps. The Banks pumps are not merely one element among many others in the SWP; they are a key facility. Their major role is to pump water from Northern California (including from rivers, Delta, and storage facilities) to canals, reservoirs, and dams for use by Californians primarily to the south. The Banks pumps, unlike other SWP pumps, do not generate electricity but rely on the CAISO transmission grid for the electricity used in pumping.

This chapter focuses on a specific question: Can unscheduled changes in electricity flows from the transmission grid affect changes in water flows, *even during normal operations* of both the electricity and water infrastructures?[1] The argument that changes in electricity for pumping affect changes in pumped water flows may look unexceptional—changing the inputs changes the outputs—but it is not for those who manage the respective systems. Since each infrastructure operates under legal, regulatory, and mission mandates to be reliable, this frequently means that there should be fallbacks and alternatives to ensure reliable supply if problems arise elsewhere. There are backup generators at Banks if regular power supplies are disturbed. Also remember that the electricity transmission grid has been designed to an $N - 2$ contingencies standard, in which a failure in one of its transmission lines would not necessarily interrupt overall power flows, since alternative routing exists. But that is only the design and technology side of the design-management continuum; there is also the management side, and that is where resilience comes in. Changes in electricity for pumping water affect the water being pumped, but those changes must be managed so end users of each service are not affected in terms of their own consumption.

As a starting point, it seems reasonable to assume that under normal conditions and over an extended time the respective water and power flows in the SWP and CAISO would be of low and slightly positive correlation: low correlation because, while the infrastructures are connected, each is designed to be reliable even if periodic trouble emerges from another such infrastructure and slightly positive correlation because, over the long haul and all else equal, one expects demand and supply for both water and power to move in the same direction with broad economic conditions and secular trends.

Our hypothesis is this: holding other factors constant, the more reliability problems in electricity flows on the transmission grid (and thus into the Banks pumps), the less water (and noticeably so) to flow through those pumps, when both infrastructures are stressed during normal operations. That is, we hypothesize a negative correlation, not a positive or negligible one, between reliability problems on the electric transmission grid as an infrastructure and the water flows at a core facility of the water infrastructure during common periods of stress.[2]

What does it mean to say that the power and water systems are under stress? Start with the case of CAISO, as the argument here is that problems in its transmission grid can affect the water flows through the Banks pumps under conditions of stress. CAISO's most critical electricity reliability requirement is to maintain balance between load and generation across the grid at any point in time and over time. More load than generation can cause the grid to collapse, leading to widespread shedding of load (blackouts and worse). Too much generation relative to load can destroy parts of the grid and cause the loss of very expensive physical assets. The balance between load and generation is monitored through the Area Control Error, which is observed on monitors by CAISO control operators. The Area Control Error is to fall within the Control Performance Standard 2 (CPS2), which are limits established by the Western Electricity Coordinating Council for intervals every hour.[3]

Our earlier indicator research (Roe and Schulman 2008) found that CAISO control operators were especially sensitive to several factors when it comes to managing CPS2 violations. For the purposes of this chapter, we focus on two. Unscheduled generation outages cause CAISO operators difficulties—that is, generation capacity that goes off-line unexpectedly puts at risk balancing load and generation, as does congestion along the transmission lines—that is, when more energy is needed to flow across lines that are already at capacity. These factors push CAISO operators to their performance edge with respect to the CPS2. The closer to their performance edge, the more stressful is that period for them and the more system-wide resilience becomes an issue. Not surprisingly, given their importance, CPS2 violations, unscheduled outages, and line mitigations are recorded on an hourly and daily basis.

To put this in the language of control variables, grid reliability is maintained by CAISO operators and support staff by controlling operating features, including when generator outages can be scheduled and routine line maintenance undertaken. Conditions making it difficult for CAISO operators to manage such control variables successfully are associated with moving to a performance edge. The ability of operators in real time to rebound from these difficult conditions is what we found to be the precursor resilience in their high reliability management.

SWP control operators also face their own performance edges associated with periods of stress when it comes to pumped water flows. The SWP is subject to regulatory and other legal standards governing water flows through the Banks pumps, and these vary by time and scale. Their constraints encompass agricultural water contracts, environmental regulations, court orders, urban water quality limits, and other standards. Conditions during certain times of the year make SWP operators especially sensitive to these constraints because their usual control becomes more difficult. We see in this chapter why *lower* water flows would be problematic during these periods, giving SWP operators "less wiggle room," as one SWP support person described it.

Our core question is how, if at all, does the effect of CAISO operators moving to their CPS2 performance edge because of unscheduled outages and transmission line congestion (mitigations) reduce water flows at the Banks pumps, when those water flows are already stressed during normal operations? This question is of interest because interconnected control variables, *even during normal operations*, can require resilient behavior on the part of the respective operations (resilience is never only time to recovery after failure).[4]

RESULTS

Start with water flows at the SWP Banks pumps. Operators contend with considerable variation over time in the amount of water that is pumped. Water exported from Banks varies substantially throughout the course of a year and between years. The time series in Figure 8.2 shows the variation in average amount of water pumped at Banks each month for 2005–2010 versus a baseline averaged for all six years.

Depending on the year, the amount of water that is pumped is highest during the summer and into early autumn. It is lowest in the spring. For reasons explained, operator stress is increased by having to match water flows with water obligations largely in the agricultural, industrial, urban, and environmental sectors. The more difficult it is for them to make the match, the greater their real-time stress, given the precluded-event standard of never shutting down the pumps unexpectedly or indefinitely.[5] Summer and early autumn can be stressful times because SWP operators draw down from reservoirs and dams, thereby diminishing water supplies during times when temperatures are at their highest (summer) or when weather is unpredictable (temperatures may remain high into September and October).[6] September and October are also

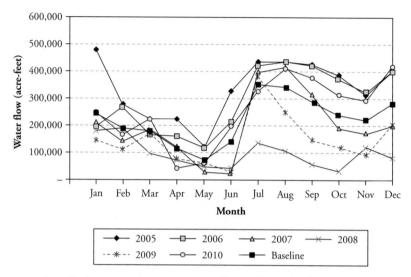

FIGURE 8.2   Banks water exports, 2005–2010. *Source:* Roe and Schulman 2012a, 199.

notable for several important environmental standards coming into force that constrain water flows further (some seek to limit the negative effect of pumping on fish survival). In other words and recognizing the great year-to-year variability, through summer and early autumn SWP operators must maintain high water flows and are under environmental constraints to ensure sufficient water for threatened and endangered species and habitat. To shut the pumps down unexpectedly during this period or deviate to lower flows than planned would be particularly stressful.[7]

Turn now to the CAISO dataset and reliability indicators. Figure 8.3 shows the average number of CPS2 violations for any month averaged over 2004 to 2008. CPS2 violations appear highest in the summer. In June and July, the average number of violations per day is over eight, compared with about six or fewer in February through April. The average is also roughly eight in October. On the basis of our research, the "shoulder months" of April and May, and September and October were found to be periods of stress with respect to operator performance. This is because these periods are of seasonal change, which make it more difficult to predict peak loads and actual occurrence, which in turn have an effect on the repair and maintenance schedules of generators and transmission lines.

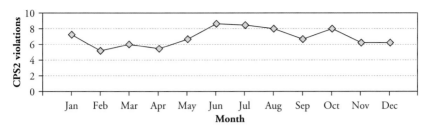

FIGURE 8.3   Average number of CPS2 violations by month for July 2004–July 2008.
Source: Roe and Schulman 2012a, 200.

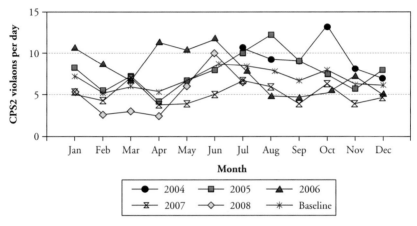

FIGURE 8.4   Disaggregated daily CPS2 violations by month for July 2004–July 2008.
Source: Roe and Schulman 2012a, 201.

    A time series of the average daily CPS2 violations by month for 2004–2008
(Figure 8.4) shows again that normal operations during summer months can
be stressful, though here as with water flows (Figure 8.2) each year differs.
When it comes to generation outages, the mean daily unscheduled outages
(Figure 8.5) are highest from summer into early autumn. The average daily
total transmission line mitigations (electricity must be rerouted because one
line is already at capacity) is higher in midsummer though rising again in autumn (Figure 8.6). To summarize, summer months and in some cases autumn
months have the highest number of outages, mitigations, and CPS2 violations.
It is also the period in which water flows through the pumps are high and
necessarily so (and thus not expected to be declining).

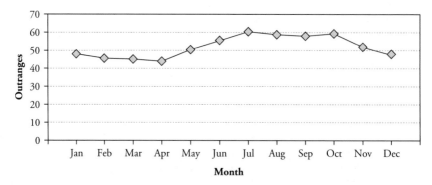

FIGURE 8.5   Average daily number of ambient and forced outages by month for
July 2004–July 2008. *Source:* Roe and Schulman 2012a, 201.

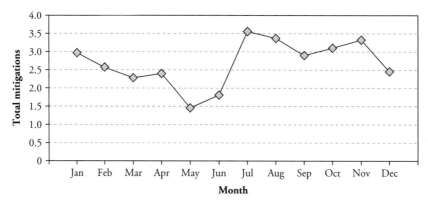

FIGURE 8.6   Average daily number of total mitigations by month for July 2004–
July 2008. *Source:* Roe and Schulman 2012a, 201.

Table 8.1 shows the correlation coefficients of the CAISO daily indicator variables when run against daily water flows at the Banks pumps. Table 8.1 also disaggregates the July 2004 to July 2008 study period into subperiods of possible stress, along with their respective correlation coefficients. In all cases we tracked for those days the actual unscheduled outages, line mitigations, and CPS2 violations to see how correlated they were with the water flow variable. As the table estimates demonstrate, some years were more difficult than others in terms of the effect of temperature and weather on water flows and power flows. We also saw how the summer months (June through August) and the early autumn months (September and October) could cause more stress for

TABLE 8.1   Correlation coefficients with water flow for all data and various subperiods

	Outages	Mitigations	CPS2 violations	Number of observations
All data (July 2004–July 2008)	**0.097**	**0.189**	**0.096**	1,479
July–December 2004	−0.079	0.210	−0.147	184
2005	0.141	0.074	0.254	363
2006	0.126	−0.034	−0.081	364
2007	0.285	0.066	0.113	356
January–July 2008	0.152	−0.077	−0.113	242
Delta Dispatch (May 1– July 15)	0.001	0.245	0.192	307
June–August	0.097	0.242	0.092	430
Shoulder months (April, May, September, October for the period September 2004–May 2008)	0.232	0.157	−0.003	486
October	0.216	**−0.181**	**−0.341**	124
September–October	0.197	**−0.223**	**−0.277**	244

Source: Roe and Schulman 2012a, 202.

control operators. There were also special activities, like the Delta Dispatch between May and July, which caused problems since water cooling temperatures of key Delta generators—and thus their availability—were regulated to ensure better spawning habitat for adjacent fish species.

Most Table 8.1 correlation coefficients are positive. That is, water flows and CAISO reliability indicators move in the same direction. This is not surprising, if—and this could be a big if—(1) over time water and power flows increase or decrease together with economic conditions or other secular trends and (2) these ups (and downs) in water flows mean more (or fewer) outages and mitigations. (To verify this conjecture would have required a much longer time series of data than we could obtain.) In any case, the overall (boldface) correlation coefficients in Table 8.1 for outages, mitigations, and CPS2 violations over the entire period (the first row in Table 8.1) are low and positive, as expected for infrastructures that spend most of their time in normal operations rather than in disruption or failure caused by the other.

Of more interest in Table 8.1 are the negative correlation coefficients (boldface in the last two rows), for these move in the opposite direction, consistent with our hypothesis. As line mitigations and CPS2 violations increase (indicating increased problems on the grid), water flows decline or lower, all else constant. Since correlation is not causation, the reverse could be argued. The

negative sign could instead indicate that, as water flows increase, line mitigations and CPS2 violations decrease on the transmission grid system, although
by means we have yet to discover.[8]

The rest of this section focuses on one subperiod, September and October, (1) when both SWP and CAISO are operating under stressors, (2) during which water flows are by and large expected to be high and not declining,
and (3) in which the Table 8.1 correlation coefficients (boldface) are negative
for line mitigations and CPS2 violations (albeit not for outages) with respect
to water flows.[9] That is, Table 8.1 suggests that from the perspective of those
water flows as the dependent variable for SWP control operators, mitigations
and CPS2 violations (but not unscheduled outages) are independent variables
in the September–October subperiod.[10]

Table 8.2 provides results of a regression analysis with daily water flows as
a function of the independent variables line mitigations and CPS2 violations
for September and October during 2004–2008. The numbers and findings in
Table 8.2 are important for our purposes. The independent variables are of the
correct sign (negative) and their respective negative beta-coefficients are statistically significant at the 0.05 level or better.[11] The overall functional relationship

TABLE 8.2   Water flows as a function of mitigations and CPS2 violations for the
September–October subperiod

Regression statistics	
Multiple R	0.305
R^2	0.093
Adjusted R^2	0.086
Standard error	3383.019
Observations	244

Analysis of variance (ANOVA)					
	df	SS	MS	F	Significance F
Regression	2	283434345	141717172	12.3826532	7.6034×10^{-6}
Residual	241	2758200350	11444814.7		
Total	243	3041634694			

	Coefficient	Standard error	t stat	P-value	Lower 95%	Upper 95%
Intercept	12058.544	369.110	32.669	1.6785×10^{-90}	11331.451	12785.638
MIT	–176.946	84.219	–2.101	0.0367	–342.846	–11.046
CPS2	–126.334	37.216	–3.395	0.0008	–199.645	–53.023

Source: Adapted from Roe and Schulman 2012a, 204.
Note: MIT = line mitigations; CPS2 = CPS2 violations; numbers are rounded up.

between the dependent variable, water flow, and the independent variables is statistically significant (the high F-statistic). The adjusted R^2 suggests that of every one hundred movements in water flows at the Banks pumps during this September–October subperiod, eight or so can be explained by the CAISO grid-wide problems in line mitigations and outages.

One way to cross-check the Table 8.2 findings is to determine if, during those years when Delta water flows had to be pumped through Banks pumps irrespective of problems on the transmission grid, the water flow rates were less sensitive to CAISO line mitigations and CPS2 violations. DWR key informants told us that in wetter years, the SWP is under pressure to pump the now more abundant water out of the Delta into storage as reserves for periods of shortages. The SWP cannot afford *not* to take advantage of a wet year when years were dry before and are likely after.

For DWR purposes, a water year runs from October 1 through September 30, inclusive, and October 2005 through September 2006 was a relatively wetter year. When we ran the water flow variable as a function of line mitigations and CPS2 violations for September–October 2005 and for the combined September–October of 2005 and 2006, the results were statistically insignificant in terms of their F-statistics and *p*-values. That is, during a relatively wet year, water flows through Banks appear to have been less connected to grid reliability problems when compared to the overall study period in Table 8.2. As our key informants insisted, large amounts of water had to be pumped that year *in spite of* problems on the grid that would have affected them in other years.

This suggests to us a possible precursor resilience on the part of the SWP during stress periods or a CAISO precursor resilience during its own normal operations. In this view, what makes the wet year of 2006 special is that the SWP seemed able to detach its management of the Banks pumps from CAISO contingencies or that CAISO seemed able to function with respect to its load without relying on adjustable Banks water flows as part of that load. Such resilience is what we observed in our CAISO research, in which control operators were able in real time to absorb perturbations in their own control variables or bounce back from those shocks while planning the next step ahead.

That number, 8 percent of variance in water flows in Table 8.2, explained by problems in the wider electricity transmission grid, may seem negligible to an outsider. But it can be very important to dispatchers in the SWP and CAISO control rooms during stress months. This 8 percent may represent something they can manage through better coordination compared to other unpredictable or uncontrollable factors affecting them during the same months.[12] By "better coordination," we mean reducing line mitigations and CPS2 violations in ways that could moderate the adjustments in water flows at Banks.[13]

The follow-on question then is are control operators and their managers coordinating for better performance during the common stress period? To answer that question would have required actual observation of SWP control operators, both to confirm their impressions about September and October being mutual stress periods, and if so, what that may have to do with CAISO grid problems. Sometimes common stress did encourage mutual cooperation, we were told: according to one CAISO manager, "We have good coordination in times of shortages with the SWP, as long as they bid pump load or generation into the market."

That said, there is no reason to assume that control operators in the respective infrastructures know that problems in one are causing problems in the other or that the same set of conditions is causing the stress in each case. To repeat, domain expertise is so intensively demanding in each infrastructure that problems have to be addressed quickly in real time as an infrastructure-specific problem. When we asked a senior manager of the SWP control room if he noticed anything out of the ordinary about September and October with respect to Banks water flows, he said it was a period of high diversions, in part because of the environmental standards coming into play those months. As for CAISO transmission grid issues, he felt CAISO was equally likely to call with instructions at any time.

IMPLICATIONS

The above findings confirm the usefulness of differentiating resilience into at least three types, as in our framework. The most familiar are *restoration resilience* and *recovery resilience*, which many end users actually see. These are the abilities of the critical service provider to visibly bounce back from disruption or failure. Another important resilience is what we have termed *precursor resilience*, which the end users do not see. This is the ability of control operators to correct and adjust normal operations in real time to keep or bring back operating conditions within acceptable bandwidths. Precursor resilience allows operators to manage stress and unexpected difficulties while still maintaining reliable service to customers. That said, it can no longer be assumed that normal and reliable outputs always entail low and stable output variance under these different types of resilience and in the kinds of interconnected settings we have been discussing (a point returned to Chapter 11).

Given this distinction and to summarize the findings, precursor resilience in water operations with respect to perturbations in electric transmission grid was very probably evident in at least one time period when both infrastructures were stressed but maintain normal operations. That is, the SWP was able with precursor resilience to ensure reliable water flows during a period of stress without a temporary loss of service (e.g., an unexpected stoppage in pumping),[14] even when CAISO control operators, the supplier of pumping electricity, were finding it more difficult than usual to ensure their own reliable operations.

The results reinforce our finding that infrastructure resilience might be better thought of as a property that extends across stages of an infrastructure's whole cycle of operations—normal operations and disrupted operations, as well as restored, failed, and recovery operations—rather than being a capacity that is turned on during disruption or worse and off the rest of the time. In the same way as it is misleading to isolate interinfrastructural connectivity only to worst-case scenarios of infrastructure vulnerability, so too is it misleading to isolate resilience only to operator behavior in disruption or failure.

Our perspective that resilience is a varying property across an infrastructure's whole cycle has substantial implications for discussions about the need for resiliency in infrastructures. First, when we move to the system level, we move away from the notion that resilience stands or falls on how well it is embedded in all infrastructure elements or facilities on their own. Resilience as a whole-cycle property compels us to ask wider questions, such as which, if any, critical infrastructures will never be resilient enough in the management of high reliability services, whatever is done to improve individual elements and structures? Furthermore, changing the operations in the control room may well affect different forms of resilience across the whole cycle. Change the cognitive models and skill sets of the reliability professionals in any one infrastructure, and you could significantly affect recovery resilience. Importantly, such change is already on the policy agenda. What would happen if proposals for a stand-alone California Delta governance structure were implemented, transferring direct control of some infrastructure elements that are collocated to the new governance structure? At the time of writing, it has been argued by policy makers and analysts familiar with the Delta that we need an authority for the Delta that can make enforceable decisions when it comes to the interconnected critical infrastructures there. But what would ensue for the reliability operations of the original infrastructures in such a major reconfiguration?

We return then to the key point that large sociotechnical systems cannot be designed to be "damned foolproof" and that highly reliable systems are managed to be *reliable beyond design*. If they were operated only according to design, they wouldn't be managed with the resilience needed for reliability. That means designers, be they engineers, policy makers, or senior executives, must trust and facilitate the skills of control room operators to add the necessary resilience to the engineered foundations of high reliability. As we see in the next case study, this is in no way assured when top-level officials introduce major technological innovations into the real-time operations of infrastructure control rooms.

CHAPTER 9

INTERINFRASTRUCTURAL INNOVATION AND ITS CONTROL ROOM IMPACTS

A Case Study of CAISO and MRTU

C ONTROL ROOMS OCCUPY CENTER STAGE IN the ICIS framework for reliability and risk offered here because of their unique organizational niche as well as their special features and capacities in ensuring high reliability for critical service provision. This means that substantially changing the control room can substantially change reliability. We present a case study of major technological change introduced into an ICIS setting through an individual control room to describe and explain its impact on the skills and special features that control rooms and their operators and support staff have evolved for reliability purposes. The case presented here brings the concepts of performance modes and comfort and precursor zones and the whole cycle of operations and precursor resilience together via the lens of the effects that new software innovation can have on real-time reliability.

No single case study could do justice to the complexity described in this book, and we make no argument that this case is representative (nor could that assertion be made for any case study). Different infrastructures have had different experiences with new software, computerized models, and hardware technologies. The virtue of this case study is that it integrates many framework concepts and findings into one illustration. It also allows us to broaden and update the longitudinal case study of a critical infrastructure presented in earlier work (Roe and Schulman 2008).

THE CAISO CASE: BACKGROUND

CAISO was created in 1998 as a public-benefit corporation to assume managerial responsibility for the newly integrated Northern and Southern California high-voltage transmission grids under a deregulated wholesale electricity marketplace. In seven-plus years of studying the California high-voltage transmission grid, we witnessed continuously fluctuating challenges to high reliability from sources external and internal to CAISO. These included the California energy crisis, with rolling blackouts during 2000–2001. Over the course of our research (April 2001–August 2008), CAISO operated within a task environment that was volatile and at times destabilized. In our experience and on the basis of our control room observations, there seldom seemed a time when CAISO policy and procedures were not changing for its Folsom, California, headquarters and control room.

CAISO's task environment was rarely stable, largely because of wider forces driving and rapidly changing the electricity sector in California, the United States, and globally. These forces included, and still do, the spread of competitive wholesale and retail markets; new computer-based information and monitoring systems; advances in switching, relay, and transmission technology; and the globalization of capital and technology. We heard from several interviewees that they had seen more change in the industry in the last years than previously in their careers. This changing environment was captured neatly in CAISO's then-new strategic plan:

As the industry continues to evolve, requirements associated with management of the grid and markets, design and implementation of products and customer support will call for the continual development of skills, especially in the area of applying new technology and providing advanced tools and systems. These include new skills in power system and transmission modeling and analysis, locational marginal pricing, energy losses, congestion management and ancillary services cost calculations. Additionally, many of the complexities anticipated in the next five years may require a better understanding of state and federal regulatory processes and access to outside experts in industry and academia as new regulatory requirements emerge and reliability standards are developed. (California ISO 2008, 24)

With so many task-environment dynamics resulting from substantial competitive pressures in the electricity industry as a regional, national, and international sector, CAISO support staff actions relative to real-time control operations took on high salience.

The role of support staff to the Folsom control room operators was pivotal under conditions of constant change. Many were responsible for finding and correcting the root causes of problems that preoccupied control room operators in real time. CAISO's support staff were not unique in serving as "wraparounds" (the adjacent or physically nearby engineering and technical staff who support control operations). Wraparounds are also present in other infrastructures we observed and provide resident technical knowledge of a system's network and interconnectivity. Support staff also buffered control room operators from direct outside pressures that would undermine their high reliability management. "Buffering" is basically running interference so things can happen quickly on the floor, one support staff member told us.

Without the buffer of support staff, control operators would have to understand and address new external or otherwise unfamiliar real-time operating standards and thus be less able to pay attention to changing grid conditions affecting their reliability requirement of balancing load and generation in real time. When pressed for time, operators were reduced to undertaking quick fixes and firefighting, relying on what they call Band-Aids, or what we have called just-for-now performance. Prolonged just-for-now behavior in the control room turned out to be the best indication we found that support staff were unable to buffer operators from surprises or other shocks in the wider task environment.

An example is helpful. We were in the control room when it was reported to us that, on a Friday afternoon, a major regulator approved a protocol for more generation procurement, an approval that included at least one major provision unfamiliar to CAISO. This notification of approval and its provisions had been e-mailed to the control room roughly around the time of the shift change that Friday evening. Saturday turned out to be one of the highest load days for that time of year, meaning that control room personnel did not have the time to read their e-mails fully. The regulatory protocol, however, became effective that weekend; no prior training in the protocol had been provided. Whatever was going on in this reported event, it was *not* a wraparound of support buffering the control room from outside turbulence.[1]

Nothing in what follows about wraparound problems is intended to diminish the professional commitment and esprit de corps of support staff. We observed entire units dedicated to assisting control room operators. Their primary customer, we heard them say, had to be real-time grid operations. Such buffering and support, however, appeared to be attenuated during our case study, which encompasses the technological change of the Market Redesign and Technology Upgrade (MRTU). What then was MRTU?

MRTU: AN INTRODUCTION

One ongoing challenge to the high reliability of CAISO operations was the introduction of and response to new and demanding computerized systems and markets. These proved demanding because of difficulties they posed for both wraparound support and control operators. At times, software and hardware challenges increased system volatility, reduced operational options, and hampered operators' maneuverability to respond to changes in volatility and options. One earlier software system for automated dispatching of generation instructions for increases or decreases, the Real-Time Market Application (RTMA), pushed operators to the edge for months before programming malfunctions could be sufficiently addressed and before they, the operators, gained RTMA familiarity sufficient to develop response scenarios (mostly in the form of work-arounds to accommodate its programming and hardware limitations).[2]

A far more ambitious and taxing development in hardware and software, MRTU, was undertaken afterward. CAISO's 2007 annual report called MRTU a "herculean effort" that "will enhance grid reliability" (California ISO 2007, 25, 26). This system would automate the process of making bids to provide power from individual generators and would introduce locational marginal pricing to "set wholesale electricity prices at 3,000 different system points (nodes) that reflect local generation and delivery costs" (Direct Energy Business 2009). MRTU was CAISO's unprecedented initiative to improve and automate the electricity markets and push more market schedules to day-ahead instead of hour-ahead or real-time commitments. The effort involved many systems and other infrastructures, both as suppliers and end-users of electricity. CAISO staff reported to us that MRTU required "replacement of the existing market systems, market interface, settlements system, and congestion revenue rights systems, followed by the integration of these with eighteen legacy applications that support CAISO markets and grid management." It was felt by some that if MRTU worked, CAISO would be at the leading edge of market innovation.[3] "We're betting the company we can take control of these markets," said a CAISO interviewee.

Many other things were happening in the CAISO control room at the same time as the upgrade. Western Electricity Coordinating Council reliability coordinators (regulatory monitors of the Western interconnection system) were being transferred out of CAISO and other independent system operator control rooms; younger dispatchers without prior or deep experience in electricity generation or distribution were replacing older experienced operators (an industry-wide phenomenon); bidders into the market continued to innovate when it came to strategic behavior; transient but major events such as wildfires throughout California inevitably preoccupied dispatcher attention; and crew numbers as well as team composition changed considerably because of a CAISO 2006 "realignment" (downsizing).

Also, nothing in what follows argues against the need to automate processes, especially as many at that time required manual entries across multiple systems, fostering errors of number transposition or accidental entry of the wrong number in the wrong place.[4] Similarly, nothing here argues that no progress was made in addressing the problems to which we turn now. In fact, the upgrade described below has been implemented, being a major focus of what CAISO described in 2011 as "a successful energy market turnaround" (California ISO 2011). When we returned to CAISO in 2012 at its headquarters for a brief visit, we were told MRTU was now working well.

A HIGH RELIABILITY MANAGEMENT PERSPECTIVE ON MRTU

As MRTU development was getting under way, a senior control room manager asked, "Do you think we're headed for a train wreck here?" In ways we explain below, the design and project management of MRTU challenged reliability mandates and processes in CAISO's control room by introducing uncertainty among operators and wraparound personnel, reducing the confidence of operators that they would be able to work around design glitches in the new system, imposing open-ended time and attention sinks for key control personnel in the MRTU development process, and adopting a design approach that required outright replacement of existing systems rather than enabling evolution into new systems.

In addition, coordinating the new system with other infrastructures necessitated setting a formal and public go-live date that, given development problems, became a series of missed go-live deadlines that strained higher-management credibility not only with external market participants but with control operators, creating major communication gaps between MRTU managers and control room personnel concerning MRTU's development and implementation. "You think you see the light at the end of the tunnel," one floor supervisor told us at the time, "and before you know it, it's a mile away again."

Why was any of this an issue for the control room? To revert to our analytic framework, operators work most reliably when able to recognize real-time system-wide patterns and apply them to the contingency scenarios they are then formulating. They do so by being connected, as crews and shifts, to others in the control room and to wraparound support staff, including real-time engineers, outage coordinators, prescheduling personnel, and IT specialists. Even though expertise may be person-based, decisions under pressure are often collective and shared among dispatchers and core support staff.

During our research period, it appeared to us (and we were informed by CAISO discussants) that MRTU did not build on these operator skills in system-wide pattern recognition and contingency-scenario formulation, as earlier troublesome initiatives like RTMA, with work-arounds, had. MRTU sought instead to substitute an automated rapid-action analysis and optimizing system for much of the pattern recognition and scenario formulation done by operators and their immediate wraparound. Optimization of electricity systems has a long history, but MRTU was to go further, not only changing the requirements for individual expertise but also remaking the network for shared management.

In the earlier RTMA initiative, operators in effect led the redesign of the software as they revealed programming shortfalls, which were subsequently corrected by engineers, for operations on the control room floor (some of these formal programming corrections were based on what engineers learned from the work-arounds of the operators). The RTMA load-forecast biasing that generation dispatchers introduced not only served as an operational work-around for RTMA but also gave the engineers information with which to undertake upgrades. In these and other ways, RTMA evolved in no small measure through the real-time pattern recognition and scenario formulation of the operators and core support staff. While originally designed one way, it had to be operationally redesigned so as to support, rather than complicate, high reliability management.

MRTU, however, was designed to replace entire portions of the pattern-recognition and scenario-formulation capacity of operators and wraparound staff by remaking the reliability space described in Chapter 3. As stated in its strategic plan, CAISO was "reinventing grid operations" with this new software and technology (California ISO 2008, 2). For generation dispatchers and others in the control room, their future roles and job descriptions under MRTU remained substantially undefined during the time of our research. A CAISO director raised the issue at a meeting of how MRTU would redefine the generation desk, and a generation dispatcher who was familiar with the MRTU design responded that the desk would have to cover two positions in his view, one handling the market and the other reliability. If so, the potential for cognitive conflict between the positions or within the one professional doing both jobs would be great. MRTU, we saw, wasn't just to transform CAISO's reliability space; it was to be the wholesale redesign of the control room's domain of competence.

IN EXACTLY WHAT WAYS WAS MRTU A CHALLENGE TO CONTROL OPERATORS?

MRTU changed the network of reliability professionals from within. Selected wraparound staff and units were now responsible for managing MRTU development and implementation and were under pressure to speed the development process to avoid more missed deadlines. Whereas once these managers and their units had had the mandate to support the control room crews, control room operators were now mandated to support the wraparound staff newly dedicated to the MRTU enterprise. While some support staff still assisted control room operators in working around the inevitable software and hardware glitches, MRTU reinforced and intensified a growing separation of wraparound elements from the control room we had been observing since 2001.

In addition, MRTU managers embedded new members and time demands into the work domain of reliability professionals. Control room operators had to leave their crews and shifts for MRTU meetings or longer assignments with vendors and contractors responsible for MRTU software and hardware development. Operators also spent floor time with consultants who experienced their own turnover. Operators expressed frustration at having to repeat information and explain things over again to a series of new consultants.[5]

Further, when the operators were in meetings with MRTU designers, vendors, and contractors, they were there for the information they added to MRTU development. They by and large were not there testing and refining prototype MRTU processes and services. This meant operators were troubleshooting software designs or protocols for which they were not in a position to develop the actual work-arounds to ensure operational reliability once it was out on the floor. No matter how effective any prior troubleshooting, operators learned never to trust a new piece of software or hardware unless work-arounds could compensate for glitches that became evident in real time.

Another challenge arose because the information operators provided during MRTU meetings was often centered on the patterns they recognized and the scenarios they formulated for then-current control systems. When MRTU designers responded by saying in effect, "MRTU will change that," operators found themselves being asked to problem solve outside their proven domain of competence. This reinforced among operators their priority of securing unavoidably necessary work-arounds from designers who were instead intent on automating processes throughout. Finally, some key control room support staff became as uncertain as control operators with respect to MRTU when they also found themselves operating outside their domain of competence.

When these concerns were raised, the counterargument was that the MRTU posed a test no greater than the challenge of creating and starting CAISO in the first place. Then, too, there were few if any preexisting patterns and scenarios for high reliability management. Yet CAISO persisted in the face of those many unknowns. Why not the same for MRTU? What was different now? we were asked by senior executives when we reported our research findings. But the challenges of MRTU and those at CAISO's start-up differed considerably.

First, the orientation of the operators in comparison with support staff had turned inside out relative to start-up and MRTU. MRTU designers frequently were not looking ahead beyond implementation of the initiative, whereas that was exactly what operators were doing in their preoccupation with developing work-arounds that had to be in place once MRTU went live. "Work-arounds have been everything for these guys," a senior grid operations manager and others told us. MRTU meant that grid operators and managers ended up taking on what had been wraparound functions. "Little did we know it ended up giving us a second job," said one operator about control room involvement in MRTU, a fact some senior CAISO executives acknowledged.

Second, both the start-up and MRTU were grounded in a twenty-first-century vision of an electricity industry allied to markets and leading-edge technologies, not just high reliability. This vision shifted, however, from being externally induced to internally induced. The problems experienced by CAISO in its first half decade were primarily from outsiders designing electricity restructuring and deregulation. The problems experienced in MRTU development were a result of what were perceived to be unrealistic project management goals and timetables *within* CAISO. "We've made this [situation] for ourselves" is how one official put it.

A third difference between start-up and MRTU was that MRTU increased the complexity of control room operations by orders of magnitude, as in the case with locational marginal pricing. The number of pricing points based on distance from generation to load (and thus the transmission burden of power generation at different locations) was to increase from a single digit to four digits. MRTU complexified control operations during the period of our research by increasing the number of elements for operators to worry about, multiplying the interconnections among these elements they had to monitor, and redefining operators' tasks with respect to these many more elements and their interconnections. In this way, the smallest component in the integrated system could become a major issue. It was as if that forty-megawatt generator, which in the past had been marginal to meeting most cases of daily load, was no longer marginal at any time. "MRTU has become finer grained. Even a difference of one megawatt can make a huge difference now," said one operator. The requirements for high reliability management were increasing with MRTU, and operators didn't see the resources for that management increasing at the same time.

Finally, MRTU meant that the transaction time of major grid operations was being speeded up, but the diagnostic time needed to figure out what went wrong with a transaction was being lengthened. MRTU, as designed, would mean cutting the time available to the operator to assess if a proposed dispatch of energy would work before finally approving it. We observed and heard reports that problems with one key component of MRTU, its new scheduling and transaction software (Control Area Scheduling, or CAS), took longer to figure out than under the old scheduling software (which indeed had its own problems), largely because of CAS's interlocking set of systems. One support staffer summed it up: "To understand CAS you have to move from the outside in. You have to start with the systems feeding it and leading from it and then move inside." This at least was not the case with the older defective software (we return to CAS in a moment). The potential for cognitive dissonance was obvious: CAISO had been directed, at least up to the point of MRTU, to *reduce* problem-solving time in the control room, not increase it.[6]

In these ways, and up toward the end of 2008, control operators were left with the prospect of having to deal with faster transaction speeds for more integrated systems and different variables requiring comparatively longer diagnostic times. With MRTU "we will have to trust more people. . . . It makes you [the control operator] more cautious; I could never do what [one support person] does, so I trust him, but if it [the solution from MRTU] does not make sense, I will ask him why it does not make sense," a floor supervisor told us. In short, it was apparent and reported to us that toward the end of 2008 MRTU had already changed the risks that control operators and their support staff had to address in their real-time high reliability management. What did all this mean in terms of the concepts introduced and developed in this book?

MRTU IMPACT ON CAISO DEVELOPMENT

MRTU designers asked us why operators were not as confident as they, the designers, were about MRTU. When the designers looked at the past performance of operators since CAISO inception, they concluded that operators would be able to make MRTU work just as they had pulled off reliability time and again before. This time around, however, operators lacked such confidence for several reasons related to MRTU specifically, including reasons connected to the operators' comfort zone, the conflicting orientations between operators and designers, and the increasing demands to operate at the same time across multiple performance modes with different risks and in new unstudied conditions.

Operators' Comfort Zone

As indicated earlier, the operators we studied were not satisfied with the kind of retrospective confidence the designers expected of them. Operators instead practiced prospective caution and vigilance. Operators know that past success always carries the risk of making professionals *over*confident and complacent. This meant that operators would be uncomfortable with MRTU as its development unfolded in real time, even if, after a great deal more work, it could be operationally redesigned into a success story. All this had a direct bearing on the control room operators' comfort zone with respect to MRTU during the study period.

Operators were very uncomfortable with MRTU because of their high sensitivity to error, which is part and parcel of their high reliability management. They expected MRTU to force operator errors because of MRTU design errors, as happened with RTMA and CAS.[7] Meanwhile their error sensitivity increased, because regulatory oversight of error was understandably intensifying during these changes. Operators were also very uncomfortable because MRTU work-arounds seemed more promised than developed.

Just as important, needed improvements, for example, in RTMA had been put off on the expectation that RTMA would no longer be needed once MRTU came online. In this way, operators found themselves between two reliability-challenging worlds—defective software in existing systems and no work-arounds to ensure the reliability of the systems to replace them. Since MRTU was a moving target (go-live deadlines continued to be missed), work-arounds were by and large not possible until some unspecified time later. Equally worrisome, time to problem solve had increased in other ways, as we have seen. According to one younger operator, "The system is getting so automated that we can't make work-arounds for it anymore. We really don't know where the system is when the computer stops doing what it is supposed to do. Before, we would know where the system was and make a decision on the basis of what we know. But now the computer does everything, and when it stops, we [have] got to figure out where the system is, and that takes time."[8]

Operators were very uncomfortable with MRTU, in sum, because reinventing grid operations meant promoting a cognitive orientation that ran counter to operator professionalism: they were being asked to make themselves less reliable while all the bugs were being worked on under the promise of making themselves more reliable once the bugs had been worked out—all in advance of having necessary work-arounds in place when new bugs were found or old ones hadn't been worked out. This posed a major professional hazard for control operators, since it meant giving up their real-time flexibility to a new system, the general design of which posed unstudied conditions but which they were mandated to manage nonetheless.

The debate between operators and market designers over relaxing constraints on transmission requirements illustrated the new risks involved. Before MRTU, operators told us, they could overschedule generation to build up power reserves and wait until real time to let the market identify cheaper prices for the scheduled energy. Under MRTU, as they understood the design at that point, they would have to schedule generation to meet *less than* the projected requirements, on the expectation that the market would find the missing energy in real time to meet the requirements. To some operators this MRTU scheduling looked like violation of a reliability constraint. To CAISO market people, this was the market doing its job.

When the research for this case study was ending, an illuminating interchange was reported between lawyers and operators in the control room. At issue was how operational flexibility for control room dispatchers was to be redefined in light of major changes taking place in the control room operations because of MRTU. In our paraphrase of the lawyer's draft definition, "operational flexibility" would be the room for maneuver provided to CAISO by transmission improvements designed in accordance with best practices and that do not lead to inefficient or unreliable operations of its grid during scheduled outages or emergencies. The head of a major operational unit concerned with control room reliability offered a different version, however: to paraphrase, the room for maneuver necessary for control room operators to provide reasonable assurance that the transmission system is secured, given the inherent uncertainties in system conditions or unpredictable circumstances, which are, thus, not specifically or fully covered by operating procedures. A control room manager reported that he would change that last clause to "which cannot be specifically or fully specified," explaining that the grid was so dynamic that all pertinent situations could never be detailed or adequately addressed procedurally. The more expansive operator's definition of flexibility makes the contrast to the lawyer's far more constricted one clear.

Operators were also very uncomfortable with MRTU because of the gap between what was promised with the advent of MRTU versus the ongoing reality of the control room. Hardware and software problems were frequent on the floor during MRTU's development and component phase in. Even before such development, the operating environment was one of periodic display dropouts and patches, fixes and Band-Aids, where one problem followed another. Multiple problems coincided because multiple systems were operating. One operator told us, "Nothing comes by itself here. Just like we learned in the Navy; we trained for things coming in pairs. Same here. One overload, one mitigation, one curtailment we can manage, but add more, and then conversation in the control room triples." One incident, for instance, posed simultaneous problems with fires, unscheduled outages, unusual electricity flows, RTMA, and poor transparency in CAS.

Even when an innovation worked in the testing (staging) environment and even when there were redundant hardware and software in case something went wrong in moving from the testing to real time, reality on the floor required firefighting.[9] What had worked in MRTU staging, for instance, was qualified by operators as having worked only "under predefined conditions." That wasn't reality. MRTU fixes couldn't be fully tested beforehand, we were told on several occasions by operators involved in MRTU development. Also important was the nature of real time itself: "Listen, you can't test real time," one senior floor manager insisted.

Another feature of MRTU disconcerting to operators was that as development lagged and go-live dates loomed, training had to be delayed because the system was still changing. Both operators and training personnel were concerned that there would not be adequate training before the system's implementation.

Finally, operators were very uncomfortable because MRTU's development added the challenge of operators having to work simultaneously in multiple performance modes. Operators were encouraged by MRTU designers to focus on just-in-case performance, and we saw operators urged and pushed to foresee all possible contingencies arising out of MRTU and translate their knowledge base of patterns and scenarios into the design of MRTU as an expert system. But MRTU protocols were creating a framework for just-this-way responses to the foreseen contingencies. Meanwhile, back in the control room, operators were every day managing just in time and, increasingly, just for now with the advent of hot weather during the 2008 summer. Having to address these four performance modes simultaneously or contemporaneously was a major cognitive challenge for operators.

To put it another way, operators were outside their comfort zone both because of what they knew—they had to manage software and hardware unpredictabilities—and because of what they did not know—where were the MRTU work-arounds to manage such unpredictabilities? Operators continually pressed MRTU designers and others to tell them how MRTU would deal with the problems the control room always had when seasons change, something happens to this or that major interstate transmission line, crucial databases and displays fail, or a transmission line has to be watched especially carefully. It may seem unrealistic to require MRTU designers to have answers for every question, but the opposite of unrealistic was precisely the issue: real-time reliability operations are all about the details; operators had to worry about unscheduled outages, daily load forecasts, other less-than-adequate tools, and problematic ramp rates—and not just when MRTU came into effect.

Conflicting Orientations on Interinfrastructural Interconnectivity

Operators appreciated that the MRTU imperative was to make things better by having day-ahead schedules drive real-time generation. But the downside of MRTU development and how this contrasted with then-current real-time grid operations were captured in the interchange of a generation dispatcher with a shift supervisor:

Dispatcher: You know each crew only remembers what has happened to them. We only have time to remember what happened yesterday for what we should do today.

Shift supervisor: It's the opposite of MRTU. We have to forget what we learned today, because it'll change tomorrow.

In 2008, it was difficult to see MRTU's promise of operators becoming better analysts. MRTU was supposed to enable operators to get to where they should have been after CAISO first started and hired personnel. The head of grid operations said, "Their [the operators'] world is going to change with MRTU. The congestion management they are doing in real time, which represents 50 percent of what they do—that will be done in day-ahead [scheduling]. This will change their world. This will allow them to do what we said they would do when we hired them: to manage at the twenty-thousand-foot level. With MRTU they can do analysis of the grid."[10]

That gap between the future promised and the present realized was palpably evident to those in the control room. "Right now, just gaining the knowledge and experience to go live is my concern," a control room supervisor reported to us, adding, "My first perception was that MRTU was a do-all application, and my job [was] to just push the one button and watch it work. As things progressed, the holes became clearer, and . . . what was needed was not all designed into it all, so it was not just one button but several buttons that had to be pushed at the same time. Now I see it as a tool that has to be manipulated."

To summarize the cognitive challenges and recast the dilemma, MRTU was different and difficult because it sought to combine without reconciling two very dissimilar cognitive orientations of designers and operators with respect to the system. Designers and operators each had a different take on interinfrastructural interconnectivity. For MRTU designers, "systems integration" meant integrating for optimal performance the major software components and subsystems among energy suppliers and end users of the transmission grid. For operators, "systems integration" meant integrating the system-wide patterns they recognized across the grid with localized contingencies to ensure high reliability across the grid. Otherwise load and generation (whatever the suppliers or end users) would be dangerously out of sync.

These two types of integration—designers talk about intersystems integration, while operators are doing pattern-scenario integration—were at odds in many MRTU meetings we attended. Designers pressed operators to troubleshoot their designs with the big picture in mind, saying, for example, "Tell us what to do, knowing that this is where MRTU wants to get to." Operators in turn pressed designers about how MRTU would actually work, if this or that contingency really happened. For operators, thinking about the next steps ahead went hand in hand with responding reliably to what was happening now. This meant that the big picture that came with intersystems integration was of use to operators only to the extent it addressed a real-time problem whose solution was core to grid reliability.

For designers, the big picture was *always* useful, whether or not it resolved any specific problem. Note that this disconnect is *not* between the big-picture global integration of a future MRTU versus a purportedly narrow and localized problem specification by operators. When it comes to high reliability management in critical infrastructures, pattern-scenario integration has its own big picture, in which a particular problem has to be managed reliably if only because that problem could ramify across the infrastructure as a system. Indeed, when we hear infrastructure managers and operators speak about their achieving a high-altitude view of operations, the picture they are seeing is more often than not the integration of patterns and scenarios key to their reliability management.

Multiple and Simultaneous Performance Modes along with
Their Risks and Unstudied Conditions

From their big-picture vantage point, the operators' four performance modes are the evolutionary advantage of pattern-scenario integration, because they enable considerable variability and flexibility (requisite variety) in crew-based behavior across changing conditions. Pattern-scenario integration generates multiple pathways to meeting the reliability requirement of balanced load and generation, thereby avoiding lock in to any single path dependency. Contrast this high reliability equifinality and operational redesign with MRTU. Not only did MRTU have no demonstrated evolutionary advantage (it, after all, was to be the first of its kind); the advantage of the then-current system was its resilience—that ability of its operators to bounce back from a shock while planning the next step ahead.

The impact of these developments was profound as CAISO moved closer to MRTU going live, in that control room operators and managers knew risk *and* other unpredictabilities were evolving in the control room in ways they had not seen before. Not only was risk (probability of hazard times the magnitude of that hazard) intensifying but uncertainty, ambiguity, and even ignorance seemed to be increasing, situations in which latent risk could not be assessed because operators faced potential hazards whose magnitude or probability, or both, they did not know. We noted a moment ago how operators had to simultaneously work in multiple performance modes. The point to remember is that each mode of operation has its own risks. Operators run the risk of misjudgment in just-in-time performance, while the major risk in just-this-way performance is that those being commanded or controlled fail to comply. This means that when control room operators worked in all multiple performance modes at the same time, the systemic risks of managing that way are amplified.

Operators now had up to four major types of operational risks to contend and interact with in real time. Or to put it the other way around, there was no dominant performance mode, which is to say there were fewer and fewer normal days in the control room in the advance to MRTU going live. At one point in mid-2008, the head of grid operations summed up the situation facing the control room operators: "Fourteen hundred [wildland] fires and counting. . . . Fires continue along the path of the five-hundred-kV lines in the north. . . . Winds are picking up. . . . Hydro is now below 50 percent capacity and 60 percent of normal—whatever that is at this time."

The consequences of having to operate in multiple performance modes at the same time or having no one dominant mode at any time were substantial. It wasn't just exhausting. It also meant too much was going on for operators to feel they owned the MRTU processes that were being developed with their involvement—and CAISO was a culture in which owning processes had been an integral part of high reliability management.

This new situation differed substantially from what we had seen earlier at CAISO. When first undertaking our research, we found the dominance of just-in-time performance in control room operations (high system volatility but still relatively many options with which to balance load and generation). When we returned for more intensive research at CAISO in 2004, we saw in the run-up to RTMA a worsening of control room conditions, with a great deal of what these operators called real-time firefighting, Band-Aids, and quick fixes going on (which we have termed "just-for-now performance," with high system volatility but far fewer satisfactory options with which to respond to system conditions—the most unstable performance mode for operators). Operators also complained that these short-term fixes were of low quality—that is, they were one-off solutions that did not represent a cumulative increase in learning, adding little to a usable inventory of patterns and action scenarios.

What we were seeing, however, by 2007 and into 2008 with the MRTU buildup and in the presence of other events affecting grid operations (e.g., summer loads, staff realignment) was not just that operators found themselves more and more backed into an operational corner, in which making one thing better could end up making something else worse later. Now the enlarged challenge was having to operate at the rock face of unstudied conditions with unpredictabilities beyond calculable risk. High volatility in the control room's task environment had become higher, while the few options to respond to volatility had become even fewer or more uncertain or ambiguous. By the end of 2007, operators seemed to us to be at a performance edge yet have all the while to manage reliably at or beyond the edge during events not seen before. They were, in brief, increasingly outside their comfort zone. Measuring just how unstudied and oscillating conditions pushed operators to their performance edges takes us to the realm of reliability indicators.

WHAT DID THE RELIABILITY INDICATORS SAY?

We have argued that MRTU development, at least in the initial stages we studied, was perceived to have increased some risks and unpredictabilities, pushed operators outside their comfort zone, and compelled operators from time to time to confront unstudied conditions. But how do we know this actually pushed operators to a performance edge? Operators have been quoted to that effect, but then how did they know that this was happening?

Here we had an example of the utility of indicators for real-time reliability, a concept introduced in Chapter 8.[11] As we were winding up our work at CAISO, a senior grid manager asked us to extend our earlier indicator analysis and investigate this new episode. He and others in grid operations wanted to see what the indicators showed for the time when CAISO implemented a major new piece of MRTU scheduling software, the aforementioned CAS system. This was a period that in turn had been marked by an early change in daylight saving time (DST), a change important to not only scheduling software but other control room software. We had also been observing the control room and interviewing operators and recording heightened concern on their part about additional unpredictabilities in CAS, concern that seemed to have been precipitated or accentuated by the advent of DST. CAISO grid operations staff credited the resulting indicator analysis with independently confirming what they had been experiencing.

We observed over several months and in meetings that, as the indicator analysis we prototyped was updated, control operators and managers viewed the results with growing concern. The indicator graphs demonstrated to them that operators were increasingly unable to dampen connections between grid conditions and CPS2 violations.[12] As a result of unscheduled outages, line mitigations, and forecast biasing, control operators were unable to keep grid conditions from leading more directly to CPS2 violations. They saw in the figures confirmation that the problems they had been experiencing with the introduction of CAS, a key MRTU component, were increasingly moving control room performance sensitivity to generator outages, load forecast errors, and line congestion to higher levels as reflected in CPS2 violations. As the DST changeover occurred in the midst of ongoing problems with the CAS introduction the month before (between February and March 2007),[13] operators saw in the updated indicator figures evidence for what they had been experiencing in the control room at that time: a level of CPS2 error sensitivity not experienced before, a level at which they stayed longer and returned to usual baseline levels of sensitivity more slowly (even when compared to what they had experienced with the July 2004 introduction of RTMA).[14] Heightened operator concern in real time over problems in CAS performance and the ongoing effects of the DST change reinforced each other in ways no one had seen or could have predicted. This was also the same period in which the control room experienced a rare but major Disturbance Control Standard (DCS) event (February 20, 2007, after the introduction of CAS but before the DST changeover).[15]

Grid operations staff took the analysis to demonstrate that fewer and fewer normal days were occurring in the control room (again, not just because of MRTU). The long-term trend in CPS2 sensitivity, which had been improving from mid-2004 to the end of 2006, now looked to them to be worsening. We heard more operator complaints about "fighting the COI [California-Oregon

Intertie]," "chasing the load," "driving to a bad number," "tricking the software," and "flying in the dark." There were days when they saw CPS2 violations increasing in hours when violations usually went down. Summer 2008 posed new problems, the DST changeover continued to be an issue, and so on. Some operators told us that the indicators had "predicted" the DCS event. It was during these times and under these conditions that the ability of operators to bounce back from new shocks was attenuated. In our terms their precursor resilience was degraded. Some MRTU designers, however, interpreted the growing concerns of operators over these developments as resistance to change.

MRTU IMPLICATIONS

As discussed at the outset of this book, older high reliability organizations (HROs) and many integrated utilities before deregulation operated within an institutional niche founded on societal dread. To lose electricity indefinitely or have a radiation leak from a nuclear power plant must never happen from a societal viewpoint. So highly consequential were the hazards that the costs of not managing them reliably exceeded any expected savings from not doing so. Societal dread, however, is neither permanent nor present across all of society's reliability mandates (for a discussion of the obstacles facing the "attempt to fear the worst," see Pidgeon 2010, 215). Even when it is agreed that certain events must be precluded—no overtopping of dams, no levee breaches because of unscheduled reservoir releases, no shutdown of the SWP pumps in response to a levee breach—these infrastructure-specific precluded events can work at cross-purposes interinfrastructurally.

After seven years of studying CAISO we had a fuller sense that organizations mandated for high reliability have life cycles, analysis of which requires both a political and an organizational perspective. Once an HRO does not mean always an HRO. Reliability is not everywhere high reliability management, a topic returned to in this book's last chapter. A high reliability management network with a focal infrastructure does not mean the infrastructure is always managing reliably or always remaining focal in importance. Prior chapters have described infrastructural change from an old normal to a new normal that was induced by events such as storms and earthquakes. Internal crises can do the same, such as may follow from executive choices made on the premise that innovation is necessary to secure an institutional niche against outside political, budgetary, and market threats. This, we believe, was the case with CAISO's MRTU at the time of our study.

From its first days as the creature of California's electricity market restructuring, CAISO had a precarious economic and political status among competitive commercial generators, large distribution utilities, federal regulators (such as the Federal Energy Regulatory Commission), state regulators (particularly the California Public Utilities Commission), and ultimately major politicians in the state. Against this dynamic background we saw CAISO, as an organization, go from its designation as the California ISO to what was for some the more appropriate official designation as the California System Operator Corporation.[16] In legal terms, CAISO remained a hybrid not-for-profit public-benefit corporation throughout.

The emerging tension between the public and the corporate was demonstrated in no better way than in the shift to MRTU. The control room was demonstrably the locus of the public-benefit side of the corporation. That was part of its special institutional niche. Someone observing the control room floor in the mid-2000s would have seen the public sector at work, in this case meeting the mandate in providing an always-on vital service without which the private, public, and not-for-profit sectors would not be reliable. It was here that the high reliability management of the grid was the priority and where ensuring the physical integrity of the grid was not to be traded off against other considerations important to the rest of the organization.

Outside the control room was where more of the corporation side was. In the corporation the chief executive officer and leadership team made a major public commitment to reduce CAISO's fees and wrote that the "introduction of locational market prices forces physics and economics to come together in the operating timeframe" through MRTU (Mansour 2008). The unresolved tension between the not-for-profit public side and the corporation side of CAISO became increasingly evident in our view.

One cannot overstate the organizational tension brought into play by housing under one roof very different mission aims: CAISO's upper management saw in MRTU the essential means to securing CAISO's institutional and market survival in the years ahead. As researchers, we'd be presumptuous to try to second-guess the merits of their understanding. One senior official was reported by our interviewees to have said that CAISO might as well close its doors if MRTU was not undertaken. In this perspective, survival was not about today's operations or today's reliability. It was about a CAISO with a future within a (more) stable institutional niche. Without that, it would be subject to continued political and legislative interventions, not to mention market unpredictabilities that made no sense for CAISO as a reliability manager. State officials, for example, mandated a standard requiring renewable energy to make up 20 percent (now 30 percent) of the state's electricity generation without any reference—at least as far as we could determine—to the reliability requirements facing the transmission grid during such a dynamic transition.

Conventional management and business schools counsel that when organization survival is at risk, leaders should take risks. MRTU was one such leadership-driven, risk-seizing initiative. Senior executives and others felt, we came to understand, that it was better to risk failure in meeting a given MRTU go-live date if it meant success thereafter in the energy markets and the industry. *But risking failure is what high reliability control room operators do not do.* As one senior control room manager put it, "Risking failure is not even in our lexicon." For the control room, risking failure was antithetical to high reliability. You do not become less reliable to become more reliable later.

It is possible that not to risk failing to meet an MRTU go-live deadline would have, in the minds of a number senior executives of CAISO, left the organization to become what researchers Marshall Meyer and Lynne Zucker long ago called a "permanently failing organization," or CAISO being stalemated indefinitely because of an "incapacity to choose strategies offering the possibility of outright success, [even if] risking outright failure" (Meyer and Zucker 1989, 97). For sure, risking failure in actual grid reliability and risking failure in meeting a go-live date so as to ensure that MRTU not fail when it actually came online are not the same things, but the point is that two very different risk orientations were at issue.

One consequence of these differing orientations to risk appeared to go to the heart of the public versus corporate sides of CAISO. Every day that grid operations successfully managed the grid was one more day corporate planners and software designers felt they could redesign the grid without adverse effect.[17] "What we've been doing is that they keep throwing things at us and we keep taking them on. It can't go on," said one senior floor manager, speaking of MRTU changes. We must emphasize here that CAISO was not alone in such pressures. Another control room official underscored that "the commerce piece drives the whole process" in his infrastructure, and others said much the same thing to us about their systems. "I think of [this facility] as a factory," said one official. "We produce train departures."

CONCLUSION

If our subsequent research for this book is a guide, leaders in infrastructures (now speaking more generally) do not fully appreciate the demands their respective business models impose on their control rooms. Infrastructures and most particularly control rooms are not plastic organizational formations to be molded to whatever end designers want. Control rooms, we argue, have special features that cannot be compromised if high reliability in providing the critical service is the priority. Control rooms are unique organizational formations for ensuring high reliability management, and their operators work within a specific design with an evolutionary advantage over other forms of design when it comes to ensuring reliability. Does this mean that control operators are always right? Of course not. Does this mean that control rooms are the only organizational formation possible for ensuring high levels of continued reliability? No, though at present we know of no other. It is far more realistic to say that control rooms are managing systems so that these systems can be operationally redesigned when required than to say that society requires systems designed so that they never need that kind of management in the face of inevitable real-time contingencies.

What actually happened after MRTU was implemented on April 1, 2009? In August 2009, CAISO reported that "the overall market experience over the past four months has been positive" with respect to MRTU (Crane 2009). In our latest round of post-2008 research, MRTU problems were mentioned by control operators in the SWP. However, data to confirm or disconfirm such reports were unavailable or difficult to obtain because of reasons related to market competition in the electricity sector. As reported above, during our short 2012 CAISO revisit, we were told MRTU was working well. It thus seems appropriate to leave the last word to the CAISO chief executive officer, who offered his perspective on MRTU upon his retirement in 2011:

"We're talking about a recreation of the market that was meant to be from the beginning," [Yakout] Mansour said. "That's why we went overboard, because there was a lot of pressure and we could not afford to fail. . . . It was the right thing to do." (Bleskan 2011)

CHAPTER 10

INTERCONNECTED INFRASTRUCTURE SYSTEMS AS A COMPLEX POLICY PROBLEM

THE FRAMEWORK PRESENTED HERE FOR analyzing interconnected infrastructures highlights five main findings for understanding reliability and the risks across the systems. First, physical choke points, jurisdictional boundaries, or formal regions are misleading as system definitions and as units and levels of risk analysis for interconnected critical infrastructures operated to be reliable. Second, an interconnected system in failure differs substantially from the system as it exists in normal operations or even disrupted operations, and the recognition of related shifts between latent and manifest interconnectivity is crucial to system reliability and risk management. Third, multiple forms of resilience are instrumental to an infrastructure's reliability over its whole cycle of operational states. Fourth, managing interconnected control variables is core to system-wide reliability among multiple infrastructures. Last, any formal all-hazards approach to emergency and disaster management is itself risky without specifying the infrastructures, failure scenarios, and interconnectivity configurations of interest. It is thus appropriate to ask do leaders and regulators understand all this?

In answer, the overall findings and framework set the stage for rethinking critical infrastructures as a policy problem in two primary respects. We must first reconsider the role and frequent criticisms of leadership and regulation when it comes to infrastructure performance. Once these are reconsidered, we are better positioned to address another policy issue discussed only briefly to this point but that needs detailed attention as a leadership and regulatory challenge in its own right: Is there a *system of infrastructure systems* to lead, evaluate, and regulate?

Consider first many of the criticisms leveled against leadership and regulation with regard to large sociotechnical systems. There is the bald claim that public and private leadership has failed to protect and improve society's infrastructures up to standards required. In addition, infrastructure regulation is regarded by many as the poster child of government failure to guarantee safety or otherwise promote the public interest. Blunt statements such as these are easily qualified, but we believe our research points to a more substantial reconsideration of these criticisms. Leadership and regulation of critical infrastructures are public policy problems but not the ones such criticisms suppose them to be.

LEADERSHIP FAILURE?

Start with periods when normal infrastructure operations have been disrupted or worse. How should we evaluate the performance of leaders during periods of crisis management? Through what ways and to what standards should we hold these leaders accountable?

Many crisis management evaluations revolve around output measures of disaster relief—most notably, the speed of emergency service delivery in disasters. But such output or overall outcome measures do not enable comparison of management efficacy, if only because each disaster and its challenges differ so. Even large fires, as we've seen, are difficult to compare, let alone crisis responses across floods or earthquakes. Assessing leadership in crisis management from the vantage point of the full operational cycle does, however, offer a basis for one type of comparative evaluation. A leadership standard in relation to infrastructures would be that of maintaining the integrity of key cognitive processes and their organizational requirements among control operators during the entire crisis cycle, including the recovery of services and the establishment of a new normal. Do the actions and performance of leaders make control operations in the major infrastructures worse or better from the standpoint of the balance between options and volatility? Are the public statements of leaders in or out of phase with control room crisis stages? Do leadership actions support the types of resilience necessary for restoration or recovery? The degree to which leaders in crises support key cognitive and managerial processes across affected control rooms is one measure of the degree to which their crisis management has been effective.

Evidence for attention to the preservation of control room capacities would be found in the functional integrity of communication channels between the control room and other parts of an infrastructure as well as communication among key control room personnel across infrastructures and with emergency management personnel, including political leaders in emergency operations centers.[1] After-event interviews can provide information concerning internal team communication and cohesion, and formal indicators of problem-solving effectiveness have been formulated from data routinely kept on control actions and consequences. But the most important evidence for better crisis management would be what is available and observable in real-time control room operations, as the operational cycle unfolds. The best way for crisis leaders to gather this evidence, while they can still act on it, is to talk to control room operators and managers in the infrastructures they oversee.

We cannot overstress the importance of early warning indicators to operators who use them in real-time and leaders who must give the public the best available information: "What we learned in the [2001] energy crisis," a CAISO manager said, "was to schedule blackouts and give advance warning. If I know it's coming, it's an inconvenience. It's major when it happens and I'm not warned." Since early warnings have a major role in protecting the cognitive competence of reliability professionals, leadership means promoting indicators and information sharing of actual use to infrastructure operators and managers in their real-time activities across their entire cycle of operations. Precursor indicators can also provide early warning to regulators and public officials about the vulnerability of critical infrastructures.

The argument here is not that safeguarding key control room processes is the only important dimension of crisis management. Nor does this analysis assume that doing well on this metric guarantees successful crisis outcomes, including recovery of reliable services after failure. But we do argue that the inability to recognize the stages of how a crisis unfolds and is dealt with in control rooms when combined with the failure to support the problem-solving resources that control operators bring to managing crises undermines the chances for successful outcomes.

Political and organizational leaders are often tempted to simplify and clarify the problem definition of a crisis for the public. Yet this clarification may not square with the problems confronted by control operators, and it may be significantly delayed relative to the crisis stage experienced by control operators. We have seen how control operators frequently know something is going wrong before others—including their own organization's executive team and political leaders—know or acknowledge it. Leaders may intervene to organize tasks and provide motivational support when control operators are already on the upward trajectory of their intensive recovery period.

It is also important for leaders to know when not to intervene in the problem solving of reliability professionals during crisis periods. In one crisis, the 1989 earthquake in San Francisco, PG&E experienced widespread losses in electrical service. The utility, responsible as it was for consumer power service, mounted a substantial service recovery effort organized largely by line crews, switching station personnel, and dispatchers. When asked about the factors leading to this successful recovery, the director of the distribution unit replied, "Mainly we supervisors just stayed the hell out of the way."

By not recognizing differences along the operational cycle of an infrastructure, leaders can inject more risk (and more uncertainty and ambiguity) into disaster response and recovery. Premature closure on a vexing problem can undermine the pattern recognition, scenario formulation, and performance mode maneuverability of operators. Although the recommendation to stay out of the way may seem self-serving, in terms of our analytic framework it is far more realistic than habituated calls for more transparency in all stages along the infrastructure performance cycle. Infrastructures are complex. A good deal of what matters by way of managing interconnectivity and surprise is not transparent and can't be made so to leaders and the public outside the control room without error.

Remember that control rooms need to adjust their control variables quickly, including instructions that override earlier ones. A senior hydrologist in the Flood Operations Center said, "It's part of my situational awareness that things can happen quite fast." Control rooms and emergency responders function in network relationships in which these rapid adjustments are needed and accepted for the situation at hand. "You can never assume a frozen case," one desk officer in the Coast Guard's command center told us.

In contrast, institutional controls that leaders have access to are more "sticky"—the decisions and policies of leaders are meant to carry momentum and can become routinized or rigidified later on. Procedural or policy stickiness can undermine the flexibility of control operators to operationally assemble or redesign options and shift performance modes and thus degrade their capacities. At the conclusion of a crisis, in the rush to affix accountability and reassure the public, it's not uncommon that new regulatory rules and restrictions are imposed on infrastructures. Some of these significantly affect control operators—restricting their options or limiting their maneuverability across performance modes. While we drew the new normal in Figure 7.1 as, we hope, above prior levels of performance, it could just as well be unintentionally lower because of counterproductive leadership. This underscores that the standard for evaluating leadership performance at any stage along the whole cycle of infrastructure operations means ensuring that those better practices identified in the crisis management literature also meet the test of supporting rather than undermining the cognitive skills and processes of control operators.[2]

Leaders should also recognize and reinforce the learning ability and resilience of control operators to make them more reliable before, during, and after a crisis. To that end, one major role for leadership in risk assessment and management lies in better understanding the distinctions between planning for reliability and reliable planning in the interconnected critical infrastructure setting. Much of infrastructure planning is dedicated to planning for a reliable grid or water supply or transportation system or whatever the critical service. Risk analysis in planning for reliability has a well-established set of regulatory and professional standards, methods, and practices with respect to many major infrastructures. But planning for reliability is only part of the challenge of better risk assessment and management.

Equally central is the challenge of reliable planning. Reliable planning means sensitivity, much as control room operators have, to possible errors of forecasting and estimation and in basic assumptions of a planning exercise. Electricity transmission planning, for example, has to estimate load, generation

resources, and policy constraints ten years in advance and sometimes well beyond. Risk assessment and planning for reliability, with their long time horizons,
necessarily face a set of widening uncertainties, ambiguities, and unstudied
conditions that require a great appreciation of latent and manifest risks in operations. Planning processes themselves must be reliable despite complexity
and unpredictability if they are to produce reliable infrastructures. How do
we render planning more reliable as unpredictability ramifies?

To answer, the driver of reliable planning is the need for realistic expectations, because many in the public (not only their leaders and regulators)
seem to take it for granted that planning for reliability is straightforward and
is itself reliable planning. The stakes in making this distinction clear are underscored by what a CAISO official said about using forecasts as a means of
expectation management:

Before I worked in [the] summer assessment, I didn't know anything about probabilistic or deterministic models, and my job is to get people to understand what is
going on and what it means [to those] who know even less about these specifics. I try
to get legislators and policy makers and others to know what these numbers mean
and how they should respond to them. The summer assessment is a tool for us to
let people know what they should know and be concerned about, what their level
of concern should be for the knowledge we have about the summer ahead. . . . One
problem is that we had this overall good summer, but if tomorrow we had to curtail
load, they would be saying to us, "But you told us it was a good year!" A summer
assessment isn't a day-to-day forecast. People need to know what the data mean and
what it means as conditions vary.

His colleague immediately added, "We try to bookend the summer assessment around a number of scenarios, but it always comes back, for them, [to],
'What's the bottom line? Just give me a number. Are we going to be okay or
not?'" A senior state water manager put the dilemma of managing expectations
this way: "You can only plan so much on the basis of forecasts. Early June a
storm was forecasted to go through, and we released Shasta [Dam] water . . .
but the storm didn't pan out."

Water releases, and not just in California, have very real opportunity costs
over a planning horizon—so much so that they're litigated expectations to be
managed for the present and future. "One time we were doing releases in light

of our forecast," a water control dispatcher told us, "and the fish people came to us and complained after the fact when the storm hadn't happened: Why did we release the water [which meant less water for the fish]? Why didn't the forecast come true? *They just didn't understand real time,* that we made the releases in light of a forecast" (our emphasis). Yet in other cases, the wrong forecast may be welcomed by the same group. A senior hydrologist told us, "In the December 2006 high rainfalls, we were projecting [so much cubic feet per second] in a reservoir, which would have meant [we'd have to release more water into a river than it could take], but then the rain stopped twelve hours before we predicted it would. We had started evacuations, and no, there was no pushback because we got it wrong."

Reliable planning, in other words, is more difficult than planning for reliability when expectations vary so along the whole cycle of operations.[3] Operators and emergency responders we talked to want plans that offer reliable options or volatility reduction when required by their reliability mandates. In that regard, it has been easier for leaders and regulators to insist on more information as a way of settling expectations than it has been for them to appreciate that their own market reforms, technology innovations, and designs have unsettled control room expectations about what information is necessary for reliable planning. "We have tons of information when it comes to planning," one emergency manager told us, though "maybe 80 percent of what you get proves irrelevant."

We were given examples of the kind of leader called for over the whole cycle: a person (male or female) who "has tremendous knowledge with respect to where we've been and how we got here—he is the guy to go to, he would know, he has a great memory." We heard this description in different words many times in the course of our discussions and observations. We believe these leaders see the big picture not only from the perspective of the operators' domain of competence, but also from the perspective of the whole cycle's vertical as well as horizontal dimensions when it comes to key participants and stakeholders.[4] Leaders should be able to focus on the cause of an infrastructure crisis and *at the same time* zoom up and across to see its effects on the entire infrastructure and other systems dependent on it. These leaders are retiring, their experience base is disappearing, and the systems they led are themselves changing, sometimes dramatically. Nonetheless, the crisis metric we propose for evaluating leadership remains relevant for critical infrastructures now and for the future.

REGULATORY FAILURE?

"We need better leaders" is frequently accompanied with the further complaint that "we need better regulation!" Yet from this book's perspective, as long as infrastructure regulation is equated with what regulators do, society will have a very myopic understanding of how regulation functions for critical infrastructures. The regulation of infrastructures is not just what the regulators do; it is also what the infrastructures do in ways that their regulator of record could never do on its own.

Contrary to conventional wisdom, it is not a criticism of regulators to say they never have the same timely information as do those operating the critical infrastructures being regulated. It's a statement of the obvious cast as a negative. Restate the obvious, but now as a positive: those who have the real-time information must fulfill regulatory functions that the official regulator cannot fulfill. How well they are fulfilling the regulatory functions depends on (1) the skills in real-time risk management of their reliability professionals and (2) where those professionals are located, which for our purposes means the infrastructure control rooms and their respective support units.

From our perspective, it makes little sense for critics to conclude that regulators are failing because formal regulations are not being complied with, if the infrastructures are managing in a highly reliable fashion and would not be doing so if they followed those regulations to the letter. Regulation, as we see it, moves beyond the regulator's macro-standards for reliability to embrace the resources and expertise of professionals who realize the regulated reliability in practice.[5] Here, as in planning, it is important to distinguish regulating for reliability from reliable regulation. In our analysis, the issue is as much about regulatory reliability as it is about reliability-focused regulations or regulators. The question of regulatory reliability becomes how does regulation function empirically, given both the differing reliability mandates and risks reliability professionals face in control rooms and across their operational states? To answer that, we must understand that regulatory functions are themselves diverse, and one important regulatory function must be to catch and correct errors in the original regulations and laws enacting them. This ability to identify and fix regulatory error takes on added salience when the infrastructure has more than one regulator, as is the case for many of those we studied.

In our analysis, regulators and their staff (and those who legislated the laws from which regulations are derived) are primarily macro-designers and the last people society should expect to catch all consequential errors in their regulatory operations. While of course important for ensuring reliability, macro-design is only the starting point and does not function reliably when applied to every single case. In fact, when macro-designers start operating as micro-operators, high reliability in critical infrastructures gets short shrift. The series of rapid regulatory exemptions and approvals by the former Minerals Management Service in the lead-up to the Deepwater Horizon explosion is just one of many such examples (Deepwater Horizon Study Group 2012).[6]

To put our point another way, operational seriousness over precluded events does not and cannot come through macro-regulation alone. Specifically, regulation cannot substitute for Background, Searle's concept discussed in Chapter 5. The Background shared by operators in their comfort zone sets the gravitas with which the operator skills in pattern recognition and scenario formulation are exercised; it adds the commitment to reliability as a foundational value and responsibility down to the level of the individual operator. We can see how important Background is when we consider cases where it is absent or voided. In the 2008 financial crisis, every cognitive function practiced by reliability professionals was evident in the financial services infrastructure—market traders recognizing patterns, formulating scenarios, reacting quickly and skillfully, and operating under macro-design standards set by the regulators—*except* that the shared Background was not there. In fact, no Background existed against which to adduce a system-wide commitment to financial reliability over and above a given market transaction. This was core to the lack of market discipline much commented on during that crisis: the absence of any shared template for identifying larger consequences of error in trading versus marketing novel financial instruments.

WE BELIEVE THESE EXPANDED notions of leadership and regulation have a greater chance of helping in an ICIS world than the current criticisms of each. In our view, regulators and leaders must better understand that the risks to be analyzed and acted on when it comes to interinfrastructural interconnectivity are far more than those related to Pf and Cf and include risks of infrastructure disruption and recovery; risks associated with operator complacency, misjudgment, noncompliance, and loss of options; latent risks associated with uncertainty and ambiguity that have yet to become manifest (or may never become manifest); and the most important risk, the inability to recognize conditions under which it is impossible to calculate one or more of the risks just mentioned. The gap between understanding this and what is actually done by way of current leadership and regulation is, we believe, considerable and is for us the real policy problem when it comes to leadership and regulation.

With these reconsiderations of how leadership and regulation should be undertaken and evaluated, we can now turn to answering that other important policy question: Is there really a system of infrastructure systems to be led and regulated?

"THE SYSTEM OF SYSTEMS": A PRECLUDED-EVENTS STANDARD OF RELIABILITY AT THE ICIS LEVEL?

If leadership is evaluated in terms of how leaders accommodate and facilitate control operations and how emergency response and recovery is handled along the entire infrastructure cycle, and if regulation is to be a set of dispersed reliability functions across infrastructures and regulators, what does this imply about the role of leaders and regulators in realizing high reliability management in the ICIS as its own system?

We have repeatedly stressed how interinfrastructural interconnectivity can create unstudied conditions for control operators within individual infrastructures. We suggest now that infrastructure regulators can help promote reliability by taking the lead in studying unstudied conditions. This would mean first that regulatory reliability must now be understood as an interconnected property when it comes to further study and action. In this proposed leadership role, regulators would find ways to consider the effects on interconnected infrastructures of regulations that are written and enforced across different regulatory agencies. This purview includes but goes beyond determining how individual reliability standards are interconnected, even at some points competing.

Regulators and their staff across these agencies would also become experts on when, how, and under what conditions *intra*infrastructural control variables can become cross correlated and linked *inter*infrastructurally in ways that individual control rooms, because of the intense knowledge demands of their own domains of competence and the proprietary nature of much information among privately owned infrastructures, cannot know or fully appreciate. If leaders must have the big picture through zooming down, up, and across, regulators in our framework must know intersystem details.

In short, regulators have a very important role as guardians of ICIS reliability. Two information security experts highlight the regulatory challenge:

Why is it, for example, that large IT projects fail? We have much better tools for managing complex projects than we did 30 years ago, yet the same proportion of big projects seem to fail—we just build bigger failures nowadays. This suggests that the causes have as much to do with incentives and organizational behavior as with intrinsic system complexity. And as systems become ever more interconnected, the temptation for system owners to try to dump reliability problems on others will increase. (Anderson and Moore 2006, 613)

ICIS reliability requires regulators to oversee and help correct these infrastructure-to-infrastructure reliability problems and perverse incentives. It also requires regulators to protect and establish legitimacy for control room reliability within infrastructures whose higher officials might well be pursuing values contrary to that reliability, such as competitive cost reductions or proprietary-information withholding in emergency circumstances. We would also expect those leaders discussed earlier to lead by enabling and monitoring this enhanced regulatory role.

All this, though, raises the question what ICIS precluded-events standard, if any, exists with which to evaluate infrastructure and regulatory performance? Which in turn raises a prior question: Is there an ICIS-specific Background, or comfort zone, without which it is impossible to imagine a control room of control rooms? Let's start answering these questions with one of our research findings about ICIS reliability: while individual infrastructure operators and wraparound staff complain about the effects of regulations on their own management efforts, the regulations on other infrastructures connected to them have been one very major reason why these control operators and support staff still manage as reliably as they do.

Most infrastructure managers we talked to would probably agree with the statement one gave us after we had pressed him for examples of any positive regulation he may have encountered: "Well, regulation restrains response capacity. I can't think of where it would help improve that capacity." This manager at the Port of Stockton, like others, found himself challenged with meeting environmental regulations. Yet activities for reliably managing transport into and out of the port have benefited from the reliability of the electricity grid, the rail system, the deepwater shipping lanes, and telecommunications—all of which in turn are regulated. One clear benefit of regulation is the extent it stabilizes the assumptions of what is reliably in place elsewhere for the port— or any other major infrastructure for that matter—to operate reliably.

Regulation clearly can support and legitimate the control room as the pre-eminent reliability unit within a larger infrastructure organization. For instance, the North American Electric Reliability Corporation protocol for ensuring that CAISO could not go into the next day planning for only 3 percent reserves (the ISOs must instead ensure adequate operating reserves for both a primary and secondary contingency) was a major source of support for control operators to enhance their strategy for reliable CAISO and interinfrastructural operations. The Coast Guard, for its part, sees its regulatory authority over ensuring the reliability of waterways and vessels in a highly positive light: "We'd be nothing without regulations," a Coast Guard official told us. In this and other cases of interinfrastructural reliability, it is empowerment, not disempowerment, that comes from state and federal regulation. Regulation of other infrastructures is an ICIS Background that individual control rooms do not always appreciate precisely because it so often goes unarticulated.

Regulators and political leaders (again, with their staff) could help in better understanding and coordinating this systemic, macro-prudential view of interinfrastructural operations and interconnected control variables and performance standards. Such a role and expertise would require more collaboration among official regulators than presently exists, which reflects, we believe, a lack of leadership that is truly worrisome. "They bring no resources and have no expertise," said one real-time infrastructure manager of some regulators.

This is a common complaint, surely, but one that must be taken very seriously from an ICIS perspective.

What is the ICIS-specific standard for high reliability, and where exactly does leadership, regulation, and performance criteria come into it? In answer, undertake a thought experiment. When considered by a levee system only, levee stretches A, B, and C are recommended for improvement next year. When considered within an ICIS context (e.g., those stretches of levees that are important for roads, preserve access to power lines, or facilitate wetlands management), the priorities for the same levee system may be the different stretches X, Y, and Z. To allocate the fixed budget on the basis of the ICIS priorities raises an immediate issue for the levee infrastructure: What about its own priorities (made under its own regulatory requirements and reliability considerations) for levee system repairs next year that would now be displaced or delayed by the ICIS reordering?

As formulated, the lack of congruence between ICIS and CIS priorities— nonalignment of the benefit-cost calculations of CIS and ICIS leaders and regulators—can be considered a principal-agent problem to the extent that the individual critical infrastructure (the agent) is setting priorities differently than would be the case were the ICIS (principal) doing so. A related collective-action problem was captured by a senior emergency manager in the Delta (with firsthand experience in the last major Delta levee breach, at Jones Tract): "Yes, the farmers may know their land; yes, the engineers may know their levee, but who is concerned about the downstream consequences of that levee failing? The farmer is only worried about his forty acres, but who is worried about the consequences of no drinking water for those in Bakersfield or those who have to purify the water in order to drink it now? And all of this because the farmer is only worried about his fifteen hundred feet of levee."

One common solution to the question of who decides is to insist that such externalities be internalized into the price of the service—in this case the critical infrastructure services in question. If, for instance, the costs of levee improvements are not shared by the electricity transmission system protected by those levees, then (all else being equal) the role of the ICIS leadership and regulators is to ensure they are internalized by apportioning those costs among the CISs involved. This, however, affords no real solution from the perspective of our analysis. We cannot assume that management at the ICIS level trumps management at the constituent CIS level. Why?

Because there is always a nonzero risk that the ICIS leadership makes the wrong decision even under the best ICIS risk assessment and management available—assuming of course that there are ICIS leaders and that they rely on better risk analysis. (Remember the methodological difficulties of internalizing comanagement of shared control variables.) These complications in turn reinforce the earlier conclusion: when mistakes are made at the ICIS level, the CISs within the ICIS should be able to absorb or bounce back from any shock arising out of such a mistake. The best remedy for ICIS mistakes is CISs resilient enough for a variety of different shocks, including ones that would have arisen from mistaken ICIS priorities.[7]

We can put the ICIS reliability management challenge another way. In principle, an interconnected infrastructure *system* is established and bounded when no other infrastructure can be coupled with or decoupled from the others without reducing the options or increasing the volatility of at least one of the infrastructures remaining. This is in effect a Pareto optimality test for an ICIS frame of managerial and regulatory reference. To insist instead that all infrastructures are part of an ICIS, because they are a priori interconnected (everything is connected to everything else), not only is misleading but does harm. It adds modeling and management uncertainty and potential error, confounding even more whatever interinfrastructural risk assessment and management is actually under way.[8] Regulators and other leaders need to understand that too limited an analytic scope, focusing on only a few interconnected infrastructure elements (one output is another's input), could well leave out too many control variables that affect cross-infrastructure management. But too broad a scope for evaluation introduces altogether more analytic and management unpredictabilities, making it far more difficult to understand relevant latent interconnectivities and shift points.[9]

Notwithstanding these by and large positive leadership and regulatory assertions at the ICIS level, we as researchers do not see a super control room for multiple control rooms as currently possible. We do not foresee superoperators sharing a single precursor zone and one comfort zone. Yes, the VTS was created, after an incident, to help manage, interinfrastructurally, both the waterways *and* the movements of vessels having their own pilots who couldn't see each other. But it may be that an organization, such as USBR, is able to have its precluded event of reservoirs not being overtopped only to the extent that it is not part of a wider and more formal system of systems.

To put the point in another way, a reservoir failure, as complex as it already is, may be more understandable and better understood than an ICIS failure. Too much ambiguity and uncertainty over what constitutes the latter would work against any ICIS comfort zone. We have seen how many varied types or features of ICISs there are, such that any system of systems can look much more like an overlay of multiple different systems with different reliability mandates than a de facto or emerging network with only one overarching reliability standard or set of standards. Managing a system of systems, each of which has no stable resting point, begins to look less and less like management when system interconnectivity starts adding new hazards without known probabilities (increasing uncertainty) or renders consequences with known probabilities much more ill defined (increasing ambiguity) or creates ignorance about both.

That said, interinfrastructural coordination is taking place and more can be expected, some of which would benefit from a more informing leadership and regulation. One area is already known and established: the need to improve effective communications among critical infrastructures. The loss of telecommunications hardware and capacity was mentioned time and again as a major concern of control operators and emergency responders. Communication concerns extend beyond hardware difficulties, though. One senior emergency manager reiterated several times the challenges posed by having some infrastructure headquarters relocated outside Northern California: "With [corporate] consolidation after consolidation, what is a major Bay-Delta problem for a local firm no longer need be for a nationwide or global firm with headquarters elsewhere in the States. For them, the levee or levee failure is a small piece of the corporate risk management strategy." We have mentioned examples in which corporate executives of infrastructures do not themselves understand the unique demands imposed on their business models by having control rooms mandated for high reliability management. Which brings us full circle: ICIS leadership under such conditions becomes very challenging, thereby representing one crucial reason why resilience must be managed as a variable throughout the entire cycle of individual infrastructure operations.[10]

CHAPTER 11

TOWARD MULTIPLE
RELIABILITY
STANDARDS FOR
INTERCONNECTED
INFRASTRUCTURE
SYSTEMS

W E START THIS BOOK BY ARGUING THAT the future reliability of infrastructures may well determine much of the future of high reliability itself. While our analysis offers evidence for the significant value added to reliability by control room operators and other reliability professionals, it highlights challenges to their skills in the domain of complex interconnected infrastructures. We reported these challenges for one infrastructure in previous work (Roe and Schulman 2008), and we now have documented other operators increasingly locked into performance that is at the edge of their own system reliability and their skill sets. It is time to connect these challenges to their implications for the future of infrastructure reliability more broadly.

First, the variety of operational states and interconnectivity configurations that modern infrastructures assume in effect define a range of output fluctuations that they produce. Contemporary infrastructures are networks consisting of multiple elements and units dispersed in geographical space. They are interconnected, as is demonstrated throughout this book, through webs of relationships to other infrastructures. They are also influenced by exogenous conditions, like the weather, and fluctuating demand to which they must respond. This means that they have a significantly high *input* variance. To limit *output* variance they cannot rely solely on low *process* variance—routines, procedures, and careful rule following. Instead they must have higher process variance if they are to be reliable, at times relying on improvisation, inventing actions and assembling options in real-time as conditions change, sometimes well beyond what has been previously experienced. We have seen this high input and high process variance again and again in our research.

What has also been demonstrated, however, is that interconnected infrastructures cannot command and control the *output variance* they present to the world, and accordingly, their operational states and interconnectivity configurations vary as well. In fact, our categorization of infrastructure states—each involving shifting manifest and latent interconnections—lays the groundwork for understanding types of reliability different from the high reliability described in classic high reliability organization models.[1] To be succinct, both the necessity and the tolerance of those additional system states differentiate reliability along several major dimensions. The six states (normal, disruption, restoration, failure, recovery, and the new normal) are each a form of output and suggest a different standard of reliability. A brief typology is presented in Table 11.1, which describes the additional forms of reliability in relation to the

TABLE 11.1   A typology of alternative infrastructure reliability across states, standards, and strategy

Reliability type	Dominant infrastructure state(s)	Reliability standard	Reliability strategy
Precluded events	Normal operations	Socially unacceptable events must not happen	Technical design, operation within analysis, and precursor resilience
Avoided events	Normal, disruption, restoration	Internally unacceptable events should not happen	Risk-benefit analysis and risk trade-offs
Inevitable events	Disruption, failure	Social acceptance of disruptions and failure as unpreventable or inevitable	Insurance, emergency response management, restoration, and recovery resilience
Compensable events	Recovery, new normal	Failures forgiven by learning and added capacities in a new normal	Technology updates, procedural revision, and reorganization

changed outputs they must embrace and the extent of their departure from the precluded-events standard for high reliability management described in this book and in the earlier work.

The precluded-event reliability standard as we have described it is grounded in societal fears and aversions. These are ongoing and often articulated in groups that maintain public and political pressure on regulators and organizations that manage risks based in that dread. Both social expectations and organizational commitments embrace the idea that these events must never happen.

The strategic features of precluded-event reliability—careful prior analysis, planning, and anticipation—are often prescribed by regulation. But infrastructures operating under high reliability mandates must go beyond regulatory and design requirements. As we have demonstrated, precursor resilience, based on prior response scenarios and the skills of reliability professionals, is an important strategy to keep operations out of, or move them quickly back after excursions into, precursor zones. Importantly, however, under the precluded-event standard of reliability it is acceptable to forgo the actual provision of service rather than risk a precluded event. It is acceptable for a nuclear plant to go off-line rather than operate in unsafe conditions or for air traffic control to close a sector of airspace to traffic when conditions threaten the separation of aircraft by controllers.

But many of today's interconnected infrastructures are not in a position to preclude events. First, the major infrastructure events and consequences of concern to modern society, as discussed in Chapter 1, are primarily *the loss of service itself and the aftermath*. Given collective dependence on infrastructure services, the loss of service can constitute a societal catastrophe. But at the same time the infrastructures cannot preclude that loss of service. Temporary disruptions and loss of service for a fair number of infrastructures are in fact not that infrequent. Under these conditions, restoration after a disruption becomes itself a service—and the reliability standard becomes how effective restoration resilience is and how quickly disrupted service can be restored.

Modern interconnected infrastructures also cannot preclude failure, the destruction of assets, and an extended loss of service after catastrophes such as earthquakes and floods. These knock out infrastructure assets and may produce concatenations of failure. As has been documented, reliability management can buffer or otherwise interrupt these concatenations and reduce their probability and consequences, but it cannot preclude them. Recovery after failure then becomes the output the public sees. Crisis management and recovery resilience become the test for reliability in an interconnected infrastructure system, and a good enough recovery relative to past performance may meet public acceptance, as seen in the Jones Tract case of Chapter 3. The new normal, for its part, poses another reliability test insofar as the new output at least attains if not exceeds the performance levels under prior normal operations. If it does, this is compensable reliability from the perspectives of regulators and the public.

For still other events societal aversion may be less strong and persistent. Refinery explosions, aviation accidents, Internet hacking, and identity theft arouse social concern, but public attention is evanescent and energized only after the event. Regulatory and managerial attention may similarly follow a cyclical pattern. When societal dread is less salient, precluded events unclear, and technical control less complete, an infrastructure may adopt an avoided-events standard for reliability. Here the infrastructure tries to avoid internal events but cannot or chooses not to preclude them.[2] These are should-avoid rather than must-never-happen events and they can occur in normal operation or under disruption and restoration conditions. For example, a natural gas distribution system seeks to avoid depressurization of its lines in both normal and disrupted operations because of the difficulty and risk of subsequent relighting of pilot lights, one by one. Infrastructures also seek to avoid industrial injuries, many of which can occur during efforts at service restoration.

Avoided events may be actively managed against, but they aren't precluded. Careful risk analysis and human factors research may be applied to these events. For example, the Coast Guard's search and rescue service we observed undertook near-real-time risk assessments for its ongoing rescue missions, updating them as conditions changed.[3] In other cases, a reliability strategy is to try to manage risks in a cost-sensitive way, when one cannot deterministically prevent the events from happening. A risk-benefit analysis may indicate to the organization that the risk of the event is less than the costs it would incur trying to preclude it. Last but certainly not least, it is possible that pursuing one avoided event may make another socially adverse event more likely. An effort by the natural gas provider to maintain line pressure to avoid costly and hazardous repressurization processes may make gas explosions more likely because of leaks.

Still another form of reliability centers on making the best of what are seen as inevitable disruptions and failures. This is reliability focused on the states of restoration and recovery. In this domain of reliability it is accepted, operationally and societally, that some disruptions and failures are impossible to prevent and thus constitute inevitable events. Earthquakes, floods, severe storms, and acts of terror induce such disruptions or failures. Rolling blackouts and service curtailments in the midst of the generation shortages and illegal market manipulations of the California 2001 energy crisis were not considered to be major failures for CAISO. These disruptions were instead accepted as part of a larger precluded-event reliability strategy in CAISO management: shedding load to prevent a complete collapse of the grid during a severe imbalance between load and generation. A major strategic focus in this domain of inevitable or uncontrollable event reliability is a focus on restoration and recovery resilience—readiness, training, emergency response, and coordination, both internally and across interconnected systems.[4]

Finally, another form of reliability centers on the new normal after failure and system recovery. Even a socially must-prevent event or an internally should-avoid event can be turned into a compensable event if the new normal, on the basis of lessons learned, technical systems redesigned, or organizational reforms, works for a higher future reliability compared to what preceded it. The Three Mile Island accident in nuclear power proved to be such a compensable event when it led to significant safeguards and safer industry practices in nuclear power. Whether an event can be compensable depends on public perceptions and political reaction as much as on learning and technical, organizational, and managerial changes that follow.

The first two types of reliability—precluded- and avoided-event reliability—are founded on preventing specific things from happening. Psychologist Karl Weick has described this reliability as "a dynamic non-event . . . continuously reaccomplished" (2011, 21). This formulation, however, does not cover the last two types of reliability. The latter—inevitable- or compensable-event reliability—are about very distinctive things happening: effective restoration or recovery to a notably improved new normal.

In sketching these additional types of reliability, we have moved beyond the domain of precluded-event high reliability. Infrastructure reliability can no longer be equated solely with the safe and continuous provision of a critical service, even during (especially during) turbulent times. Yet as we have seen, this does not mean that service reliability and reliability enhancement no longer have meaning for these large sociotechnical systems. It's scarcely appropriate to insist that if an infrastructure is not highly reliable, it must by definition be unreliable. Nor is it appropriate to call organizations "reliability seeking" when they are actually reliability achieving. For as the typology in Table 11.1 underscores, service reliability can still encompass the following actions:

1. Undertaking prior planning and strategy as well as restoration resilience (including performance mode flexibility) to limit disruptions in time and in their probability of proceeding to failure

2. Having emergency procedures for failure and effective recovery resilience (here crisis management metrics can be reliability indicators)

3. Devising strategies to protect against degradation (or indeed promote the enhancement) of the new normal across new system states

4. Ensuring thoughtful efforts to reduce the likelihood of human errors (including misperception, misestimation, and mis-specification) in all operations throughout the various system states

5. Being mindful of ICIS connectivity, both manifest and latent across operational states, at least with respect to common control variables and the downstream effects on the other infrastructures of actions taken

Such distinctions must be kept in mind, given the presence of those who still insist that (1) reliability is all about trading off specific risks (no, reliability is first about setting and achieving system-wide standards from which different risks emerge), (2) the infrastructure crisis is primarily one of underfunding and underinvestment in physical assets (only true as far as it goes, but it most certainly does not go far enough in prioritizing the system-wide management challenge for reliability and resilience), and (3) the most dangerous interconnections arise from the physical proximity of collocated infrastructure elements (most certainly not always so). Multiple reliability standards for interconnected infrastructures argue against reductionist scenarios centered on the physical or technical to the detriment of the managerial.

IMPROVING INFRASTRUCTURE RELIABILITY
AND RESILIENCE IN ITS MULTIPLE FORMS

Given the range of states to which infrastructures are subject, the key question more and more has become just how resilient are infrastructures *as systems* in the face of these variations? Again, resilient elements or robust components alone do not add up to a resilient or robust system when it comes to managing their complex interconnections. But when you combine the existing portfolios of known scenarios and patterns with the skills to think ahead, we believe that in "control rooms" society has a foundation for the interinfrastructure resiliencies (plural, not singular) needed to provide a socially acceptable answer to that question.

If control rooms are prospective grounds for future improvements, it is at the same time true that researching reliability and risk management in control rooms is itself becoming more difficult. Access to the control rooms of large sociotechnical systems, never an easy matter in the United States, is closing in too many cases. As researchers, we were fortunate to have begun our high reliability studies early on and established our bona fides well before the events of 9/11. "9/11 changed everything," a senior Coast Guard emergency manager told us, and we couldn't agree more. When you add homeland security to the existing restrictions on control room access because of proprietary and market reasons, it is no surprise that entry into, continued observations of, and long-term analysis of the reliability management of U.S. critical infrastructures has become complicated to say the least.[5] The challenge of continued research is great particularly since longitudinal studies, not point-in-time or short-term investigations (so favored by funding agencies and consultants), are needed to capture shifting interconnectivity configurations as well as assess the stability of reliability mandates. Without steady control room access by researchers and scholars, we believe that the reliability management of infrastructures will continue to be a black box lying outside careful analysis and deep understanding by policy makers, regulators, and the public. Note that this point isn't just another call for more research; the call is for more access to continuously observe and document critical control room functions during all stages of operations.

Notably, the research insights to be gained run both ways. In our case, while it has taken months and even years to understand what specific reliability professionals are doing, they without fail report to us that we've helped them see their activities in different ways. It has been our privilege not just to learn so much from them and share it with others but also to develop with these reliability professionals concepts and vocabulary that lend them new insights about what they are doing. Much more needs to be done by many more in order to better address the infrastructure crisis identified in this book.

Various publications on today's infrastructure crisis include future disaster scenarios, which their authors tell you could happen if things are not set right soon. We too have participated in the scenario frenzy (Roe and Schulman 2008). Yet on further reflection, we believe that many crisis scenarios of cascading infrastructure failure are beside the point. Yes, such scenarios may be useful in emergency planning exercises; yes, disaster scenarios may be an integral part of the what-if game. But the point this book has stressed is that infrastructure control rooms are society's last line of defense against the unknown unknowns. These unknown unknowns have always been the Achilles' heel of any formal risk assessment and management strategy. Control rooms have to manage these surprises in real time and under very demanding reliability mandates. That again is why reliability comes before risk. Do the operators succeed all the time? Of course not, but they succeed more than doomsayers suppose. Moreover, they succeed because risk does not take priority over reliability in the sequence of key questions that preoccupy reliability professionals: What is the system to be managed? What are the standards of reliability to which the system must be managed? What are the risks (including uncertainties and ambiguities) to be managed that follow, including those of managing that way?

If we are right, then all of us should be spending less time trying to think the unthinkable and instead answer this: Who are the enemies of control rooms? One great irony in the current debate over cybersecurity attacks on critical infrastructures is the focus on outsiders doing the attacking. Certainly, terrorist attacks are a growing danger. But a close reader of this book knows there are other adversaries. What about protecting critical infrastructures from the following lineup?

The infrastructure CEO: Forget the Neanderthals in the control room, if we don't risk failure by cutting our costs we'll never maintain market share.

The economist: Trust me, electricity is no different than corn syrup.

The politician: Not to worry; when things go belly-up, we'll hold someone accountable.

The planner: There's nothing like a disaster to clear the table so we can start fresh.

The risk assessor: Nothing's wrong with our models; it's just that events happen that are twenty-five standard deviations from the norm.

The technology innovator: There's no progress without risk, and what better place to promote innovation than with what we depend on most.

The infrastructure regulator: If it takes fining them on the silly stuff to get their attention and to do what we say, so be it.

The public: The whole point of paying taxes is not to have to worry about whether the lights turn on or the water comes out of the tap.

This line-up, it seems to us, is doing quite well in undermining infrastructure security all by itself. The sooner the United States has a research-based strategy to protect infrastructure reliability from *all* its enemies, the better we can hope to be in *managing* both reliability and risk.[6]

APPENDIX
Research Methods

I N GATHERING THE DATA USED IN THIS
book, we used multiple research methods along with a re-
view of literature, meetings with hundreds of people, and many hours of direct
observation of control rooms and their operators. We started with a literature
review of interconnected critical infrastructures, including current conceptualizations, case studies, and databases that are public. The literature review
clarified that our initial focus on the California Delta water and energy infrastructures would have to be expanded to include transportation (not just roads
but rail and shipping), telecommunications, and other large sociotechnical
systems, including emergency response. Subsequently, our research strategy
focused on informal discussions with key informants in those organizations
and other infrastructures.

None of the discussions were tape-recorded; we took notes during the meetings and wrote them up most often immediately afterward. Discussants were
asked questions, some prepared beforehand and others more open-ended, that
followed the discussion format used in our previous work with control operators. As in the earlier work, informants are not named in the text. They bear
no responsibility for the way we have interpreted their points, and any errors

in transcription are ours alone. Key informant discussions proceeded by the snowballing technique, in which new discussants were identified as persons we should talk to by previous informants. Except for a few cases, all discussions were face-to-face and lasted an hour or more.

We directly observed control operators over many hours at the Contra Costa Water District in Concord, California, at the Coast Guard's Vessel Traffic Service (VTS) and Interagency Operations Center (command center) on Yerba Buena Island in San Francisco Bay, and at PG&E's Gas Operations Control Center in San Ramon, California. Those with whom we talked had positions that included, at Contra Costa Water District, director of operations and maintenance, manager of water operations, operations control administrator, water resource manager, and senior engineer (operations and maintenance) and, at the Coast Guard, lieutenant commander, chief of command center, command center supervisor, VTS director, VTS training director, vessel traffic management specialist, security specialist, and lead command center controller.

In the case of the California Department of Water Resources' (DWR's) State Water Project (SWP), Port of Stockton,[1] and PG&E's Vacaville Electrical Operations Facility, we discussed control operations at length with real-time dispatchers and managers on different occasions. Their positions included, at DWR, security coordinator, chief dispatcher, water and power dispatcher, chief of operations support office, and emergency preparedness and security manager; at the Port of Stockton, operations manager, environmental manager, director of facilities maintenance and construction, port chief of police; and, at PG&E, system dispatchers. We discussed control operations as well with key managers at Union Pacific's Roseville, California, facility (including its general director, operations and safety, and the general superintendent of the Roseville Service Unit) and emergency response measures with state and federal officials responsible for emergency management in their respective units (among whom were regional administrators and emergency services coordinators). We also facilitated an August 2010 tabletop exercise between control operators of different infrastructures and emergency responders as part of the Resilient and Sustainable Infrastructure Networks (RESIN) project of the University of California, Berkeley. To summarize, we have been fortunate during the course of our research to have discussions with over seventy-five control room operators, emergency responders, support staff, and management in operations of multiple water supplies (county, regional, and state), energy (electricity and natural gas) transmission and distribution, transportation (shipping, navigation, port, and rail), and telecommunications, most prominently.

Save for the exceptions explicitly noted, the bulk of the discussions took place between mid-2009 and mid-2013. Discussions were supplemented by material gathered during a November 2009 site visit to Sherman Island and the August 2010 tabletop exercise. These events were attended by officials, area specialists, and stakeholders, and the minutes of the events are available in RESIN's digital archive at the University of California, Berkeley, Center for Catastrophic Risk Management. The case study of the initiative by CAISO discussed in Chapter 9 is based solely on our research up to the end of 2008, after which we no longer had research and consulting access to CAISO's Folsom control room.

Chapter 8's data analysis of electricity and water flows at the SWP's Banks pumping station uses a specific research methodology described fully in "Case Study of Interconnected Critical Infrastructures in the Sacramento–San Joaquin Delta" (2011) by Benjamin Baker, Emery Roe, and Paul Schulman. Briefly, DWR provided records for how much water the Harvey O. Banks Pumping Plant pumped and how much energy it used to run the pumps. These data span more than six years (June 2004–December 2010) of hourly energy records (MWh) and daily pumping flows (acre-feet). The CAISO power reliability metrics regarding daily CPS2 violations, generation outages, and transmission line mitigations for four years (July 2004–July 2008) were drawn from Roe and Schulman's *High Reliability Management* (2008). Our study period for the case study was primarily mid-2004 through mid-2008 for several reasons. First, anything more recent meant that figures might be revised in light of later measurements becoming available through regular reporting updates and after-action reports following our research. Second, it was important to choose a period of analysis that was not so distant in the past that control operators couldn't recognize our findings but not so recent that the operators (or others) could be "blamed" for the findings.[2] Third, while both CAISO and the SWP have had major changes since 2008 affecting their real-time operations, the methodological approach could be updated to the present by their own staff in light of their respective proprietary, security, and market competition concerns. To determine if and the extent to which electricity problems affect water flows during normal operations, we relied on the analysis of variance (ANOVA), which includes correlation and regression analysis for the combined dataset.

With respect to the Chapter 3 Jones Tract case study, discussions with Chris Neudeck and Bill Darsie of KSN Engineering; Dave Huey and Jimmie Abbott of the Contra Costa Water District; Sonny Fong, chief of DWR Emergency Security and Preparedness Operations; and Don Boland, executive director of California Utilities Emergency Association, helped frame and highlight our understanding of that recovery effort. The usual disclaimers apply, as the interpretations and any errors made from material gathered from all discussions remain ours.

Last, we have used material from articles and a book chapter published earlier as part of our research. These publications are acknowledged here:

Roe, E. 2011. "Surprising Answers to Rising Sea Levels, Storms, Floods, Desertification, Earthquakes and Ever More Environmental Crises in California's Sacramento–San Joaquin Delta." *Journal of Contingencies and Crisis Management* 19 (1): 34–42. © 2011 John Wiley & Sons Ltd. We thank the journal and John Wiley and Sons for permission to republish material from this article.

Roe, E., R. G. Bea, S. N. Jonkman, H. Faucher de Corn, H. Foster, J. Radke, P. Schulman, and R. Storesund. Forthcoming. "Risk Assessment and Management (RAM) for Interconnected Critical Infrastructure Systems (ICIS) at the Site and Regional Levels in California's Sacramento–San Joaquin Delta." *International Journal of Critical Infrastructures* 12 (1–2). We thank the journal and Inderscience (which retains copyright for the original article) for permission to publish material from the article.

Roe, E., and P. R. Schulman. 2012. "Risk Management of Interconnected Infrastructures." In *Risk and Interdependencies in Critical Infrastructures*, edited by P. Hokstad, I. B. Utne, and J. Vatn, 189–209. London: Springer-Verlag. © Springer-Verlag London 2012. We thank the editors for the opportunity to publish the chapter and Springer for permission to publish material from it.

Roe, E., and P. R. Schulman. 2012. "Toward a Comparative Framework for Measuring Resilience in Critical Infrastructure Systems." *Journal of Comparative Policy Analysis* 14 (2): 114–125. We thank the journal and the Taylor and Francis Group for permission to republish material from this article.

Roe, E., and P. R. Schulman. 2015. "Comparing Emergency Response Infrastructure to Other Critical Infrastructures in the California Bay-Delta of the United States: A Research Note on Interinfrastructural Differences in Reliability Management." *Journal of Contingencies and Crisis Management*, March 6. doi:10.1111/1468-5973.12083. © 2015 John Wiley & Sons Ltd. We thank the journal for permission to republish material from this article.

Schulman, P. R., and E. Roe. 2011. "A Control Room Metric for Evaluating Success and Failure in High Reliability Crisis Management." *Policy and Society* 30: 129–136. We thank *Policy and Society* and Elsevier for the opportunity to publish this article.

NOTES

CHAPTER ONE

1. For more details, see Longfellow 2013; Ohio River Valley Water Sanitation Commission, n.d.; Schneider 2012; and Neff 2010.

2. Of course, not all critical infrastructures, as officially classified, have control rooms (e.g., education).

CHAPTER TWO

1. Cumulative effects may also emerge from normal operations of the collocated infrastructure elements rather than because of any disruption in one affecting the other (see, e.g., Dekker, Cilliers, and Hofmeyr 2011, 942; Saleh et al. 2010, 1109; Richman and Pant 2008). Some parents might look at Figure 2.2, for example, and worry about possible electric magnetic field impacts, if any, on children attending the school.

2. For details on our research methods and interviewees quoted throughout the book, see the appendix.

3. These forms of interdependency are described in a classic analysis by organization theorist James D. Thompson in *Organizations in Action* (1967) and elaborated by Todd LaPorte in *Organized Social Complexity* (1975).

4. For one such example (among many), see Quill 2012.

CHAPTER THREE

1. For an analysis of "predictable" surprises and their causes, see Bazerman and Watkins 2008.

2. As one engineer we interviewed in an earlier round of research exclaimed proudly, "I try to design systems that are not only foolproof but damned foolproof, so even a damned fool can't screw them up" (Roe and Schulman 2008, 11).

3. In 2009, one of us gave a presentation to an overseas meeting of a natural gas provider that had consolidated part of its infrastructure with another's. After the presentation a planner for the consolidation came up from the audience and asked, "If I understand you right, you're saying we should have consulted with the control rooms before we did this?"

4. A senior hydrologist working with the DWR Flood Operations Center agreed with USBR: "What we worry about here as well is losing control of the reservoirs. With reservoirs, you need to be 100 percent reliable."

5. "Reconstructing the dam [after overtopping that led to failure] would be a bureaucratic nightmare," a USBR official told us. "Not just environmental regulations—if [a certain dam] failed, . . . a huge quarry would be needed [for reconstruction], and could that happen today? All the expertise to build large dams has disappeared or is fast disappearing [or going] overseas." Said another USBR manager, "A large dam failure here would suck up all the dam engineers in the U.S."

6. An experienced VTS traffic manager felt that new trainees tended to keep to the rules more. The experienced manager would follow the rules until he couldn't (for example, when there was no rule for the event being faced). He also felt that a particularly important time for trainees was just before they qualified, because senior traffic managers "had to listen harder, since [trainees] were sounding more confident about what they were saying, which still could be wrong." In this way, one curb on complacency in experienced operators may be having to attend to overconfidence in newer ones.

7. Organization theorist James March has drawn a useful contrast in this regard between decisions guided by a "logic of consequences" and those guided by a "logic of appropriateness" (2009, 57–58).

8. It may be that motivational near self-sufficiency in the control room is an evolutionary adaptation to a predicable loss of attention and erosion of sense of urgency that follow an initial period of high-intensity disaster prevention or emergency management. Louise Comfort, Michael Siciliano, and Aya Okada note, "In communities that have experienced disaster, the . . . urgency of danger directs the priorities for action, and organizations and individuals voluntarily act cooperatively to meet immediate needs, representing a first step toward resilience. Yet, their sources and energy committed to a shared effort to meet immediate needs generated by the extreme event slowly give way to entropy, or the dissipation of attention, energy, and resources that leads to a consequent loss of efficiency in risk reduction" (2011, 1). This suggests that control rooms can also be an organizational adaptation against entropy within a context of disaster prevention and recovery.

9. This coordination is in terms of a deep understanding of causal processes or a focus on signature events (such as shifts in the electricity frequency) that guide reliability requirements even in the absence of full causal understanding of the system (Roe and Schulman 2008; Dekker, Cilliers, and Hofmeyr 2011). For a discussion of control variables in the context of control theory, see Powers 1990.

10. For an initial discussion on the gap between probability risk analysis and high reliability approaches, see Saleh et al. 2010.

11. Much of the operators' cognitive approach to real time is described in the "recognition-primed" model of decision making (Klein 1999, 8; Kahneman and Klein 2009) as well as in elements of human-factors approaches (see, e.g., Woods and Hollnagel 2006).

12. "A great deal of my training [of] new staff," the senior hydrologist told us, "is directed to getting them out into the field. . . . Seeing it is important for overall situational awareness." Some operators—though again and importantly not all—did not and could not have firsthand experience with their respective systems' coverage area. One instance serves for many: "[Our] operators don't have on-site familiarity with all the areas, so that makes it difficult for them to visualize all the terrain. But does it affect our response? Maybe," said a control room operator in another infrastructure. Last, cognitive limitations may be in the form of inexperience in how backup technologies or subsystems are to be used: "How can it be redundant if you don't understand how to use it?"

asked a different control room operator. That question must be very worrying from a high reliability management perspective.

13. For good reviews of the psychological findings on cognitive biases and limitations, see Bazerman and Moore 2012 and Kahneman 2012.

14. To put the point differently, promoting reliability professionals to senior executive positions in no way ensures they continue as reliability professionals, since they no longer remain part of the same network from which they were drawn.

15. For more detailed analyses of "requisite variety," see Ashby 1966 and Weick 1995; for a more specific discussion with respect to one critical infrastructure, see Antonsen, Skarholt, and Ringstad 2012. Note that "bandwidth" is not "threshold." Specific threshold, or trigger, points can convey the impression that risk is on-off with respect to the specified point. We find in our research that what matters is whether the observed risk falls within or outside ranges of risk (see, e.g., Jonkman 2011; Jonkman et al. 2012).

16. In another context (aviation safety) Carl MacRae (2014) has used the term "risk resilience" to describe a similar process.

17. A prior effort to differentiate infrastructure interconnectivity across multiple states of operation is in Rinaldi, Pereenboom, and Kelley 2001.

18. As reported to us, some difficulties faced in real time were daunting. The Army Corps of Engineers refused to participate in repairing the breach because the levee did not meet Public Law 84-99 construction standards. The Corps also refused to armor the related Trapper Slough levee (although they did participate in heightening the levee to protect the nearby State Highway 4). The BNSF railroad was said to have refused to allow certain work under its railroad trestle through which lower Jones Tract was flooding for fear it would disrupt train crossings across the trestle, and finally, the fill purchased by the Corps from the Port of Stockton to protect highway 4 was later determined to have had some toxic contaminants.

CHAPTER FOUR

1. In this book, "interinfrastructure connectivity" and "interinfrastructural interconnections" are synonymous and interchangeable.

2. These figures should not be confused with a Venn diagram union-of-sets analysis, since the infrastructures remain different and their interaction (unidirectional or bidirectional) is an empirical question for analysis.

3. Nothing in our definition of sustainability implies that sustainability equates to the permanence of physical structures or to a static-state condition. What matters is, for example, the persistence of reliable water supplies, not permanence of existing structures of pipes, canals, and dams.

4. The concept of requisite variety has been used in the theory of control systems (Ashby 1966) and more recently in the area of organizational management (Weick 1995). The central idea is that it takes some degree of complexity to manage and control complexity. Translated into our framework of high reliability management, it takes high process variance (e.g., options variety) to convert high input variance into low output variance (reliability).

5. Engineering colleagues argue that deterministic interconnections are still probabilistic, with the probability of 1.0. We agree they are equivalent, but for our purposes "deterministic" is more meaningful for infrastructure managers.

6. Delta reclamation districts vary considerably in their capacities. One emergency manager cautioned that some "are really nothing more than a couple of people, a duck club, and they are not really responsible for the full levee but only their part of it, leaving the rest to someone else." A number of Delta island residents see flood prevention and risk reduction as the responsibility of government.

Other reclamation districts are more professionalized (we were told the Port of Stockton is basically the reclamation district for its Rough and Ready Island).

7. The Coast Guard in Northern California has other reliability features in addition to being a focal infrastructure: presence of redundant real-time monitoring and communication channels; an unusually strong command and control authority when needed (i.e., just-this-way management by the captain of the port, including waiving of certain procedures and regulations); use of a risk management protocol in command center search and rescue activities; ongoing regular coordination with other infrastructures, including Army Corps of Engineers, ports, and private or public entities; a legal mandate to focus on resilience, especially safeguarding supply chain navigation to and from ports; and the focus on a key control variable shared with other infrastructures, the rate and amount of water flows. One possible complication is the routine and at times high turnover of personnel within the VTS and command center as new trainees come and go. That, however, has made the Coast Guard supportive of training and exercises involving other key personnel in interinfrastructural operations and emergency response.

8. Interinfrastructural cascades can obviously be induced or accelerated by management error (just as cascades can be more granular than commonly supposed). These errors, however, do not pose the same risk as does the worst-case endpoint of automatic, unmanageable cascades across fully stressed infrastructures.

9. For more on alternative routing in Delta transportation, see Delta Protection Commission 2012, 215.

10. A water control operator distinguished smooth days from and rough days: "If things remain smooth, then it's maintenance. 'Smooth' means meeting the parameters of the facility the water is going through. . . . Say[, however,] we don't want to be pulling water from [one usual facility], so we make a change and decide to pump from [another]. Well, the pumps don't come off and on instantaneously; nor do the valves. All this takes time, which means that the actual amount of water flowing into the canal as we shift between one source to another means the water flows go down. . . . When that kind of thing happens, it can mean you are making adjustments through a whole shift. That is rough; that means watching and doing a lot of changes, opening and closing the checks. My decisions during these times will affect the guy who is working after me."

11. Our research uncovered many examples of shift points with respect to vulnerabilities and resilience, including the Jones Tract levee breach discussed in Chapter 3. The normal sequential interconnectivity among Northern California and Delta water infrastructures, controlling the flow of water from pumps to reservoirs and then through release channels, was transformed with that breach into a pooled interconnectivity as potential saltwater intrusion threatened Delta water quality and flows in and beyond the Delta. When latent interconnections become manifest factors in recovery, they can alter incentives for interinfrastructural cooperation over shared control variables (in this case related to water flows). If a pooled or reciprocal interdependency were to emerge from what had been before a sequential interconnectivity, knowledge that such a shift would occur might encourage cooperation beforehand.

12. Of course, failure is always a possibility, but so is managing to prevent failure, if not one specific failure, then others. The need to have real-time indicators of system precursor resilience is crucial in tracking how the managed event of nonfailure or nondisruption actually occurs.

13. Management through communications is doubly important for emergency responders who by definition work across infrastructures. When we asked control operators and emergency responders at the August 2010 tabletop exercise what would really screw up their day during a major storm, they told us levee failures, barge shortages, and problems in communications. One Cal Fire official reported, "What amazes me is this thing [*looking at his cell phone*]. It means immediate communication. We

had a case when the governor was flying south and saw a fire from the plane and wondered what it was, and in minutes he had the message from our director that it was this fire. Our system reports from the ground all the way up to the director on events, and in these days where budgets are cut, look how it can matter that the governor gets his info when he wants it."

CHAPTER FIVE

1. The natural language of many people, including some experts, is to conflate these four types of unpredictabilities and their respective importance (see, e.g., Spielgelhalter, Pearson, and Short 2011).

2. Consequently, from a high reliability perspective, one must be very chary of proposals to put risk assessment and risk management into separate organizational risk enterprise units decoupled from real-time control operations. Once decoupled, risk analysis can easily become an analytic exercise neutered of considerations that require more granularity (again in terms of time horizons as well as variables) for actual management purposes.

3. When risk analysts undertake a formal risk-benefit analysis of a very complex infrastructure project, they frequently end up specifying discount rates and time horizons and monetizing many other intangibles. This places them far closer to uncertainty, ambiguity, or ignorance than they themselves may concede or can appreciate within multiple ICIS settings.

4. "We don't have a clue of what financial stability actually means," concluded an International Monetary Fund chief economist five years after the 2008 financial upheaval (quoted in Porter 2013, B1). "We were never in calm waters," admitted a head of the European Central Bank (quoted in Atkins 2011, 5). Evidently the financial services infrastructure did not have a reliability strategy to keep out of ignorance: they knew neither probabilities nor consequences. Yet one key response to the 2008 financial crisis has been to call for "better" risk management, as if managing Pfs and Cfs had been going on all along, albeit ineffectively. In actuality, it is not clear even now that risks can be calculated in relation to major probabilities or consequences in this sector. If they can't, financial service providers have no high reliability management expertise whatever.

5. Such procedures need not be written down or codified. A senior manager told us that they had determined there were some sixty steps in his part of port operations: "This is probably the first time these steps have been written down. They're not formal procedures but what we've learned on the job. It's what I actually do; it's what we do. [Another experienced port manager] would write out the same steps."

6. This acute awareness of the limits of their skills and knowledge is a trait psychologist Gary Klein (1999) asserts is a common distinction between experts and amateurs.

7. Complacency is also a very major risk from the high reliability perspective because it is directly counter to the precluded-events standard of reliability arising out of a persisting social dread about which few if any can ever be complacent.

8. This need and ability to maneuver seems obvious, but it contrasts with conventional wisdom that those in the bureaucracy who follow the rules can't go wrong. If they follow procedure, meet their job requirements, and work within the chain of command, no one can accuse them of doing the wrong thing. Yet from the perspective of high reliability management, just-this-way performance (as in follow-the-rules compliance) can cause havoc when conditions require instead just-in-time or just-for-now performance to meet even the regulatory reliability mandates.

9. In the banking and investment sector, "turbulence is defined as much by abnormal correlation of returns as it is by abnormal volatility" (Horan 2010).

10. This applies as well to the many retrospective assessments of reliability made by upper-level executives in infrastructure organizations. "We've done it successfully in the past, so what's the problem?" This retrospection is especially dangerous when associated with unsuitable indicators of

overall reliability and risk. Regulators and executives of BP took the absence of slips, trips, and falls on the Deepwater Horizon rig to be an indicator of overall reliability and safety of the Macondo well operations (Deepwater Horizon Study Group 2011).

11. The prospective orientation of reliability professionals is not limited to control room operators and their immediate support staff, the subject of this research. When it comes to reliability and risk, other professionals in the respective critical infrastructures might well be very proactively focused, for example, on what the resulting risks of abruptly disrupting or suspending ongoing programmatic investments in infrastructure reliability are.

12. For an economist or engineer, innovation is undertaken to replace what went before. The virtue of operational redesign is that it is directed to maintain reliability throughout any such flip over or transition. If, as a well-known historian put it, "the ambition of the inventor is to contrive something which shall be fool-proof" (Oliver 1931, 85), reliability professionals know that management is always required because of such true believers in the foolproof. These reality checks have not stopped engineers or economists from recommending otherwise, however. Referring to computer crashes and electronic glitches affecting the financial markets, MIT economist Andrew Lo comments, "The solution, of course, is not to forswear financial technology but to develop more advanced technology—so advanced that it becomes foolproof and invisible to the human operator" (2012).

13. We offer a case study illustrating ineffectual practices in project management in Chapter 9.

14. That Union Pacific's major central control room is in Omaha indicates a national grid being managed. We were told of a case of the Omaha control room remotely accessing control equipment at the Union Pacific drawbridge crossing Carquinez Strait in Northern California and finding that a sensor had failed there.

15. One of us (Roe 2013) has long advocated bringing ecologists or other environmental specialists directly into real-time control room operations for water and energy, given reliability mandates for better ecosystem management and restoration.

16. One information-gathering meeting we had on Delta infrastructure vulnerabilities began with a senior emergency specialist telling us of confidential discussions on such vulnerabilities later being ruled by a California court to be matter of public record. Such concerns over imparting information are responses to homeland security restrictions, market and proprietary factors, and transboundary issues such as found in the European Union (Comfort, Boin, and Demchak 2010).

17. For example, the California Delta Stewardship Council has the coequal goals of ecosystem restoration and water supply reliability. The council's website explains, "The Delta Stewardship Council was created in legislation to achieve . . . state mandated coequal goals for the Delta. '"Coequal goals" means the two goals of providing a more reliable water supply for California and protecting, restoring, and enhancing the Delta ecosystem. . . .' (CA Water Code §85054)" (Delta Stewardship Council 2015).

CHAPTER SIX

1. According to the TNO-DUT summary, "The energy sector initiates more cascades than it receives. Interdependencies occur very infrequently. . . . Fixed telecom disruptions affect ATMs and electronic payments (financial sector), the mobile phone base stations–base station controller links, governmental services, and internet and telecom services. Within the energy sector, most dependencies (61) occur between power generation, transmission and distribution" (Luiijf et al. 2008).

2. In a strict sense, the ability of CIS_2 always to avoid the interconnection of its control variables with CIS_1 is equivalent to Pf_{CIS_2} being statistically independent of Cf_{CIS_1}. Chapter 8 returns to what this means for control variables.

3. The work of sociologist Ronald Burt (2010) is exemplary here.

4. "I know I can speak for the entire crew when I tell you we were simply doing the job we were trained to do," Captain Sully Sullenberger said after having piloted his aircraft to an emergency landing on the Hudson River in which all survived (quoted in McCartney 2009, 7).

5. A similar shift in the definition of safety as things going right has begun to replace the prior focus in safety management that safety can be defined and measured by the absence of negative events (see Hollnagel 2014).

6. One former senior grid manager told us, "It was also important for my career that when I was at [a California utility] I was also working closely with the gas people. We were on the same floor. Knowing the gas operations was crucial for [the utility's] power plant operations, so I knew a lot about interoperability issues when I got to [a senior management position elsewhere]."

7. For an introduction to the multiple standards that the Central Valley Project and SWP must meet, see the DWR website, at http://www.water.ca.gov/swp/operationscontrol/docs/bay_delta standards.htm.

8. In his research on train operations, Steenhuisen found that "as soon as [traffic] controllers identified a deviation, they buil[t] plausible scenarios that may have negative consequences" (2014, 161).

9. The executive director of the U.S. National Association of Water Companies made this point from the opposite direction: "Four years ago, the American Society of Civil Engineers issued a report card giving water and wastewater infrastructure a D minus, and this year we moved up to D. But nobody's water is ever a D or D minus. It's an A until one day it's not. It's F and you're out of water for hopefully half a day and then it's back to an A for the next ten years" (Michael Deane, personal communication 2013).

10. This is not a one-of-a-kind finding. "Our analyses suggest that effects of diversity-dependent ecosystem feedbacks and interspecific complementarity accumulate over time, causing high-diversity species combinations that appeared functionally redundant during early years to become more functionally unique through time" (Reich et al. 2012, 589).

11. A slow leak over decades became one of the largest oil spills in the continental United States (Beamish 2002).

CHAPTER SEVEN

1. We discuss indicators of recovery resilience in Chapter 10.

2. For more on zooming down, up, and across, see Roe et al., forthcoming.

3. For more on the special importance that the temporal dimension has in high reliability activities, see Shrivastava, Sonpar, and Pazzaglia 2009a, 2009b.

4. Or to come to this point from the other direction, we as reliability researchers appreciate just how little we still know about these infrastructures.

CHAPTER EIGHT

Case material in this chapter is adapted from Baker, Roe, and Schulman 2011 (with the assistance of Doanh Do and Robin Torres). A more detailed version of the chapter has been published as Roe and Schulman 2012a.

1. Such interactions are not unique. When one of us visited the operation center of the Contra Costa Water District, operators reported they had been busy that morning with pumps being reset and backup generators needing field checks because of an outage in the PG&E system.

2. In any case, we expect non-negligible but not large correlations because the stress variables we use for the grid reflect many more issues and performance conditions than those that connect directly with the Banks pumps.

3. CPS2 requires that CAISO dispatchers minimize fluctuations of the Area Control Error within a maximum bandwidth every ten minutes. The standards also require a monthly 90 percent performance rate within these bandwidths and allow a daily quota of fourteen ten-minute CPS2 violations. If monthly averages fall below 90 percent, the regional reliability organization can impose a fine.

4. Our data sources, period of study, and statistical methods are discussed in the appendix.

5. Depending on the time of year, an unplanned shutdown of the pumps with an unspecifiable return to service could mean major disruptions and consequences for urban, agricultural, and environmental water users in the Delta and south of the Delta. Closing the European Union airspace in 2010 because of ash from Iceland's Eyjafjallajökull volcano comes to mind as an analogy.

6. Recurring and one-off factors have also been involved, such as major fires in October 2007 in Southern California, regulatory requirements for endangered smelt and salmon, and gearing up to meeting Army Corps of Engineers flood-control reservation requirements in major reservoirs. It is also evident in 2010 and 2011 data that tidal action and the operations of a major reservoir played a role in the gap between the planned and actual daily allotments of water flow. While mathematical tide is fairly predictable in terms of moon and gravity effects, tides are also affected by barometric pressure and wind direction. Depending on the water level inside a major reservoir, SWP operators may have only one to two feet of clearance to work with to ensure the allotment is taken into that facility. A mismatch of pumping patterns and gate opening times can impede the operator ability to take in the full planned allotment. We thank DWR's Andy Chu for his help in this matter.

7. Unsurprisingly, the amount of water pumped was proportional to the electricity it took for Banks to run the pumps (details are in Roe and Schulman 2013).

8. For example, we wondered if hydropower produced by the SWP pumps at high-flow periods could have some such effect on the CAISO grid, but those whom we asked did not see how. More generally, that correlation is not causation may not be as much a methodological issue as it first seems. In earlier chapters, we discuss the need to distinguish latent and manifest interconnections and the implications for risk analysis. If "latent" means that the interconnectivity is waiting to happen (i.e., waiting to be triggered into manifest), then a precursor or signal that latency could exist is a statistical correlation, an indication of some kind of resonance between two infrastructures.

9. Table 8.1 suggests that 2006 may have been a stressed year for water and electricity infrastructures. Over 15 percent of the movements in daily water flows through Banks that year were matched by 2006 movements in daily CPS2 violations on the CAISO grid. Note, however, that a calendar year is *not* the water year for the SWP planning purposes (more below).

10. Preliminary analysis suggests that unscheduled generation outages might have had a statistically significant effect on Banks pumps' electricity usage during on-peak hours during July 2004–December 2005 (the only period for which we had on- and off-peak hourly data). We were told that considerable SWP generation is done during on-peak hours.

11. The beta-coefficient is the amount of change induced in the dependent variable by one unit change in the independent variable. If the beta-coefficient is not significantly different from zero, the effect would be to multiply zero against any line mitigation or CPS2 value, thus rendering the variable as having no effect on the dependent variable, water flow.

12. An important next step in research would be to determine how well the daily relationship holds when we drill down to the hourly level for September and October. To do so would require hourly water flow data, for which we have only daily values. Access to such information was restricted for security and competitive market reasons.

13. It is interesting to note that those fifteen days when Banks was shut down for scheduled maintenance and repair were also days (with respect to water flows) and hours (with respect to electricity inflows) when CAISO operators managed to have fewer line mitigations and CPS2 violations

compared to study period averages. That said, the 8 percent variation during normal periods of operation for both infrastructures could be a precursor indicator of more direct and powerful control variable connections that become manifest *only* during periods of *unexpected* disruption or failure for one or both of these systems.

14. None of the days of zero water flows through the Banks pumps occurred in September or October for the study period.

CHAPTER NINE

1. In describing this event's personnel repercussions, one control room operator told us, "I go home and sit in my chair and think about the kind of stress I have here and ask is it worth it. At [my previous job] I got about the same pay but nothing like the stress I have here now. It's inhumane. . . . Look at what I have to keep in my head during the shift—you know, all the kinds of things I have to do." One reason that prolonged just-for-now performance is so unstable may be that cognitive demands on the operators are high precisely when viable options are scarce (for research on scarcity's effects on cognitive loads, see Shah, Mullainathan, and Shafir 2012).

2. A detailed analysis of this example is in Roe and Schulman 2008.

3. An infrastructure that has cutting-edge technology does not necessarily use all its functionality. A control room operator in another infrastructure described the screen-to-face interface at his console as a "Porsche stepped down to a Honda."

4. A generation dispatcher compared manual and automatic handling of market dispatches and prices: "Prices are more reliable if computed automatically. If we go to a manual process, we can't be as reliable for prices as it would be on automatic. When we are issuing manual dispatches, it won't be running as smoothly, since we'd be taking one big unit [to provide all the energy needed] versus RTMA's ten smaller units [that would provide an equivalent total]."

5. It was obvious that MRTU designers should consult with control room operators when designing software—we ourselves recommended so early on. But taking operators off the floor where and when they were needed had consequences. During our research we found ourselves concurring with the view that, because MRTU issues appear so fast and so late, not all affected parties were being consulted on the solutions. But we also had to concede that, when the affected parties were consulted, it meant removing them from the control room at critical times. A shift supervisor told us, "I never minded grid ops being mushrooms; we don't need to know everything. We have to be hived off from the rest of the organization so we can maintain reliability." This view points again to control rooms as unique organizational formations.

6. This problem exists well beyond CAISO. "We have gone from fairly simple computing architectures to massively distributed, massively interconnected and interdependent networks," one expert says in the *New York Times*, to which the correspondent adds, "Flaws have become increasingly hard to predict or spot" (Schwartz 2007).

7. We were told that there were basically two types of operators: those, typically older, who didn't see the sense in changing what was working and thus resisted new untested applications and those, typically younger, who were more willing to trust new applications. The experience with CAS and RTMA reinforced the view of the first type and made the second more skeptical (for more on the role of trust and distrust in automated systems within high reliability contexts, see Schöbel 2009).

8. A younger dispatcher, who had just taken an MRTU training module, told us that it was good to have locational marginal pricing explained. In his view, only a handful of people knew and understood locational marginal pricing fully, and he was happy to have the opportunity to learn his part. What was left unsaid were the implications of building a system that is difficult to explain, let alone analyze when it goes wrong.

9. As someone in the control room told us, "The culture here is to bury problems, and now you have people standing on a mountain of problems and not knowing which one will reach up and grab you. We have problems with [one critical piece of software] that are unresolved for the current system, let alone for MRTU."

10. It has never been clear to us how control operators could manage for reliability at the much-vaunted twenty-thousand-foot level if they can no longer understand how and why a system operates as it does in real time.

11. See also Roe and Schulman 2008, chap. 11.

12. A CPS2 violation is incurred when a small excursion from a tight load-and-generation balance is sustained for over ten minutes. CAISO was allowed ninety-three CPS2 violations per month without a fine.

13. CAS was introduced for its first full day on February 14, 2007, and DST that year occurred on March 11, 2007.

14. In their *Science* article, "Anticipating Critical Transitions," M. Scheffer and colleagues suggest that an early warning signal of a transition in complex systems is a system "slowing down near tipping points"—that is, "in the vicinity of many kinds of tipping points, the rate at which a system recovers from small perturbations becomes very slow" (2012, 346).

15. The DCS is a metric of a balancing authority's (such as CAISO's) ability to balance resources and demand with contingency reserve and thereby return the interconnection frequency back quickly within defined limits, following a reportable disturbance.

16. For a broader discussion of corporatization in a critical infrastructure, see Lofquist 2010.

17. This process of resetting the perceptions of normal has been termed the "normalization of deviance" in an analysis of NASA's drift away from reliability commitments in its space shuttle program (Vaughan 1997).

CHAPTER TEN

1. Emergency operations centers are part of the U.S. national and state incident command structures.

2. For more on the lessons learned in crisis management, start with Rosenthal, Boin, and Comfort 2001; Boin et al. 2005; and Boin, McConnell, and t'Hart 2008. For more on problems with leadership, see Kellerman 2012.

3. For example, PG&E is mandated by regulation to have a duty to serve. This has been interpreted to mean that PG&E really cannot plan for failure in the sense of planning to be off-line indefinitely.

4. It has been our impression that key stakeholders often left uninvited to the table when discussing changes in a critical infrastructure are those other infrastructures that are interconnected to it. It may indeed be that these other infrastructures are *key* stakeholders if only because they are not going to disappear any time soon (as do some other stakeholders). If so, then the interconnectivity can be a positive source of stability for discussions and not just negative points of vulnerability.

5. For example, we would say on-site regulatory supervisors and inspectors (as found in financial services more today than before) bring resources if they have both a global view of better practices with respect to the operations being supervised or inspected and a local view that adds deep contextual knowledge of what's being supervised or inspected.

6. For more on the issue of regulatory capture, see Rourke 1969 and Bernstein 1955. A great deal of the literature on regulatory capture insists that the regulator and regulated organizations be independent if not adversarial entities, even though reliability functions might of necessity require cooperative relations between them (Levine and Forrence 1990).

7. Ensuring the functional resilience of any critical infrastructure at the system level, remember, is a very difficult task under mandates of high reliability. We know from our discussions that some

CISs have specific infrastructural elements and locations that cannot be rerouted around easily or for which there is no at-hand alternative—each of these systems as systems have their own choke points. It is important to be mindful that, while not all elements in an infrastructure are choke points, some elements can be—but that determination is an empirical issue and not an assumption.

8. Note how this criterion differs from the stopping rule used in conventional risk analysis, namely, you stop adding factors to the analysis or expanding the scale of analysis when doing so makes *no* difference to the estimation of Pf and Cf. With our standard, you stop the risk analysis at the point when adding infrastructures *undermines* the estimation of Pf and Cf in terms of understanding manifest and latent risks, system volatility, and the options with which to respond to them by the control operators involved.

9. In other words, managing on too broad or too narrow a scope leads to manager ignorance about system behavior. An example is a former U.S. district judge's attempt (in a major California Delta court case related to an endangered fish species) to operationally manage real-time water flows affecting interconnected water supply and ecoinfrastructures. Nothing from the high reliability literature with which we are familiar would indicate that a court mandating daily water-flow levels and rates, which it has no real-time capacity to monitor, let alone manage, would achieve the legally mandated high reliability.

10. Because resilience is a system property to be managed, we see companies and firms that insure or otherwise indemnify critical infrastructures (again, many of which are privately owned) as having an even more important role when it comes to leadership and performance evaluation.

CHAPTER ELEVEN

1. For one alternative exploration of differing reliability or safety regimes, see Amalberti 2013.

2. In effect many precursor events and conditions identified and managed under a precluded-event standard are avoided events for the infrastructures in question.

3. A Coast Guard manager said of search and rescue missions, "You have to go, but you don't have to come back." Trying to manage probabilistically rather than deterministically by way of managing reliably comes closest to the conventional engineering definition of reliability: the probability that a system achieves and retains, over a given time period, the intended level of quality and functionality. We, however, resist the engineer's temptation to define reliability as the probability that the system will not fail in that time period, as if there were only two system states of real issue.

We have spent considerable time trying to convince our engineering and economist colleagues that high reliability is not a probability or a variable cost to be trade-off against other factors. When we talk about management to engineers and economists, they almost invariably hear *mis*management; when they talk to us about design and technology, we see almost invariably find ourselves in the presence of hubris and the baked-in defects of theory. Our experience has been that working together across disciplines at best produces a shared situational awareness of the infrastructure—for example, we are all seeing the levee the same way—but even that does not overcome our different Backgrounds.

4. We describe reliability in the context of crisis management in Schulman and Roe 2011, 2012b.

5. It is still possible for high reliability researchers to find a welcome in control rooms in the United States. We're told the same holds even more in Europe. Perhaps most importantly for the future, the BRICS (Brazil, Russia, India, China, and South Africa) are countries where infrastructure reliability is clearly of growing centrality. Brazil with its export agriculture and offshore oil production sectors, Russia with its transboundary natural gas production and distribution systems, India with its biotechnology and software infrastructures, China with its massive high-speed-rail system (far more ambitious than other nations combined), and South Africa with its major electricity sector all merit close study, if only to identify better practices for reliability management and more comprehensive theories of life cycles in infrastructure reliability.

6. More familiar are the calls for a national infrastructure bank to fund major repairs and renovation of the nation's deteriorating infrastructures. If our framework and analysis are correct, we would also need a national academy of reliable infrastructure management to ensure that future management skills match the tasks and demands of our infrastructures. In particular, infrastructure-wide stress tests, along the lines of those for the U.S. financial services infrastructure after the 2008 financial meltdown, might be required as interinfrastructural interconnectivity intensifies. Such stress tests would necessitate that infrastructure engineers and analysts develop far more informed ICIS-failure scenarios along lines such as discussed in this book.

APPENDIX

1. We focused on the Port of Stockton rather than the Port of West Sacramento because the former has recently been more significant in terms of actual annual cargo tonnage (see, e.g., Delta Protection Commission 2012, 213). We observed this differential use of ports as well in our VTS observations.

2. For a discussion of the counterproductive nature of blaming in high reliability organizations, see Povera, Montefusco, and Canato 2010.

REFERENCES

Amalberti, R. 2013. *Navigating Safety*. New York: Springer.

Anderson, R., and T. Moore. 2006. "The Economics of Information Security." *Science* 314 (5799): 610–613.

Antonsen, S., K. Skarholt, and A. J. Ringstad. 2012. "The Role of Standardization in Safety Management: A Case Study of a Major Oil and Gas Company." *Safety Science* 50: 2001–2009.

Ascher, K. 2007. *The Works: Anatomy of a City*. New York: Penguin Books.

Ashby, R. 1966. *Design for a Brain*. London: Chapman and Hall.

Atkins, R. 2011. "ECB Skipper Braced for More Stormy Waters." *Financial Times*, October 7, p. 5.

Baker, B., E. Roe, and P. Schulman. 2011. "Case Study of Interconnected Critical Infrastructures in the Sacramento–San Joaquin Delta: The Interconnectivity of Water and Power Flows at the State Water Project's Harvey O. Banks Pumps, near Tracy California." RESIN Activity 2.6 Report, University of California, Berkeley.

Bales, R. 1953. "The Equilibrium Problem in Small Groups." In *Working Papers in the Theory of Action*, edited by T. Parsons, R. Bales, and E. Shils, 111–161. New York: Free Press.

Bazerman, M., and D. Moore. 2012. *Judgment in Managerial Decision Making*. New York: Wiley.

Bazerman, M. H., and M. D. Watkins. 2008. *Predictable Surprises: The Disasters You Should Have Seen Coming, and How to Prevent Them*. Cambridge, MA: Harvard Business Review Press.

Bea, R. 2006. "Reliability and Human Factors in Geotechnical Engineering." *Journal of Geotechnical and Geoenvironmental Engineering* 132 (5): 631–643.

Beamish, T. 2002. *Silent Spill*. Cambridge, MA: MIT Press.

Beck, U. 1992. *Risk Society: Toward a New Modernity*. New York: Sage.

Bernstein, M. 1955. *Regulating Business by Independent Commission*. Princeton, NJ: Princeton University Press.

Bleskan, K. 2011. "Retiring CEO Says His Goals for California ISO Were Surpassed." *SNL Electric Utility Report*, April 18.

Boin, A., P. t'Hart, P. Stern, and B. Sundelius. 2005. *The Politics of Crisis Management: Public Leadership Under Pressure.* Cambridge: Cambridge University Press.

Boin, A., A. McConnell, and P. t'Hart. 2008. *Governing After Crisis.* Cambridge: Cambridge University Press.

Boin, A., and M. J. G. van Eeten. 2013. "The Resilient Organization." *Public Management Review* 15 (3): 429–445.

Buffett, W. 2003. "What Worries Warren Buffett." *Fortune*, March 3. http://www.freerepublic.com/focus/news/855968/posts.

Burt, R. 2010. *Neighbor Networks: Competitive Advantage Local and Personal.* Oxford: Oxford University Press.

California Department of Water Resources. 2009a. "Delta Risk Management Strategy: Executive Summary, Phase 1." http://www.water.ca.gov/floodsafe/fessro/levees/drms/docs/drms_execsum_ph1_final_low.pdf.

California Department of Water Resources. 2009b. *Jones Tract Flood Water Quality Investigations.* Sacramento: California Department of Water Resources.

California ISO. 2007. "2007 Annual Report: A Decade of Powerful Growth." http://www.caiso.com/Documents/2007CaliforniaISOAnnualReport.pdf.

———. 2008. "Five-Year Strategic Plan—Planning Horizon: 2008–2012." http://www.caiso.com/1f8f/1f8fc5a81c632.pdf.

———. 2011. "California ISO President and CEO Announces Retirement." April 5. http://www.caiso.com/Documents/CaliforniaISOPresidentandCEOAnnouncesRetirement.pdf.

Comfort, L. K., A. Boin, and C. Demchak, eds. 2010. *Designing for Resilience: Preparing for Extreme Events.* Pittsburgh, PA: University of Pittsburgh Press.

Comfort, L. K., M. D. Siciliano, and A. Okada. 2011. "Resilience, Entropy, and Efficiency in Crisis Management: The January 12, 2010, Haiti Earthquake." *Risk, Hazards and Crisis in Public Policy* 2 (3): 1–25.

Crane, M. 2009. "Cal-ISO Fine-Tunes Market Structure in Wake of MRTU Launch." *SNL Power Week West*, August 17.

de Bruijne, M. 2006. *Networked Reliability: Institutional Fragmentation and the Reliability of Service Provision in Critical Infrastructures.* Delft, Netherlands: Delft University of Technology.

Deepwater Horizon Study Group. 2011. "Final Report on the Investigation of the Macondo Well Blowout." March 1. http://ccrm.berkeley.edu/pdfs_papers/bea_pdfs/dhsgfinalreport-march2011-tag.pdf.

Dekker, S., P. Cilliers, and J.-H. Hofmeyr. 2011. "The Complexity of Failure: Implications of Complexity Theory for Safety Investigations." *Safety Science* 49: 939–945.

Delta Protection Commission. 2012. "Economic Sustainability Plan for the Sacramento–San Joaquin Delta." http://www.delta.ca.gov/res/docs/ESP/ESP_P2_FINAL.pdf.

Delta Stewardship Council. 2015. "Coequal Goals." http://deltacouncil.ca.gov.

Direct Energy Business. 2009. "CAISO MRTU: Frequently Asked Questions." https://directenergybusiness.com/folder_icons/CAISO_MRTU_FAQ.pdf.

Egan, M. J. 2007. "Anticipating Future Vulnerability: Defining Characteristics of Increasingly Critical Infrastructure-Like Systems." *Journal of Contingencies and Crisis Management* 15 (1): 4–17.

ELCON (Electricity Consumers Resource Council). 2004. "ELCON Study Reviews Impact of August 2003 Blackout on Facilities." *ELCON Report*, no. 1, pp. 1, 4.

FERC (Federal Energy Regulatory Commission) and NERC (North American Energy Reliability Corporation). 2012. "Arizona–Southern California Outages on September 8, 2011: Causes and Recommendations." http://www.ferc.gov/legal/staff-reports/04-27-2012-ferc-nerc-report.pdf.

Fischenich, J. C. 2011. "Stream Restoration Benefits." In *Stream Restoration in Dynamic Fluvial Systems: Scientific Approaches*, edited by A. Simon, S. J. Bennett, and J. M. Castro, 45–68. Washington, DC: American Geophysical Union.

Frischmann, B. M. 2005. "An Economic Theory of Infrastructure and Commons Management." *Minnesota Law Review* 89: 917–1030.

Giddens, A. 2002. *Runaway World*. New York: Routledge.

Graham, S. 2009. *Disrupted Cities: When Infrastructure Fails*. New York: Routledge.

Hamedifar, H. 2012. "Risk Assessment and Management for Interconnected and Interactive Critical Flood Defense Systems." PhD diss., University of California, Berkeley.

Hanemann, M., and C. Dyckman. 2009. "The San Francisco-Bay Delta: A Failure of Decision-Making Capacity." *Environmental Science and Policy* 12 (6): 710–725.

Healey, M. C., M. D. Dettinger, and R. B. Norgaard, eds. 2008. *The State of Bay-Delta Science, 2008*. Sacramento, CA: CALFED Science Program.

Hokstad, P., I. B. Utne, and J. Votn. 2013. *Risk and Interdependencies in Critical Infrastructures*. New York: Springer.

Hollnagel, E. 2014. *Safety I and Safety II: The Past and Future of Safety Management*. London: Ashgate.

Hollnagel, E., D. Woods, and N. Leveson. 2006. *Resilience Engineering: Concepts and Precepts*. Aldershot, UK: Ashgate.

Hopkins, A. 2014. "Issues in Safety Science." *Safety Science* 67: 6–14.

Horan, S. 2010. "Measuring Volatility in the 'New Normal' Era." *Financial Times*, October 31. http://www.ft.com/intl/cms/s/0/3f397a48-e387-11df-8ad3-00144feabdc0.html.

Huler, S. 2010. *On the Grid*. New York: Rodale Books.

Huntington, S. P. 1952. "The Marasmus of the I.C.C.: The Commission, the Railroads and the Public Interest." *Yale Law Review* 61 (April): 465–509.

Ivergard, T., and B. Hunt. 2008. *Handbook of Control Room Design and Ergonomics*. Boca Raton, FL: CRC Press.

Jardin, A. 1988. *Tocqueville: A Biography*. Translated by L. Davis with R. Hemenway. New York: Farrar, Straus, and Giroux.

Jonkman, S. N. 2011. "Technical Report: Risk Analysis for Interconnected Critical Infrastructure Systems; Applications to Flood Hazards and a Case Study for the Sherman Island Flood Risk Management System." RESIN Activity 2.8 Report, University of California, Berkeley.

Jonkman, S. N., L. Hiel, R. Bea, H. Foster, A. Tsioulou, P. Arroyo, T. Stallard, and L. Harris. 2012. "Integrated Risk Assessment for the Natomas Basin (California): Analysis of Loss of Life and Emergency Management for Floods." *Natural Hazards Review* 13 (4): 297–309.

Kahneman, D. 2012. *Thinking, Fast and Slow*. Princeton, NJ: Princeton University Press.

Kahneman, D., and G. Klein. 2009. "Conditions for Intuitive Expertise." *American Psychologist* 64:515–526.

Kammen, M. 1997. "Wrecked on the Fourth of July." *New York Times*, July 6. http://www.nytimes.com/books/97/07/06/bookend/bookend.html.

Kellerman, B. 2012. *The End of Leadership*. New York: HarperCollins.

Klein, G. 1999. *Sources of Power*. Cambridge, MA: MIT Press.

Kumar, P., M. Verma, M. Wood, and D. Negandhi. 2010. *Guidance Manual for the Valuation of Regulating Services*. Nairobi, Kenya: UN Environment Programme (UNIP).

LaPorte, T. R. 1975. *Organized Social Complexity*. Princeton, NJ: Princeton University Press.

LaPorte, T. R., and P. Consolini. 1991. "Working in Practice but Not in Theory: Theoretical Challenges of High Reliability Organizations." *Public Administration Research and Theory* 1 (1): 19–47.

Leveson, N., N. Dulac, K. Marais, and J. Carroll. 2009. "Moving Beyond Normal Accidents and High Reliability Organizations: A Systems Approach to Safety in Complex Systems." *Organization Studies* 30 (2–3): 227–249.

Levine, M. E., and J. L. Forrence. 1990. "Regulatory Capture, Public Interest, and the Public Agenda: Toward a Synthesis." *Journal of Law, Economics, and Organization* 6:167–198.

Lifelines Council. 2014. "Lifelines Interdependency Study Report." http://www.sfgsa.org/modules/
    showdocument.aspx?documentid=12025.

Lo, A. 2012. "Finance Is in Need of a Technological Revolution." *Financial Times*, August 27. http://
    www.ft.com/intl/cms/s/0/107466e2-ed2f-11e1-83d1-00144feab49a.html.

Lofquist, E. A. 2010. "The Art of Measuring Nothing: The Paradox of Measuring Safety in a Chang-
    ing Civil Aviation Industry Using Traditional Safety Metrics." *Safety Science* 48:1520–1529.

Longfellow, R. 2013. "Back in Time: The National Road." U.S. Department of Transportation, Oc-
    tober 17. http://www.fhwa.dot.gov/infrastructure/back0103.cfm.

Ludy, J., M. Matella, and E. Roe. 2010. "Activity 1.4 Progress Report, May 2010: Eco-Infrastructure
    and Sherman Island Levees." NSF-UCB RESIN-Activity Report Series, RESIN/CCRM,
    Berkeley, CA.

Luiijf, E., A. Nieuwenhuijs, M. Klaver, M. van Eeten, and E. Cruz. 2008. "Empirical Findings
    on Critical Infrastructures Dependencies in Europe." http://critis08.dia.uniroma3.it/pdf/
    CRITIS_08_40.pdf.

Luiijf, H. A. M., A. H. Nieuwenhuijs, M. H. A. Klaver, M. J. G. van Eeten, and E. Cruz. 2010. "Em-
    pirical Findings on European Critical Infrastructure Dependencies." *International Journal of
    System of Systems Engineering* 2 (1): 3–18.

MacRae, C. 2014. *Close Calls: Managing Risk and Resilience in Airline Flight Safety*. London: Pal-
    grave Macmillan.

Majone, G. 1978. "Technology Assessment in a Dialectic Key." *Public Administration Review* 38 (1): 52–58.

Mansour, Y. 2008. "Announcement Regarding ISO Executive Leadership—Message from Yakout."
    CAISO eCurrents.

March, J. G. 2009. *A Primer on Decision-Making*. New York: Free Press.

May, E. 2013. "The Power of Zero: Steps Toward High Reliability Healthcare." *Healthcare Executive*
    28 (2): 16–18, 20, 22, 24, 26.

McCartney, S. 2009. "Training Is Key to Flight Safety." *Wall Street Journal*, January 27, p. 7.

McLuhan, M. 1966. *Understanding Media*. New York: Signet.

Meyer, M., and L. Zucker. 1989. *Permanently Failing Organizations*. Newbury Park, CA: Sage.

Michaels, D., and A. Pasztor. 2008. "Air Safety's Quality Control." *Wall Street Journal*,
    May 8, p. B4.

Min, H. S., W. Beyeler, and T. Brown. 2006. "Modeling and Simulation of Critical Infrastructure
    Interdependencies." http://www.sandia.gov/nisac/downloads312.

Min, H. S., W. Beyeler, T. Brown, Y. J. Son, and A. Jones. 2007. "Toward Modeling and Simulation
    of Critical National Infrastructure Interdependencies." *IIE Transactions* 39:57–71.

Mohammad, A. B., J. P. Johansen, and P. G. Almklov. 2014. "Reliable Operations in Control Cen-
    ters, an Empirical Study." In *Safety, Reliability and Risk Analysis: Beyond the Horizon*, edited by
    R. D. J. M. Steenbergen, P. H. A. J. M. van Gelder, S. Miraglia, and A. C. W. M. Ton Vrou-
    wenvelder, 249–258. Boca Raton, FL: CRC Press.

Neff, E. T. 2010. "Ohio River as Underutilized Transportation Asset for Shipping Commodities to
    Global Markets." https://www.dot.state.oh.us/engineering/OTEC/2010%20Presentations/43B
    -Neff.pdf.

Nesse, R. 2013. "2013: What *Should* We Be Worried About? The Fragility of Complex Systems." *Edge*.
    http://www.edge.org/response-detail/23811.

NIAC (National Infrastructure Advisory Council). 2009. *Critical Infrastructure Resilience: Final
    Report and Recommendations*. Washington, DC: U.S. Department of Homeland Security.

Nieuwenhuijs, A., E. Luiijf, and M. Klaver. 2008. "Modeling Critical Infrastructure Dependencies."
    http://www.irriis.org/Filee79c.pdf?lang=2&oiid=9213&pid=952.

Noyes, J., and M. Bransby. 2002. *People in Control*. London: IEE.

Ohio River Valley Water Sanitation Commission. n.d. "River Facts/Conditions." http://www
.orsanco.org/river-factsconditions (accessed July 13, 2015).

Oliver, F. S. 1931. *The Endless Adventure*. Vol. 2. London: Macmillan.

O'Neil, P., and K. Kriz. 2013. "Do High-Reliability Systems Have Lower Error Rates? Evidence from
Commercial Aircraft Accidents." *Public Administration Review* 73 (4): 601–612.

Ostrom, L. T., and C. A. Wilhelmsen. 2012. *Risk Assessment*. New York: John Wiley.

Palfrey, J., and U. Gasser. 2012. *Interop: The Promise and Perils of Highly Interconnected Systems*. New
York: Basic Books.

Perrin, C. 2005. *Shouldering Risks*. Princeton, NJ: Princeton University Press.

Perrow, C. (1984) 1999. *Normal Accidents*. Princeton, NJ: Princeton University Press.

Pidgeon, N. 2010. "Systems Thinking, Culture of Reliability and Safety." *Civil Engineering and Environmental Systems* 27 (3): 211–217.

Porter, E. 2013. "Economists Agree: Solutions Are Elusive." *New York Times*, April 24, pp. B1, B4.

Povera, B., A. Montefusco, and A. Canato. 2010. "A 'No Blame' Approach to Organizational Learning." *British Journal of Management* 21: 1057–1074.

Powers, W. T. 1990. "Control Theory: A Model of Organisms." *System Dynamics Review* 6 (1): 1–20.

Quill, E. 2012. "When Networks Network." *Science News*, September 22. http://havlin.biu.ac.il/Pdf/
press12sciencenews_interdependentnetworks.pdf.

Reason, J. 1990. *Human Error*. Cambridge: Cambridge University Press.

Reich, P. B., D. Tilman, F. Isbell, K. Mueller, S. E. Hobbie, D. F. B. Flynn, and N. Eisenhauer.
2012. "Impacts of Biodiversity Loss Escalate through Time as Redundancy Fades." *Science* 336
(6081): 589–592.

Richman, S. H., and H. Pant. 2008. "Reliability Concerns for Next-Generation Networks." *Bell Labs
Technical Journal* 12 (4): 103–108.

Rijpma, J. A. 1997. "Complexity, Tight Coupling and Reliability: Connecting Normal Accidents
Theory and High Reliability Theory." *Journal of Contingencies and Crisis Management* 5 (1): 15–23.

Rinaldi, S. M., J. P. Pereenboom, and T. Kelley. 2001. "Identifying, Understanding and Analyzing Critical Infrastructure Interdependencies." *IEEE Control Systems Magazine* 21 (6): 11–25.

Roberts, K., ed. 1993. *New Challenges to Understanding Organizations*. New York: Macmillan.

Rochlin, G. 1993. "Defining 'High Reliability' Organizations in Practice: A Taxonomic Prologue."
In *New Challenges to Understanding Organizations*, edited by K. Roberts, 11–32. New York:
Macmillan.

Roe, E. 2011. "Surprising Answers to Rising Sea Levels, Storms, Floods, Desertification, Earthquakes
and Ever More Environmental Crises in California's Sacramento–San Joaquin Delta." *Journal
of Contingencies and Crisis Management* 19 (1): 34–42.

———. 2013. *Making the Most of Mess: Reliability and Policy in Today's Management Challenges*. Dur-
ham, NC: Duke University Press.

Roe, E., R. G. Bea, S. N. Jonkman, H. Faucher de Corn, H. Foster, J. Radke, P. Schulman, and
R. Storesund. Forthcoming. "Risk Assessment and Management (RAM) for Interconnected
Critical Infrastructure Systems (ICIS) at the Site and Regional Levels in California's Sacra-
mento–San Joaquin Delta." *International Journal of Critical Infrastructures* 12 (1–2).

Roe, E., and P. R. Schulman. 2008. *High Reliability Management*. Stanford, CA: Stanford University Press.

———. 2012a. "Risk Management of Interconnected Infrastructures: An Empirical Study of
Joint Stress Conditions." In *Risk and Interdependencies in Critical Infrastructures*, edited by
P. Hokstad, I. B. Utne, and J. Vatn, 189–209. London: Springer-Verlag.

———. 2012b. "Toward a Comparative Framework for Measuring Resilience in Critical Infrastructure Systems." *Journal of Comparative Policy Analysis: Research and Practice* 14 (2): 114–125.

Roe, E., P. Schulman, M. J. G. van Eeten, and M. de Bruijne. 2005. "High Reliability Bandwidth Management in Large Technical Systems: Findings and Implications of Two Case Studies." *Journal of Public Administration Research and Theory* 15 (2): 263–280.

Rosenthal, E. 2010. "Our Fix-It Faith and the Oil Spill." *New York Times*, May 29. http://www.nytimes.com/2010/05/30/weekinreview/30rosenthal.html.

Rosenthal, U., A. Boin, and L. Comfort. 2001. *Managing Crises*. Springfield, IL: Charles C. Thomas.

Rourke, F. E. 1969. *Bureaucracy, Politics and Public Policy*. Boston: Little, Brown.

Saleh, J. H., K. B. Marais, E. Bakolas, and R. V. Cowlagi. 2010. "Highlights from the Literature on Accident Causation and System Safety: Review of Major Ideas, Recent Contributions, and Challenges." *Reliability Engineering and System Safety* 95: 1105–1116.

Sanne, J. M. 2000. *Creating Safety in Air Traffic Control*. Lund, Sweden: Arkiv Forlag.

Scheffer, M., S. R. Carpenter, T. M. Lenton, J. Bascompte, W. Brock, V. Dakos, J. van de Koppel, I. A. van de Leemput, S. A. Levin, E. H. van Nes, M. Pascual, and J. Vandermeer. 2012. "Anticipating Critical Transitions." *Science* 338 (6105): 344–348.

Schewe, P. F. 2006. *The Grid*. Washington, DC: Joseph Henry Press.

Schneider, K. 2012. "Steel Leads Revival in Ohio River Valley." *New York Times*, September 5. http://www.nytimes.com/2012/09/06/us/steel-shipments-reviving-ohio-river-valley.html.

Schöbel, M. 2009. "Trust in High-Reliability Organizations." *Social Science Information* 48 (2): 315–333.

Schulman, P. 1993. "The Negotiated Order of Organizational Reliability." *Administration and Society* 25 (December): 353–372.

———. 2004. "General Attributes of Safe Organisations." *Quality and Safety in Health Care* 13 (suppl. II): ii39–ii44.

———. 2013. "Procedural Paradoxes and the Management of Safety." In *Trapping Safety into Rules*, edited by M. Bourier and C. Beider, 243–256. London: Ashgate.

Schulman, P. R., and E. Roe. 2011. "A Control Room Metric for Evaluating Success and Failure in High Reliability Crisis Management." *Policy and Society* 30:129–136.

Schwartz, J. 2007. "Who Needs Hackers?" *New York Times*, September 12. http://www.nytimes.com/2007/09/12/technology/techspecial/12threat.html.

Searle, J. 1983. *Intentionality*. Cambridge: Cambridge University Press.

Shah, A. K., S. Mullainathan, and E. Shafir. 2012. "Some Consequences of Having Too Little." *Science* 338 (6107): 682–685.

Sheffi, Y. 2005. *The Resilient Enterprise*. Cambridge, MA: MIT Press.

Shrivastava, S., K. Sonpar, and F. Pazzaglia. 2009a. "Normal Accident Theory Versus High Reliability Theory: A Resolution and Call for an Open Systems View of Accidents." *Human Relations* 62 (9): 1357–1390.

———. 2009b. "Reconciliation Can Lead to Better Application: A Rejoinder to Perrow (2009)." *Human Relations* 62 (9): 1395–1398.

Spielgelhalter, D., M. Pearson, and I. Short. 2011. "Visualizing Uncertainty about the Future." *Science* 333 (6048): 1393–1400.

Stanton, N., P. Salmon, D. Jenkins, and G. Walker. 2009. *Human Factors in the Design and Evaluation of Control Room Operations*. Boca Raton, FL: CRC Press.

Steenhuisen, B. 2009. "Competing Public Values: Coping Strategies in Heavily Regulated Utility Industries." PhD diss. Delft University of Technology, Netherlands.

———. 2014. "Cutting Dark Matter: Professional Capacity and Organizational Change." *Journal of Organizational Ethnography* 3 (2): 152–168.

Stirling, A., and D. Gee. 2002. "Science, Precaution, and Practice: Viewpoint." *Public Health Reports* 117 (November–December): 521–533.

Suddeth, R., J. Mount, and J. Lund. 2008. "Levee Decisions and Sustainability for the Delta: Technical Appendix B." In *Comparing Futures for the Sacramento–San Joaquin Delta*, 1–39. San Francisco: Public Policy Institute of California.

Thompson, J. D. 1967. *Organizations in Action*. New York: McGraw-Hill.

Turner, B. A. 1978. *Man Made Disasters*. London: Wykeham.

Urbina, I. 2010. "Workers on Doomed Rig Voiced Concern on Safety." *New York Times*, July 22, pp, A1, A16.

URS. 2007. "Technical Memorandum: Delta Risk Management Strategy (DRMS) Phase 1—Topical Area: Impact to Infrastructure." http://www.water.ca.gov/floodsafe/fessro/levees/drms/docs/Impact_to_Infrastructure_TM.pdf.

U.S. Geological Survey. 2011. *Overview of the ARkStorm Scenario: Open File Report 2010–1312*. Reston, VA: U.S. Geological Survey.

van Eeten, M., A. Nieuwenhuijs, E. Luiijf, M. Klaver, and E. Cruz. 2011. "The State and the Threat of Cascading Failure Across Critical Infrastructures: The Implications of Empirical Evidence from Media Incident Reports." *Public Administration* 89 (2): 381–400.

Vaughan, D. 1997. *The Challenger Launch Decision: Risky Technology, Culture and Deviance at NASA*. Chicago: University of Chicago Press.

Venturi, R. 2002. *Complexity and Contradiction in Architecture*. New York: Museum of Modern Art.

Vogus, T., and K. M. Sutcliffe. 2007. "The Impact of Safety Organizing, Trusted Leadership, and Care Pathways on Reported Medication Errors in Hospital Nursing Units." *Medical Care* 45:997–1002.

Volcker, P. 2011. "Financial Reforms: Unfinished Business." *New York Review of Books*, November 24, pp. 74–76.

Waters, R. 2009. "World-wise Web?" *Financial Times*, March 4, p. 9.

Weick, K. E. 1995. *Sensemaking in Organizations*. Thousand Oaks, CA: Sage.

———. 2011. "Organizing for Transient Reliability: The Production of Dynamic Non-events." *Journal of Contingencies and Crisis Management* 19 (1): 21–27.

Weick, K. E., and K. M. Sutcliffe. 2001. *Managing the Unexpected: Assuring High Performance in an Age of Complexity*. San Francisco, CA: Jossey-Bass.

Woods, D., and E. Hollnagel. 2006. *Joint Cognitive Systems: Patterns in Cognitive Systems Engineering*. Boca Raton, FL: Taylor and Francis.

Zimmerman, R. 2004. "Decision-Making and the Vulnerability of Interdependent Critical Infrastructure." In *2004 IEEE International Conference on Systems, Man and Cybernetics*, vol. 5, 4059–4063. The Hague, Netherlands: IEEE.

INDEX